Running South America

www.5000mileproject.org

Running
South America

with my Husband
and other animals

Katharine Lowrie

Whittles Publishing

Published by
Whittles Publishing,
Dunbeath,
Caithness KW6 6EG,
Scotland, UK

www.whittlespublishing.com

© 2017 Katharine Lowrie

ISBN 978-184995-362-7

Printed by Short Run Press Ltd.

David and Katharine's fantastic journey across the South American continent, travelling over 6,500 miles on foot, is a stunning example of dedication to showing the importance of conserving our ecosystems on this fragile planet.

Ed Smith, Former Chairman World Wildlife Fund UK

Darwin's Frog   Rhinoderma darwinii

It seemlessly merges into the forest leaf-litter

Contents

Thank You

There are countless people I would like to thank for their incredible support, kindness and generosity during the expedition, during all the planning that surrounded it and more recently for the sage words of my three book advisers, Ted Lean, John Davidson and Jake Burnyeat. Your help was invaluable. Jake was also the master-mind behind the title and has been a constant sounding-board during my quest for a publisher – Burnyeat, I salute you! Duff Hart-Davis was my inspired editor and to him I am hugely grateful. I would also like to thank Keith Whittles, who believed in my story and wanted to publish it. Thank you.

Below is a list of some of my remarkable helpers, in no specific order. Thank you: you are amazing.

Maria Elisa Pelletta, our indefatigable and inspiring translator who accompanied us vicariously through her beloved South America translating our outpourings – from ecology articles, to blogs and webpages and now for applying her eagle's eye to the Spanish phrases in this book. Thank you so very much; Maria Abud, who attempted to do what no other has done and persuade the border police to let us cross the Andes on foot in winter; Ellen Birrell Hutchins, our marketer and 'voice of America'; Jonno Gibbins, our exceptional barefoot coach, without whose skills we would probably still be hopping the continent; Lucy Clayton who, when our laptop faltered before the final hurdle, told the world we had achieved our dreams; Mike Wells and Gary Oliver, who advised on bird survey methods; Karen Johnson, our yoga advisor; My sister, Lucy Land, who created our first promotional film; Dave's Mother and Father, Anne and Brian Lowrie, who sent shoes and sundry oddities all over South America at the shortest of notice; David and Geraldine Simson, our Uruguayan family who tucked us under their silky wings, fed us and allowed us to sleep – you are always with us; Loli and Raffa Afterlion who stored our kit and took us in on the long running road; Claudia Milet, who found friends for us in Patagonia;

David Burnett, my wise and wonderful publishing mentor; Fiona Lowrie and Octavio Nef, for providing the much longed-for breaks during the expedition, and Octavio for his Spanish and self-defence advice; my wonderful cousin Marga Mercadal for translating a very long press-release into Spanish – you are a star! Doug, John and Laurie Lowrie for organising our run through London and talk; Jala Macazoumi, Tom Hamilton, Claudia Herrera, Stuart McCarthy, Camila Nef Videla. And of course my Mum, Carole Land. You are an utter star and have always been there for me, no matter how large your chick has become!

I would also like to thank the hundreds of people in South America who shared their food and homes, or imparted kind words, a much-needed wave or smile that helped buoy our spirits. We hope we can return that gratitude one day.

I would also like to give a huge thankyou to all our sponsors (see kit list) but in particular: Berghaus, Swarovski, Vivobarefoot and Inov8 who told everyone about our expedition and helped organise events for us when it was all over. Above all, I would like to thank our three trusts: Sculpt the Future, Transglobe Expedition Trust and the John Muir Trust's Bill Wallace Grant, which supported us financially and psychologically by having faith in our idea and ambition from the start.

Finally, I would like to thank David, my husband, fellow runner, conspirator, inspiration and so much more. You are extraordinary.

Preface

The *Concise Atlas of the World* lay open on the saloon table, gently rocking with the motion of the boat. South America stared at us and we stared back. Our eyes ran down its jagged Andean mountain chain, traced the course of its almighty Amazon River, alighted on Lake Titicaca, searched for the land of the Pampas, followed its intricate maze of Chilean fjords and eye-balled the Antarctic Ice Sheet at its tip and the coral-filled Caribbean Sea at its top.

Mind-boggling biodiversity and wilderness fill South America's land and water: the largest rainforest on earth, the greatest river, the longest mountain chain, the biggest wetland, the highest waterfall and the driest desert. It is home to the greatest number of bird, amphibian and monkey species in the world and its coastal waters are a breeding ground for the largest living animal on earth, the blue whale.

Could this continent really be traversed on foot – by two runners whose longest runs to date were forty-five miles, not hundreds and thousands of miles? Could we survive running through the ravages of hurricane force winds, hail stones the size of bricks and temperatures ranging from below –0°C to over 40°C. We would have to traverse mountains, cross deserts, run through crime-ravaged towns, in over 100% humidity, accompanied by swarms of insects and dangerous animals. We would have no support, beyond our own feet and a home-made trailer carrying everything we needed to survive, while sleeping in a ditch or hiding in the rainforest each night.

No one had done it before. But we were adamant we could prove it possible. It would take huge amounts of planning, severe re-training, and the faith of a team of charitable trusts and companies who were willing to gamble on a pair of runners with no form, but barrels of determination.

We hope our tale will transport you on an intimate journey through this extraordinary continent, viewed on the hoof, allowing you to inhale and bask in some of South America's most remote and undiscovered regions. It is soaked in nature – with observations and revelations about the animals whose lives we encountered – and in the nature of running – barefooted, free-thinking, wild and exhilarating. It's a story for anyone but especially runners, wildlife enthusiasts, travellers, and anyone fascinated by South America.

It is also a journey of tremendous joy and excruciating pain and sorrow. It explores how we are all linked to this far-off land and how its wildlife and wildernesses are adjusting to this global influence. Above all it's a story of hope and triumph; a demonstration of how tough the human mind and body can be, how running and movement are crucial to human physical and mental health and how with small steps we can tackle seemingly insurmountable challenges. It is not too late to protect the world's remaining unspoilt ecosystems, but time is running out.

List of Illustrations & Maps

All maps and illustrations by Katharine Lowrie

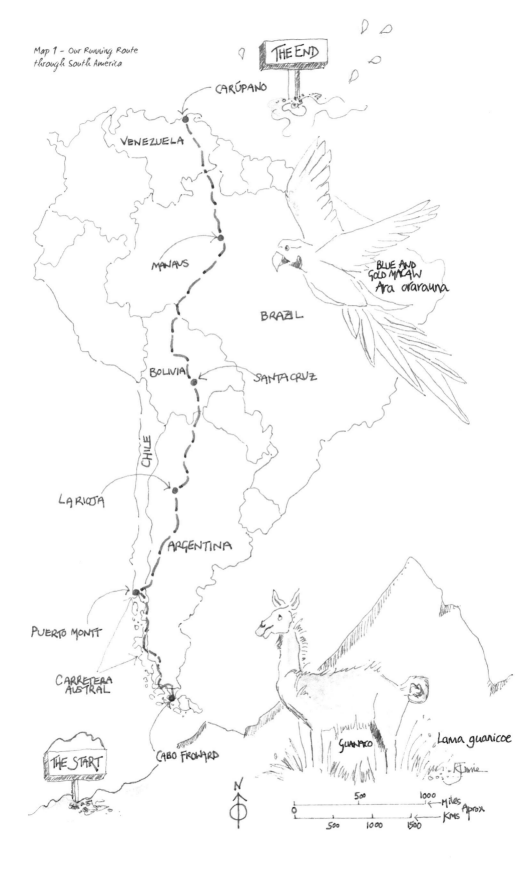

Map 1 – Our Running Route
through South America

THE END

CARÚPANO

VENEZUELA

MANAUS

BLUE AND
GOLD MACAW
Ara ararauna

BRAZIL

BOLIVIA

SANTA CRUZ

CHILE

LA RIOJA

ARGENTINA

PUERTO MONTT

CARRETERA
AUSTRAL

THE START

CABO FROWARD

GUANACO

Lama guanicoe

N

0   500   1000
                         ← Miles Aprox
    500   1000   1500 ← Kms

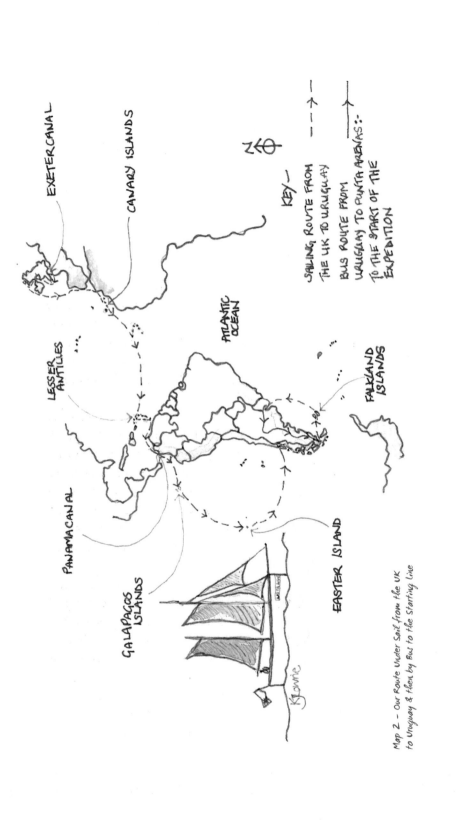

EXETER CANAL

CANARY ISLANDS

KEY:-

SAILING ROUTE FROM
THE UK TO URUGUAY

BUS ROUTE FROM
URUGUAY TO PUNTA ARENAS:-
TO THE START OF THE
EXPEDITION

LESSER
ANTILLES

ATLANTIC
OCEAN

FALKLAND
ISLANDS

PANAMA CANAL

GALAPAGOS
ISLANDS

EASTER ISLAND

K.Bowie

Map 2 – Our Route Under Sail from the UK
to Uruguay & then by Bus to the Starting Line

A snow-white adult, resplendent
with canary-yellow stockings

1 To the End of the Earth

The Magellan Strait stretched iron-grey to our left, soon to merge with the Southern Ocean. Black-browed albatrosses and giant petrels soared effortlessly over the foaming waves. Rising behind them, indigo mountains, jagged and snow-covered, marked the southern extent of the Andes. On the shingle beach a duo of juvenile kelp geese preened their feathers on an exposed boulder, under the eyes of a snow-white adult, resplendent with canary-yellow stockings.

This was Cape Froward, the southern-most point of the South American mainland. We had stepped into a winter wonderland at the bottom of the world. At first sight the soft snow-scene appeared meek, but we were fully aware that it was charged with treachery and that within hours it could transform itself into a raging beast. And that was precisely why we were there. We craved such savage and unpredictable places; where we could shed the safe skin of civilisation and re-connect to the delicious senses on which our lives once depended. Where maybe, just maybe, we might share a fraction of our existence with a puma, a hump-backed whale or a Magellanic penguin.

Here: where boundaries blurred between sea, mountain, ice-melt river and wizened southern-beech forest; to the fecund wetlands of the north of the continent pulsating with giant birds, colossal rodents and dagger-toothed reptiles; to the Amazon rainforest – the ultimate ecosystem on earth, vibrating 24 hours a day with supercharged life. South America intoxicated us and was our motivation for running its immense length: to barb our days with opportunities of glimpsing, inhaling and touching its wild animals and extraordinary wildernesses; to scratch the surface of their complexity, to seek out the drivers of their change, to understand how even we, hailing from distant shores, could be impacting on their extent and dynamics.

Like no other form of passage, running would allow us to penetrate the moods of the land and its creatures. With only a couple of millimetres of 'barefoot' shoe-soles separating us from the earth's heartbeat, often only our unshod skin, we would move silently, stealthily, creeping up on wildlife, a whisper away from discovery, a step from the unknown and unexpected.

I love the exhilaration of running: my heart pounding, the warmth spreading through my chest, my arms pulling me forward, my legs straining, my feet instinctively feeling their way, my head willing me on; my body purring with fitness. I feel naked, stripped of kit, reality, concerns, barely conscious of the drip, drip, dripping-away of stresses and anxieties. No wonder: it's what our bodies were made for, after millennia of evolution, when we stepped down from the trees and began pounding the sun-baked plains of Africa, relentlessly pursing our prey.

But for me the crucial piece of the running jigsaw is running wild; running with wildlife and wilderness, sensing the raw, natural elements within and without myself like never before, as my body and being tingle with life and vigour.

I wait under a sycamore tree near the entrance to Halifax Hall, Sheffield University. Frost coats the pavement. My stomach lurches. 'He's not coming,' I mutter to myself.

Suddenly I catch sight of a mousy, tousled head. A six-foot-four, lanky figure crests the hill – the guy I had spoken to the night before. He's followed by two other chaps, but I hardly notice them. My heart hammers; he's remembered me!

We set off fast, pounding down the road, sweeping into Ecclesall Valley Park. The river rushes past; a kingfisher blurs orange and turquoise; a coot protests, splashing into the reeds; russet leaves silently eddy into our receding footsteps. Words flow, but they have no significance, bear no resemblance to the way I'm feeling – which is on fire, flaming from my toes to the tips of my ears. My body heaves, my breath catches. Sweat mixes with mud, and ardour floods my chest, bursting my lungs.

We have no idea that our paths will diverge, that there will be other loves – but nothing like the one that waits for us seven years later, when we meet again on the forgotten moorlands of the Forest of Bowland. Now I am following invisible GPS lines over the windswept heaths, as I survey breeding birds. A mutual University friend and her boyfriend suggest we all meet for a bike-ride. I haven't thought about David in years, but as I peer from the top window of the reservoir flat at the wild-looking fellow below, I feel the same fire rushing through me.

We talk and laugh all night, and I know without a doubt he's the one I've been waiting for. Lying back on my horse's rump as a teenager, watching blue tits flit through the canopy above my head, I know he's the man I dreamt of then and have dreamt of all my life. Next morning we climb Ingleborough. I feel his fingers interlace with mine as we gaze over the rolling folds of the Dales.

And we run, entering races together: the 'Grizzly' – a 21-mile extravaganza over the beaches and cliffs of Devon; the 'Exmoor Stagger', a 16-mile woodland and moorland hill-fest; the 'Chevy Chase' – 20-mile bog-trotting in Northumberland, with far-reaching views to the North Sea; The 'Four Inns' – a 45 mile race over the bogs and 'edges' of the Peak District in the company of mountain hares. We're not running for any particular reason, apart from the need to be in wild places: to soak them up, unhindered by equipment, just us and a pair of shoes. We splash through streams, summit hills, bound over boulders and tussocks, mud-streaked and sweat-soaked, fuelled by adrenalin, rolling head-first, flying like kites, ignoring the pain; we have never felt more alive.

Three years pass.

A babble of chatter curls through the church gateway from the smiling gathering. Hatted and welly-booted, in floral dresses and long trousers, they watch two figures running away through a fine May drizzle, down a deeply-sunken Devon lane foaming with cow parsley and hawthorn blossom. The wedding bells are still pealing, but we are gone, swinging hands as we spring down the road, up over the ridge, to hurtle down a pot-holed track. We are effervescing. We can't stop giggling. Words gush from our mouths, like the river beside us, and with each foot-fall the cloud of wild garlic intensifies, filling our nostrils and purging our lungs.

For seventy glorious minutes we are alone, indulging in the first minutes of our new life together: splashing through mud and puddles, ducking under ash-branches, jumping over brooks alive with frogs, winding our way to the cider-orchard, where our friends and family will await us.

That was David and I, the year 2008, the beginning of our lives together. We both tolled 30 in the grand game of life. We both left our long-term jobs, David as a management consultant for Accenture, I as an Ecologist for the Royal Society for the Protection of Birds (RSPB). Our objective: nature conservation and adventure. Destination: the world. Exactly what adventure and what type of nature-conservation was not altogether clear. So we ran. What else would we do? We both adore running. It's what we do to relax, re-charge, go wild and ignite ideas. I think the lure is the freedom. Every vista holds something new; a peregrine free-falling through the sky; a hare dashing over the hilltop. Thoughts flow and ebb through your mind, sometimes conscious, sometimes lurking beyond. They move in time with the rhythm of your footfall and the exhalation of your breath. It's as if your senses are freshly-tuned, tingling and raw, as your feet feel the ground beneath you and the wind and rain pulls at your body. The boundary between your physical self and the land blurs as you sense its form, its contours, its being. Your thoughts move between the earth and another world, and ideas form.

Run-fuelled ideas bubbled through our heads. Of an epic, human-powered adventure, in which we would push our minds and bodies to the extreme, leap barriers, forge through the unthinkable; a first – something that would make our eyes water, and the world's. And the scene for this adventure? It had to be South America, the continent I've been entranced by all my life.

I remember standing among towers of dishes, pans and saucepans, and forests of felled cutlery cross-hatching the draining board. I was the 14-year-old dishwasher at the local pub. My hands worked through the bubbles and my eyes gazed through the steamy window, but I didn't see the swallows slicing through a cloud of midges. I saw trunks as wide as houses disappearing into the sky; an iridescent tree-frog carrying her baby tadpole on her back; giant river-otters cavorting in a stream the colour of tea, and a clan of hoatzin birds ruminating on a platter of leaves. I saw the Amazon, and for as long as I can remember, I have been obsessed.

So the setting would be South America. But to reach it, there was just the matter of a few thousand miles of ocean to cross. As our means of traversing it, David chose 'the sailing ship.' As my maiden name was Land, and I had never set foot on a sailing boat, the prospect of living for weeks on end at the whim of a savage and unpredictable ocean terrified me. But there appeared no way of avoiding my fate, for David had grown up sailing, and saw nothing unusual about living on water. I would just have to stiffen my upper lip, grow some webbed feet and get on with it.

Being a practical chap, he decided that a small, ocean-worthy fibreglass boat would suit our needs. So we streamed out of the Exe Estuary, in the south-west of England, aboard our 73-year-old whale of a wooden hulk. *Lista Light* couldn't have been further away from David's ideal craft, but he had fallen head-over-heels for her. I understood. She was utterly beautiful, even though the dizzying web of rope suspended above our heads filled me with horror. How on earth would I ever work out what was what or what did what?

But if Lista Light lacks ease and manoeuvrability, she more than outshines her modern rivals in pedigree. She's 50 feet long, 15 feet wide and 35 tonnes. In short, David reassured me that we had a whale of a beast, fit for fighting whatever the sea and weather gods might hurl at us. So, to keep fit, I strapped a discarded rowing machine to her deck, filled her holds with lemons and oranges (to ward off scurvy and the departure of our teeth, a possibility to which we were sensitive, David's aunt having succumbed on her pregnant passage to Cape Town), and David fitted solar panels to her cabin-top and invested in a wind-come-wake turbine to create energy.

We sailed thousands of miles: to the Caribbean, surveying the eastern-most islands for breeding seabirds, writing an atlas about their populations, and then bursting into the Pacific through the Panama Canal, bound for the Galapagos, Easter Island and ultimately South America. In April 2011 we dropped anchor into the frigid and opalescent waters of southern Chile. Along the way we had been struck by lightning, dismasted and grounded. David had been imprisoned and I had survived open surgery to my bum on a pitching southern sea. David, being of Scottish descent and from a long line of sailing folk, phlegmatically confirmed these to be 'Unfortunate Incidents.' I called them 'Appointments with

Death'. But amid the heart-stopping fear was sublime beauty: the largest animal to have lived on earth, the blue whale, gracefully diving below our home; white-tailed tropic birds cackling above our heads in the turquoise sky of the Atlantic Ocean, and my first meeting with a flying fish, slap-bang in the centre of my right eyeball, in a hail of scales, as I read by torch-light.

It took us three years to sail to South America. Now that we had reached our goal, we were ready to begin the greatest adventure of our lives. And a couple of weeks later we finally decided what it would be: we would run, run the entire continent, with and for wildlife. Through our feet, we would connect people around the world to South America's extraordinary biodiversity, and prove that with small steps one can tackle seemingly insurmountable challenges. It's not too late to protect the world's remaining unspoilt ecosystems, but time is running out.

BARILOCHE

CHILE

PUERTO
VARAS

PUERTO
MONTT

DARWIN'S RHEA
Rhea pennata

COYHAIQUE

ARGENTINA

COCHRANE

ATLANTIC
OCEAN

PACIFIC OCEAN

VILLA O'HIGGINS

EL CHALTÉN

PUERTO
NATALES

TAPI AIKE

CULPEO FOX
Pseudalopex culpaeu

PUNTA
ARENAS

CHILE

ARGENTINA

N

CABO
FROWARD

Map 3 – Our Running Route through
Chile & Southern Argentina

That evening we finally saw the animals we had been searching for: three huemul quietly grazing the slopes of the pass

Huemul
Hippocamelus
bisculus

2 Running on Water

If you could design the worst training plan imaginable to prepare for a long-distance run, what would it look like? (asked David) You would limit the amount of training miles the competitors could run. Ensure they were physically exhausted by the time they arrived at the start-line. Perhaps you would remove elements of their diet, prevent them from training with the equipment they would be carrying, and distract them from training with hundreds of other tasks.

Not only did we have to prepare for the expedition: we also had the sticky issue of finding a home for our boat while we skipped off to run the continent. After much investigation, it transpired that the only safe haven would be Uruguay, on the other side of South America, some 3,000 nautical miles away, through the most tumultuous seas in the world, from our current position in Puerto Montt on the coast of Chile. Thus we set off on a four-month voyage, down the coast of Chile, through the Beagle Channel, and up to a muddy creek in Uruguay.

Adaptation being the rock of human survival, we felt we could make a plan. We were also convinced that one doesn't have to run 26.2 miles to train for a marathon. Not to say you can't, but you don't have to. Somehow we needed to be physically prepared, with flexible joints, well-exercised heart and lungs, and preferably the right conformation of muscle-tissue. Physiotherapists know that the majority of running injuries are to do with muscle and vital ligament condition, rather than cardio-vascular fitness. The latter affects your times, but you won't even finish if you get an injury.

We found a seven-by-six-foot clear space of deck on which we could stretch. It was easier in port, yet in all but the grimmest conditions it was also possible under sail. Whenever we anchored, we tried to set off on foot into the hills, but often this was made impossible by a lattice-work of impenetrable shrubs and trees, whose limbs twisted and coiled into knots of vegetation that smothered entire islands and rendered crawling, let alone running, almost impossible. So we would interval-train on a small section of beach. If there was no beach, we took to the decks of our little ship and ran in a tight circle. It looked demented, guaranteed, but it was reasonable training, given a change of direction now and then. This we interspersed with skipping, which is fantastic for core-stability, creating a thoroughly knackering training-session on, not in, the comfort of our own home.

For a couple of days we anchored in Chile's Pumalin National Park, and on one of the mornings I sat in the grass outside the reserve office with my laptop on my knees, willing an internet connection. Finally an email downloaded. It was from Ruari, a mate from home, whose friend, Jonno Gibbons, was a barefoot-running coach. Apparently he would be happy to give us some tips.

My initial thought was, 'No way!' The very concept of going barefoot sounded suicidal to our goal of running a continent. Years of being measured and fitted for school shoes, on the premise of providing maximum support, had rooted deep into my subconscious. The idea was abandoned. But on arrival in the muddy, terrapin-filled backwater of Uruguay that became our temporary home, I eyed a book that had remained forgotten in our bookshelf: *Born to Run,* by Christopher McDougall. Stepping into its world, I was blown away. McDougall asserts that humans are innate long-distance runners, evolved to out-pace our prey with 'springy legs, twiggy torsos, sweat glands, hairless skin, vertical bodies that retain less heat - no wonder we're the world's greatest marathoners.' With my initial doubts cast aside, I hastily wrote to Jonno, explaining how reading *Born to Run* had been like finding a secret bible.

Jonno described how cushioned running-shoes prevent the 200,000 nerve-endings in the sole of each foot from sensing the forces acting on the body, (proprioception) causing runners to heel-strike. He offered to assess our running techniques, instructing us to send across some video-clips. The results were damning. 'In a nutshell, you're both heel-striking, have slow cadence, poor posture, braking with every step. Potential for injury is high … Your feet will be weak due to constricted shoes and calves and your Achilles shortened due to heel-lift'.

There seemed only one cure for our disastrous state; we had to learn how to run, and we had three months to pull it off. It was no longer a matter of putting one foot in front of the other. We were one-year-olds again, learning – and yet I never thought you had to *learn* to run in the first place. We began thinking about every footfall: short and quick, running tall, looking ahead, maintaining loose wrists, ankles and shoulders. How do you keep your ankles loose?! I found myself running with my tongue out, rigid with concentration, along dusty gravel tracks, oblivious to the creased eyes peering at me from lone farm-shacks, or the driver of the 1950s motorbike splashing the contents of milk-churns from its little wooden trailer, as people craned their necks to watch me. I aimed on hitting the ground with my toes. Apparently this wasn't right, either. Jonno warned me that if I tried to land on the balls of my feet I would over plantarflex, murdering my calves.

Running barefoot-style in cushioned trainers was proving impossible. So we ripped the insoles out of our old shoes and started mixing runs with short, shoeless sessions, only minutes at first. The Uruguayan grandparents *Primavera* (Spring) and *Angelito* (Little Angel), who lived in a small stone building on the river-bank above our boat, wrapped in woollen jumpers and hats, looked on in horror as the two crazy *gringos* padded barefoot over their frosty, thorny pasture, ready for the daily training-session. We avoided the desolate, sandy beach that lay half a mile to the south, whose dunes were swathed in shimmering pampa grasses and haunted by long-winged harriers hunting the frogs and snakes which lurked in the damp hollows. Instead we chose the age-old stony tracks that wove through gently-undulating arable fields and eucalyptus plantations. Hard ground provided better feedback from our foot sensors, reminding us to adjust our technique on our six- to sixteen-mile training sessions.

As the weeks passed, we followed drills of bouncing on the spot at 180 beats per minute (think Masai warrior – odd sight), walking everywhere barefoot and 'third world' squatting. But it wasn't going to be a doddle; as our bodies had adapted to 34 years of running incorrectly, it would take time to re-train them, and our minds.

A boost arrived one morning when Primavera shouted over to us from the river bank that a parcel had come from our sponsor Vivobarefoot. Inside the box were six pairs of perfectly-formed, bendy little shoes. They were as light as feathers and as snug as slippers: soon we were floating on air, springing down the road like new-born lambs. Jonno's words fell into place: everything felt simpler, the shoes were a revelation, and the thought of running a continent barefoot was beginning to seem possible.

Meanwhile, David researched survival kit for extreme climates and remote and wild areas. Hurricane-force wind, hailstones the size of bricks, relentless rain, -22°C to +40°C temperatures, snow, ice and near-100 per cent humidity would be part of everyday life. We would be running unsupported, so we had to be completely independent, carrying all our equipment. We would also have to stave off infections from parasites while camping and running in rainforests and swamps.

The planets were aligning, the start date was approaching; kit was arriving thick and fast in Uruguay, whence we posted or sent it on by bus to a network of friends pinpointed along our overland route. Extra water-filters, vitamins, first aid, new shoes, socks, tops and shorts were pre-dropped in Chile and Argentina. We opted for two distinct sets of equipment: one for the cold, wet south, the other for the hot, dry north.

We called our adventure *The 5000-Mile Project*. This was the distance David calculated to be the length of South America. Being sailors, we work in nautical miles, with one degree on an ocean chart equating to 60 miles. David added up the degrees from the Cape Froward to the Caribbean Sea, with a healthy dollop of mileage added on for the meandering roads and tracks we would have to follow.

Since the main object of the adventure was to draw attention to the great biodiversity of the continent, science and education were woven into the expedition. We created the Big Toe Classroom, producing lesson-plans, blogs, games and quizzes, question-and-answer sessions and an option for live chats, so that schools could join us, vicariously meeting the wildlife, people and landscapes we had encountered along the way. The run would become a 'mega transect' – an enormously long line along which we would record the birds and animals we saw.

The name *The 5,000-Mile Project* also gave us an opt-out clause; if our bodies packed up, we could find some other human-powered way of getting from one end of the continent to the other. Through all the long hours of training burnt the perpetual, gnawing unknown. Could we really manage this? Would our bodies cope with relentless day-on-day running in hostile environments? Our families were deeply concerned, reminding us that we weren't athletes, and that our project was foolhardy, unnecessary and darn-right dangerous.

They were right. We were just every-now-and-then enthusiasts who had a lust for running in wild places. We had competed in fell-runs, but taking on marathons day-after-day was something else. No one ran for a year on end. Professionals trained furiously, but with planned breaks to rest and rejuvenate their bodies. How could we avoid injury? Unease racked us.

One night the words of an SAS friend seeped into my mind: 'You will never die'. We would be living and running for weeks on end in the Amazon among wild animals, potentially-hostile locals and life-threatening diseases. He was adamant that, against the odds, we would survive. I must admit, until entering South America, I hadn't considered that we might die. But in the months to come, his words often resonated, as we confronted one of the most threatening challenges of our lives.

David was the chief engineer of our two-man team, and the problem of how we would carry all our gear was consuming him. I would catch him in his sleep with an outstretched arm, fingers measuring the size of the bars that would support our belongings. We knew the American ultra-runner Dean Karnazas pushed a pram across the States, while Britain's Rosie Swale Pope pulled a four-wheeled trailer (which converted into a bed) on her epic round-the-world run. We reasoned that pushing would mean that our arms were engaged, rather than doing their job of propelling our bodies forward – even if the idea of hurtling down a hill behind a liberated pram presented a certain attraction! Thus David focused his research on pulling. Curiously, after a full Internet search, nothing popped up on the screen. Walking trailers, biking trailers, even skiing trailers were all present, but not running trailers.

While David was grappling with the specifics of transport, I left the laptop over which I had been hunched all day and lowered myself into the kayak to go ashore for a midnight run. Mud squeezed between my toes as I padded into a wall of darkness. The farm track was familiar to me now, even in its cloak of black. The gravel that had been spiky and sore when we first started running unshod was now like pumice, gently massaging my feet.

I didn't feel like running. I was stiff, and expedition logistics filled my head like cotton wool. I hardly heard a barn owl's blood-curdling screech, scarcely felt the earth beneath my feet. Even the night that cocooned me had faded against my thoughts. Then a wire suddenly whipped across my stomach. I gasped at the electric fence dangling at my feet and tuned back into the world.

I reached the T-junction, the start of the run. The rain had cleared, and toads and cicadas were tuning up: whining, croaking, belching, clicking. My feet switched between pebbles and grit, damp earth and cushions of grass. Without sight, I felt my way forward, inhaling the heady fragrance of moist soil and eucalyptus. Suddenly a light flashed in the bush at my side; another light winked at the top of the hill, then another in the herbs by my foot: three milky green lights that turned on and off, off and on. Was someone signalling to me?

But it was nothing to do with me. As I ran up the hill, the track exploded into a supernatural light display. Hundreds of fireflies were taking to the air, flaunting their luminescent bums at their suitors in the scrub below. The combination of rain and the velvet night had transformed the dreary diurnal livery of the beetles into the dazzling costumes of dancing queens. I was bewitched, flying through the night in the glittering trails of these enchantresses; watching and inhaling a completely different world from the one I had run through yesterday.

Back on board, David was still plagued by the prospect of creating a trailer. He knew that it had to be ultra-light, collapsible and packable, super-strong and efficient, with zero downward load on the runner, and with minimal drag on many different surfaces. But how would he fulfil these criteria?

Then one day Sandy and Max miraculously turned up in our hidden creek, half the world away from where we had first met them. They are an extraordinary couple, who choose to follow a contrary course through life: one that is utterly sublime. They have lived together in their 40-foot floating castle since they first built it and set sail from Australia a good handful of decades ago. Together, they have wandered, watched and worked their way round and round the world.

Their arrival was impeccably timed for solving our quandary – for Max is an engineer, and an amazing one at that. Having considered the problem for a few minutes, and after making a few sketches, he gently smiled and stood back a little, straightening his spine. 'So you want low friction?' he asked in soft Australian. 'And it's got to take the pain away from you and allow the body to twist in motion? You want to be able to fix it anywhere? You don't want it stolen? And the expedition is about having a low impact on the environment? Bamboo and bike tyres: that's what you need!'

We all paused. Bamboo made perfect sense for many reasons. First, it's immensely tough, with superb strength-to-weight ratios. Second, it's available everywhere, not just cheap but free, and subsequently unattractive to a thief. Third, it's easy to work with. In many parts of the world it's an invasive crop or an abundant native species; either way, using it has a low ecological impact. The idea of the trailer was born.

In minutes David had a prototype mashed together with some old wood, bungee clips and a lifejacket harness. Long bicycle inner-tubes would connect the bamboo platform to the runner's rucksack belt, ensuring that the trailer (rather than David or I) absorbed any shocks, and that the runner could move with free arms. Our old bike wheels and forks would be lashed to the platform and our bags secured to that. Simplicity was the key. There would be no expensive parts, and we would be able to repair the contraption anywhere in South America.

As the weeks sped past, our preparations grew ever more frantic. But no matter how meticulously we planned, one spectre threatened to overshadow the entire expedition: violence. Everyone we spoke to warned us that we would be unlikely to get out of South America alive. Venezuela and Brazil were nestled at the top of the polls for the most villainous countries in the world. Added to this was the fact that Hugo Chavez, President of Venezuela, had announced elections, sending the country into turmoil.

We desperately re-consulted the maps, trying to work out alternative routes that would allow us to avoid Brazil and Venezuela. It was futile. The southern section of our run was straightforward, with Chile and Argentina filling the bulk of it. If we insisted on going through the Amazon (which I did), we would have to take the only road that ran south-north through the world's largest rainforest – and that would pass through both Brazil's and Venezuela's bad-lands (See Map 1).

Our original plan had been to run from north to south, but late in the day we decided to turn the route on its head. Rather than starting on the Caribbean in Venezuela, we would begin in the south. This would allow us to complete the first part of the expedition in the relative safety of Chile, Argentina and Bolivia. By the time we reached the crime hot-spots of the north, election furore should have died down in Venezuela. Besides, our kit would be battered, making us less of a target, and we would be more savvy to dangers.

Rotating the route translated to us hitting Cape Froward in under four weeks and plunging into a Patagonian winter. When we checked the weather, it was a balmy -2°C, expected to reach -5°C by the following morning. Instead of basking in the tropical sun on a Caribbean beach, we would have Antarctic winds boring into our bones. A serious kit and logistics rethink was required.

Thousands of families huddled in Buenos Aires' central bus-station. School-holiday traffic, added to snow-falls blocking Andean passes and a Uruguayan airliner belly-flopping, had created chaos and enormous delays. Ticket-booths shut down. The army was billeted in for crowd-control. A slow hand-clap rippled around the station. The chances of reaching Cape Froward by 28 July, the first day of the London Olympics and our elected start-date for our own Olympics, were rapidly disappearing. It wasn't just the Olympics timing that mattered: we realised that our preparations could continue ad infinitum, but we had neither the budget nor enough life to procrastinate any longer! We had been away from home for five years already. The run would add another year onto that, and the sail home at least a year on top of that. With thoughts of starting a family and achieving life-goals, we had to get on.

In a series of truncated bus-journeys, and in an increasingly foul-tempered semi-torpor, we crawled south and then west. We were carrying huge quantities of heavy luggage, including two bicycle wheels, which had not yet been fashioned into our trailer. On top of this, we found out that the cold-weather kit we were due to pick up, which was critical to survival in a Patagonian freezer, had gone AWOL.

A flicker of hope shone through the proceedings when David's sister, Fiona, who was living in Chile, unearthed a coat I could use until another materialised. She also decided to accompany us to Cape Froward and stand in as camera woman, to record the first steps of our run. On 23 July, we at last reached Punta Arenas, the southern-most city of the continent, 90 miles north of our start-line (See Map 3). With my voice hanging by a thread, we endeavoured to talk to BBC Radio about the impending expedition and our concerns.

'We have no idea whether our bodies will stand the constant battering of running every day, day-on-day, while pulling a trailer,' I said. 'We're really worried that we've focussed too much on the kit, the education, blogs, website, wildlife-surveys … everything but the run and preparing our bodies. Our bodies are totally untested, and to top it all, to reach the start line, we have to ford three freezing rivers, fed by glacial melt-water. If we don't get it right, they'll mark the end of our expedition and potentially us. I'm scared!'

Decrepit windscreen wipers fought against the whirring snowflakes that emerged like spectres from the blackness. The amber lights of Punta Arenas and the clutch of scattered settlements had long since expired. Along with Fiona, David and I huddled together in the shell of a rattling mini-bus. Everyone had alighted except us and a small, gnarled man in the front with the driver. Too soon he announced the end of the road. Our numb fingers grabbed the heap of bags, bits of trailer and food, and we watched the bus disappear into the distance.

We stood covered in snowflakes and by the enormity of what lay ahead. There was no time to linger. Practicalities took centre stage; we had to find somewhere to stay, fill our bellies and get warm. We crunched through snow. Following the road through bare woodland, we found a seemingly-abandoned *cabaña*. 'The owners must have long since gone north,' I said. 'No one's going to come down here on holiday at this time of the year. I doubt they could physically get here, anyway.'

We climbed the wire fence and searched for a camp-site. A shed looked perfect, so under the loom of our head-torches we assembled our tent beneath its roof, away from the thickest of the snow, and started cooking pasta on the petrol stove. With food in our stomachs, we slipped out into the night to scrub our teeth. Countless stars twinkled from an immense southern sky. Later, huddled together in our down sleeping-bags, three in a two-man tent, we listened to the wind creaking through the trees and released our thoughts to ride through our dreams.

Our plan was to complete this first section to the start-point in 'mountain-marathon' style: as quick and as light as possible, taking four days to run there and back. We would carry only kit crucial to survival in three small rucksacks. Our most pressing concern was to find Cape Froward. We had no maps, and Google Earth showed no path. The only directions we had – and they were pretty sketchy – came from an unidentified man who had posted a blog on the internet after walking the headlands one summer. We were worried by the comments of a friend, who had once lived down there, and explained that there was no real path, and that what we were trying to do was impossible in mid-winter. Also, a hurricane-force storm was forecast in five days' time. We had four days to find the Cape and to sprint like hell away.

Evergreen southern-beech woods clung to the teeth of wave-cut platforms. Stunted and wind-torn *bandera* trees marked the most exposed promontories, bending their resolve to the 'furious fifty' winds that had sculpted their branches to topiary. We were reaching the end of the earth, a savage yet stunning place. It surrounded us on all sides – and we knew that this exceptional wilderness represented the very essence of our expedition.

We followed a path through forest high onto a hump-backed hill. Only the very tops of the stunted *guaitecas* cypresses nosed out of the snow. It seemed amazing that these trees can survive being buried alive, that they and the southern-beech, in their quiet, lichen-encrusted hangers below, had evolved to flourish perfectly in this hostile terrain. At times the snow clutched at our waists, with each step sucking huge quantities of our diminishing energy. The hoof-print of a deer, the endangered *huemul* (about the size of a fallow), had barely indented the soft snow; the hind appeared to be going our way. I compared its print to the laboured trenches we were excavating, and realized how ill equipped we were to survive in such a wild environment.

Further tracks revealed other residents in whose home we were trespassing. Two sets of huge paw-prints spelled the passage of a puma. He was no doubt prospecting for an easy meal washed up on the strand-line. Next a line of *chungungo* or sea-otter's prints. The last time we saw this guy, he was floating on his back, carefully excavating the prickly pink flesh of a sea urchin from between his paws.

Our first river-crossing was a doddle; a tree straddled the stream's narrow width, allowing us to crawl across without wet feet. The second wasn't in the notes and proved deeper than on first impressions. We scoured the river for an alternative crossing-point, but nothing was visible. So we pulled off our trousers and dumped our packs on our heads, allowing the icy water to lap around our tummy-buttons.

The third river was a monster. Snow blanketed its sides. Our thermometer read 0°C. A blizzard tore at our faces. We could barely see the opposite bank of the metallic slick of water that rushed menacingly past us. We followed the river's course for half a mile, trying to find a narrower section, and then returned to where we had started.

'So this is it……?' My feeble, half-hearted question was whipped from my mouth by the horizontal snow. I knew crossing there was our only option, but the reality was hideous. David was already unpacking the rope, walking it in long loops, checking that it would run smoothly. We stuffed our kit into two dry bags. 'OK, I'll go in first,' David volunteered. He was the strongest swimmer, had the greatest chance of success. 'I'll swim hard to the other side,' he said. 'Then I'll pull over the bag with my clothes, the safety blanket and stove.' With that he stripped off, looped the rope round his waist and leapt in.

We fed the rope out through mittened fingers, watching his shoulders and neck recede through the snow that stuck to our eyeballs. Suddenly he was out: yelling above the wind, scrambling for the rope, pulling at the bag with the rush of adrenaline that surged through his body and snatching at clothes to insulate his freezing frame.

Next it was my turn. My fingers and toes were already ice-blocks. I could barely open the dry bag that David had shot back across the river for us to fill again. Hesitantly, I started to remove layers of clothes; too soon I was naked, my flesh made raw by the freezing wind and snow. As I stepped into the river, a flame of pain scorched my body. 'This is agony!' I howled. 'Oh my GOD!'

The rope tugged at my waist, my feet dug into the gravelly river bed, scrabbling to keep my body above the torrent, but soon the icy water licked around my breasts and I was swimming. There was no sanctuary. David was so far away, I could barely hear his voice above the roar of the wind. I felt myself slow down; a voice was whispering, instructing me to stop: 'Give in to the water, feel its tranquillity.'

It must have been only for a split-second, because suddenly I felt the snatch of the rope around my waist, 'Swim! You have to keep swimming! Don't stop!

SWIM!' I could just make out the words David was yelling. I burst forward, terrified of the voice in my head, terrified that I had listened. My arms flailed in the water, crazed strokes, desperate to rid myself of the river's icy claws. Then I felt pebbles scraping over my knees, I could stand up, I had done it! I crawled out, shaken and freezing. David enveloped me in the survival blanket. Fiona was already posting the dry bag across, and within minutes David had it open and was pulling socks and clothes over my blue limbs.

Finally it was Fiona's turn. She stripped and crammed everything into the dry bag, willing her hands to work, as she tied it to her rope. We started pulling the bag across as she threw the loop at the end of the rope over her body. Then she was off, belting across the river, as if her life depended upon it – which it did.

We could still feel the effect of that nude, glacial swim hours later. My fingers and toes were white-tipped and my lips purple. I was suffering the effects the most, partly because I was still locked in the clutches of a pestilent cold, partly because my circulation is rubbish at the best of times, and partly because my borrowed jacket was totally inadequate: rather than repelling water, it was wicking it into my freezing core.

'Here, get this down you.' David pressed a bowl of steaming milk into my hands.

Losing no time, we started south-west, picking our way inland over headlands, crawling through stunted cliff-top woodlands or wading through snow in the saddles of hills. The jagged shore-line was our reference: as long as we followed it, we would reach Cape Froward; but often this was impossible, with the land dropping vertically into the sea. Occasionally we would stumble across a path and follow the hoof- or paw-prints that had made it. Sometimes it became strong and was clearly used by a large number of animals, but often it would peter out. Then it was the turn of the compasses swinging around our necks to keep us on course, until we joined the sea again, to skate over wave-polished pebble-beaches and clamber over boulders and the carcases of wind-torn trees.

The fourth and final river was thankfully a mere wading effort. Now accustomed to the drill, we stripped off to the waist, clutched our rucksacks on our heads and gingerly stepped across.

Winter days in Patagonia are short. We had hoped to have reached Cape Froward by the end of the second day, but time was evaporating. We stumbled over rocks in the gloom, determined to cover as many miles as possible. The roots above our heads provided a finger- hold as we slid on a slimy, algae-smothered ledge above the snapping sea. Suddenly my foot shot from under me and I plunged into the icy water. Hands grabbed at my shoulders and wrenched my sodden, salty body from the waves. It was becoming dangerously dark, and I was seriously cold. We badly needed somewhere to camp, and so started to search in earnest on the hill behind us. Fiona and I clambered up it, pushing away snow-covered foliage that whipped at our heads. Meanwhile David prospected down below on the beach.

'It's no good,' he said, 'there's nothing down there. We'll have to sleep here, in this clearing on the hill.'

Our sleep was predictably awful. All night long we wriggled and writhed in an attempt to prevent ourselves falling into a heap at the bottom of the tent. I was freezing. I felt as if icicles had rooted into my body. There was no way I could sleep. Fiona felt me shivering. It was sometime near midnight when she crawled out to start the stove, heating some snow. We sipped hot chocolate, and then she filled our water bottle with boiling water, and I clutched it to my tummy and slumped into a few hours of sleep.

We all sighed with relief as the first soft colours of dawn snuck through the tent. At least now the ambient temperature would begin to rise. We mixed some oats, raisins, milk powder and water for breakfast. Food stocks were already dangerously low. We had been careful only to consume the allotted portion for each meal, but this proved woefully inadequate. I had based the number of meals on the portions indicated on the packets of dried pasta and rice. But these must have been designed for a vertically-challenged, chair-bound granny, not for three freezing walkers, burning through energy reserves at a worryingly quick rate. Even with the addition of packet-soups, we soon found that eight meal-portions barely sufficed for three.

On the bright side, if all went according to plan, we would only have to survive one further night before returning to Punta Arenas and re-stocking there. But that was where our optimism departed. We had four freezing rivers awaiting us on our return; my cold was turning into bronchitis and in two days a forecast storm would hit us.

We brushed away thick snow that had fallen on the tent during the night and quickly packed. As we rounded the final headland, at last we saw it, between curtains of falling snow: a cross marking the tip of South America and the start of our expedition. Standing above the frothing waves and shouting through the wind, David verified our GPS position. It was Sunday, 28 July 2012, the day a shot from the Olympic gun was set to resound through the streets of London.

'We're at 53' 53. 5 south and 71' 6 west,' David told the small camera that Fiona fixed in front of him. 'This is the tip of South America, the end of the landmass of the continent, and we can go no further. There's a marker on the hill. You can't see it, because of thick snow, but really we've got to start running now.' And with that, we started.

'Hooray!' I shrieked into the wind, 'South America, we're coming.'

At last we were travelling north. Our progress was erratic, as we waded through snow drifts and slid over boulders. In the evening we recorded how many miles we had walked, how many miles we had run barefoot and how many miles we had completed in the bare-foot and 'transition' shoes (running shoes with a very slight heel designed to help the transition to barefoot running). We planned to keep recording these details every single day of the expedition, along with the mean temperature, camp site, running surface, weather and bird count.

We had a day to ford all four rivers and to run to San Isidro, the lighthouse that marked the start of the path. Under a sliver of moon we phone-casted to our audio sponsor, who would deliver our first message to the world. The words would form the start of our story, from the snow-laden depths of a Chilean wilderness.

Our immediate need was to return to re-provision in Punta Arenas. The plan was to catch a lift back to the city, drop Fiona off, buy food, return by bus to the exact spot where we had jumped into the vehicle, and mark the spot on our GPS watch. This was crucial, to prove that we made no gain during the expedition by any means other than our own four feet.

The only vehicle we had seen in days came driving towards us, heading south – a white pick-up crammed full of people. To stop it we motioned towards the tiny silhouette of a bird in the bare branches above our head: an Austral pygmy-owl rotating its little head almost 360 degrees, apparently oblivious of us.

The driver drew to a halt by our side.

'¡Mira! Qué lindo ¿no?' (Look! How lovely, no?) we said.

'Sí, sí. ¡Qué lindo!' the passengers replied.

All eyes stared up. Suddenly, another owl flew on to the branch and without a nod or a word of greeting hopped on to the seated owl's back, and they bonked! The romance was perfunctory; seconds rather than minutes, sealed by a squawk, after which both parties fluttered into the night. Twenty minutes later the pick-up whizzed into view again, going the other way. I waved frenziedly. Recognising the owl-fanciers, the guy in the passenger seat flashed a smile and pushed open his door. 'Jump on up!' he said as he helped to haul us and our bags into the back with some dogs. 'Hey, what are you doing all the way down here?'

'We've just started running… South America,' I said. He looked quizzically at me for a second. 'Run? South America?' We nodded. 'You're crazy!' he laughed and jumped back into the cab. We made a quick GPS fix, huddled into the deep coats of the huskies and screeched off into the night.

An odour that was a mix of fruits, spices and must, wafted through our running steps

Humboldt's Hog-nosed Skunk
Conepatus humboldtii

3 The Kindness of Strangers

The trailer's skeleton lay scattered over the ice-rink road that would carry us north. Two bike wheels, various *colihue* (solid Chilean bamboo) lengths, David's red-and-black rucksack that had accompanied him up and down dales since a nipper, old bike inner tubes and one bar of relic steel (from our random stash on the boat) were the components of our life-support wagon.

It took about two hours to lash the segments together with the inner tubes. Then we piled the three bursting dry-bags onto the bamboo platform, and stuffed water, snacks and binoculars into our rucksacks and onto our backs. The GPS watch marked the point where we had caught the lift to Punta Arenas, trading wheels for feet. The orange beast was born and we began pounding the road with our trailer. We looked less 'born to run', more 'born to fail', as we slid and jolted over a thick layer of ice. The rucksack rubbed on my neck, and the soles and arches of our feet quickly began to ache.

Over-grazed pastures, sliced up by lines of redundant fences, merged into the grey of the road, which washed into the black ink of the sea beyond. Trees and shrubs were sparse. Those that had fought for a foothold were torn into bizarre, wind-whipped shapes. Not a soul stirred around the tin houses under the flutter of proud Magellan flags. A small bird was sent rocketing through the air by the wind.

Pulling the trailer was brutal – so much tougher than I had imagined. Every footstep was a battle. Even the hills appeared to jeer at the improbable pair as we puffed up and then winced down them. We were carrying far too much weight: we had to consolidate our kit, but couldn't imagine shedding anything – it was our lifeline. At least for the first three miles. Then I watched from behind as the trailer rolled over a boulder and split in two. 'Shite.......!' I yelled. David was fuming, 'I knew it couldn't take all that weight. Crazy carrying it all. All the work I've invested in it, for what? Bloody thing!' But within less than an hour he had re-strapped our wagon and we were on the road again.

We managed 16 miles that first day, nursing the bandaged trailer along and avoiding the potholes and rocks that threatened to snap it in two again. The road was hemmed by fencing and *'No pasar, recinto privado'* (keep out, private area) signs. This was something we hadn't considered, assuming that we would easily find places to pitch the tent each night. I grew to loathe those signs and the ranks of hostile fences that barred us from resting our exhausted bodies.

So on the first night we slept by a fly-tip, near heaps of plastic bags and shards of glass. A ginger dog appeared, sitting by our side as we devoured our meal, damp eyes pleading us to share it with him. The next evening we spotted a small house on the horizon. I summoned all my courage and finest *Chileno* Spanish to apply for a piece of the garden in which to make our home. The owners said 'Yes', and another hound turned up, this time sleek and cream, but with the same hunger.

In the morning Chilean flamingos flew in long skeins along the coastline and Magellanic oystercatchers screeched on the cobbled beach, their flame-red beaks flashing in perpetual chatter. Even a willow tree shuddered with life under the weight of over 100 black-chinned siskins.

On the third day we ran into Punta Arenas, the small city which we seemed destined to return. Plastic bags thrummed in the wind, impaled on barbed-wire fencing. Lorries piled high with rubbish sped past in clouds of debris, losing half their cargo to the sea and air. A pack of dogs hurtled towards us. I snarled, baring my teeth and growling. They slunk away.

Our hips and knees were groaning. Pain, exhaustion, filth and hunger had sharpened our senses, while adrenalin extinguished the pain, as we sped along the choked city roads. Chileans are better known for their reserve and stoicism than for their charisma, but as we ran past, they shouted and hooted. Then suddenly we saw the city centre. 'We've done it'! I shouted. 'We've run over 100 kilometres'. We had bagged Punta Arenas, our first milestone. David was smiling, grabbing me, elated. We sunk onto a bench. Further movement seemed impossible. But soon we mustered the energy to drink, eat, wash and sleep; fulfilling the most basic of human needs. And never did they seem so good.

> My feet are agonising. Shots of pain ricochet through my knees, my thighs and each tiny joint in my toes. My face is numb, my fingers ice-tipped. Water is streaming down me like I'm a river bed, filling me up, scouring and saturating me. There are no edges now between the wind, the rain and me. I'm oozing into the night, invisible, except for the pain of it all and the flashing red light from David's head torch that I'm following. I'm numb to the cars and lorries; the tyres that scorch past centimetres from my feet, barely clearing the trailer, smothering my legs in oily spume. But one thing is certain, one thing above everything else; we will never give up. We never do give up.

We had left Punta Arenas too late, but we had to keep running to get out of the city. In the flickering lights of the passing traffic we could just make out the landscape around us: sprawling housing-estates and high fences circled fields and conifer plantations. Even the grassy laybys were too steep to camp on. I channelled my hope into a solitary light shining in the distance. It belonged to a bungalow in a modest garden surrounded by fields. David was uneasy about approaching it. Why should the occupants allow us to sleep anywhere near their house? But I was adamant.

I crossed the road, heart in mouth, and knocked at the white plastic door. Music was playing. Several people were moving about inside. A tall, teenaged lad came to the door. He smirked at my Spanish, eyeing my dripping, filthy clothes. Others came to stare. Their eyes insinuated, 'She must be poor, feral, perhaps a gypsy or some other outcast.' They were all shaking their heads. 'No, no, you can't stay here. You must return to Punta Arenas. You'll find somewhere there,' and they turned to close the door. I jumped forward, my fingers clawing at it. 'But we can't return. It's miles. We're exhausted,' I pleaded. 'We're running the length of South America, hoping to be the first in the world to do it. It's only for one night. We have a small tent and will be gone tomorrow.'

I was running out of steam, grasping the futility of it all. I hung my head. Silence. Their mouths gaped. Their faces were stunned. Eyes ran over the odd, dishevelled *gringo* in front of them. I started to turn away. Then something extraordinary happened: the mother nodded, 'OK, you can stay here, over there beyond the cars.' I thanked her profusely, elation overwhelming me.

Now that we were friends, the teenager came out and showed us the sleeping spot. It was not very appetising, being gravel plastered with dog-turds. We eyed a paddock just beyond and hopped across the barbed wire fence. Perhaps it wasn't their land, but at least they knew we were there and we could probably plead ignorance to an irate farmer.

David untied his shoelaces and yelped in pain as he eased his swollen feet, which were the size of turnips, out of his shoes. He was seriously worried. 'Perhaps I've broken a bone? Something's not right. I'm worried I'm permanently damaging my feet; that I won't be able to complete the run.' He swallowed another Ibuprofen and a Paracetamol. We were both knocking them back. We don't usually take pills, but they seemed to be working, because our various twinges would subside after a couple of miles into the running day.

We had been wearing our barefoot shoes full-time, and we started to question the wisdom of this. Perhaps they had triggered the foot problems – too many miles without heels too soon? Then there was the trailer. There was nothing natural about it. Primeval man was a natural barefoot runner, but he wasn't pulling a trailer. Our bodies had to incline forward to drag the extra load, with the angle even further exaggerated up hills. This was at odds with the tall, straight, light gait of the barefoot runner that we were trying to achieve. It also significantly stressed our Achilles tendons. So we agreed that in future, when pulling the trailer, we would wear our transition trainers, which had half the heel of a normal shoe and would hopefully conter the unnatural stresses on our feet and Achilles.

We dined like kings on a pan of rice and cheese that tasted as if the gods themselves had lovingly prepared it. Two seconds later, after bundling together a pillow of jumpers, David collapsed into a torpor. Although the temperature outside was minus two degrees Celsius, we were warm and snug in our sleeping-bag, bivvy-bag, feather-jackets, fleeces, thermals and socks. After the Cape Froward expedition, David had found two sisters in Punta Arenas who agreed to stitch together both our sleeping-bags and bivvy-bags. He returned to a snowstorm of goose down, which wafted in drifts over everything in their wood-smoked room. Sitting in the centre were the unfortunate sisters, who had turned grey under the thick mat of feathers that now clung tenaciously to them. Nevertheless, our double sleeping-bag was a revelation, even if it lacked a large part of its stuffing.

The new sleeping-bag allowed me to benefit from David, an important component of a warm night's sleep. He's a six-foot-four streak of a guy, and his metabolic rate is exceptional, booting out heat in industrial proportions. I conversely have poor circulation and a near-death pulse-rate. My fingers, toes and lips frequently turn purple and stubbornly resist efforts at re-heating. Lying by the side of a human furnace proved essential to the maintenance of my own core-temperature, allowing me too to drift into a desperately-needed sleep.

The night was punctuated by barking dogs and honking traffic, and long before daylight cockerels were crowing and ducks quacking, sawing our sleep into tattered chunks. David heralded the day with a line of greenish vomit, mainly comprising Ibuprofen and Paracetamol. We were shattered, and the thought of running was horrid. Nevertheless, we eventually extracted ourselves from the tent, waved goodbyes to our hosts and trotted up the road through a moonscape of mustard-coloured tussock-grasses.

David was eyeing the side of the road, his magpie eyes glinting. He stopped by a discarded bungee-cord, picked it up and tied it around a trailer arm. In the course of the next couple of hours we cleared the road of eight bungee-cords and five inner tubes. We now had ourselves a decent set of spares.

The road joined the sea again, with huge, expectant tankers waiting to discharge their loads, mingling with small fishing vessels. Then, as if on cue, one of the illustrations at which I had been longingly gazing in our bird book walked out of its pages and into the grassland by our side: a Darwin's rhea (or ñandu in Chile) and a slightly smaller relative of the ostrich. We could have easily run straight past it, for its soft ochre, grey and white-flecked plumage perfectly merged into the steppe. Then, as if to prove how good it was at camouflage, it multiplied into three, all grazing quietly, metres from the road.

In rhea society it is the male who does most of the work once the female and any other wives have deposited their eggs in a single nest on the ground. With laying complete, the females absent-mindedly dawdle off in search of new shoots or juicy invertebrates. Meanwhile, the loyal and long-suffering male begins his incubation. Only when all his brood have hatched does he lead them out into the steppe, a group of fluffy, striped chicks, scurrying behind his three reptilian toes. He will fiercely guard his charges for at least a year, until they can fend for themselves.

In those wind-battered plains we became increasingly concerned about finding cover for the night. We'd been running alongside an *estancia* (large farm) for several miles when at last we came to elaborate gates and a three-quarter-mile drive leading to a cluster of houses and outbuildings, above which rose a coil of smoke. Should we go on running, not knowing when or if a possible camp-site might appear, or should we finish the run early, losing valuable miles that would prove difficult to make up next day? First I had to establish whether or not we could stay. Was it worth risking the long track for a 'No'? The lack of options made the decision for us, and so we started to lift the trailer over the gate – and snapped one of its arms. David slumped to his knees in despair and I started walking.

As we were setting up camp against a shed-wall (for protection from the wind) a gaucho appeared carrying a small, crackling radio. He was rotund, with a thick red beard and liquor-inflamed cheeks. He clocked our beleaguered trailer and plodded away, muttering something inaudible. Within minutes he had returned with a bundle of wire ready to whip around its arms. We were amazed at his generosity, but motioned our worry about the extra weight the wire would add, versus our recycled, super-light inner tubes. He seemed unconvinced, 'But wire is strong. This is no good,' he pulled at the torn inner tubes and broken bamboo. 'This will keep you safe.'

We gazed at miles of fences that stretched from the hub of the *estancia*. Our benefactor's enthusiasm for wire was clear. He stayed with us for over two hours, working methodically on the trailer with David. We asked him about the *estancia*. 'The owner lives in Punta Arenas,' he said. 'He prefers city-life to being stuck out here in the middle of nowhere. He employs a manager to run the place, and we do the day-to-day work on the farm. It's the same in most *estancias*; they aren't owned by the people who actually work and live on them. That's fine by us,' he chuckled. 'We get some peace!'

He said the *estancia* was 20 miles long, with over six million sheep. He seemed pleased to have company and re-appeared later on, still clutching his radio, to invite us to see the sheep. He then dumped a bag of mutton into our laps, and our evening meal was transformed. That night we watched a purple sunset fade behind the fences as bugling flocks of upland geese glided into the golden fields around us.

The lack of cover from wind in these enormous steppe-lands was troubling us. Our tent was robust, but it had to last for months, and few tents are made for that level of usage. The generosity we had been shown gave us faith that people would offer us shelter, but it was clear that things would be easier if we asked before dark. The difficulty lay in the fact that most *estancia* buildings were far from the road, often over ten miles away. Over the following days the kindness of strangeness blew us away and became an integral part of our life – something we hadn't anticipated. A policeman plunged home-made bread into our hands as we passed his lonely outpost, and countless drivers offered us hot drinks and food and their houses to sleep in.

The next city on our route was Puerto Natales, 167 miles away: the next goal towards which we were channelling our efforts. Dividing the expedition into manageable chunks was crucial to our psyche. To have concentrated purely on the finishing line would have suffocated us; the enormity of the challenge impossible. It wasn't just the next city or 100-mile stretch on which we focused; we filled each day with tiny hurdles. 'We just need to get through the next five miles,' we would will one another. Or if that was too far to contemplate, 'If we can only run the next mile, to the next bend... over the summit of the hill.' David worked out that every one hundredth of a mile represented the length of our boat. So he ran her wooden decks at each click of the GPS watch, and was able to visualise his shifts in boat-lengths, making them possible. We found that the run was shaping into a metaphor for life. 'With small steps it is possible to achieve extraordinary feats,' David scribbled in his diary. We would divide our run into bite-sized morsels: thousands of mini-races that, strung together, would span a continent.

We began each day with a bird-survey, then a vigorous one-mile, warm-up walk, downing breakfast and cleaning teeth on the hoof. This avoided wasting time in camp and helped prevent injuries from forming. Even so, the first couple of miles must have looked a comical affair, as two wooden figures trotted along like clock-work toys. Then, by about mile fifteen, old aches would begin to resurface. And no matter how fast we ran, it always seemed to be late afternoon before we found somewhere to camp, what with swapping the trailer and shoes every five miles and breaking for food.

Occasionally we stumbled across a winter paradise – as when we ran through a *lengŭa* forest on a gravelly minor road. The trees were short, wrinkled and bent over, like old magicians with silver beards of lichens and cobwebs of lemon-green mistletoe, their branches laced with a filigree of snow. Pulling the trailer off the road under their arms was like entering a magical kingdom, with their twisted shapes silencing the wind. We dug our tent into the snow, collected water from a transparent brook nearby, where dagger-shaped icicles had set a mini-waterfall, and contemplated the roof over our heads. These forests were ancient, just like the *coihŭe* beech forests we had passed under on our way to Cape Froward, with generations standing in the same spot since the last ice age over 10,000 years ago. Hundreds of plant and animal species had evolved to benefit from their cover and food – as we were doing now.

What was so sad was that the trees were dying. Below the forests, cattle, sheep and horses grazed. They rubbed on the old trees, squeezing out their last breath, trampled over their roots, nibbled away new seedlings and bashed through the understorey once populated by shrubs and herbs. Woodland after woodland had been attacked, leaving a graveyard of a former ancient forest.

During the night further snow fell. We awoke to find our tent and trailer covered in a thick, white duvet. Tiny vole-prints peppered the surface in spidery trails. Diamond paw-prints marked the passage of a fox. We had been arguing a lot recently: bickering about how to put the tent up, the time it was taking us to get out of bed, about who could use the laptop first (whether David for tapping in the daily mileages and stats or me to update the wildlife records), whether one or other of us wasn't putting enough effort into running, the time it was taking us to run, who had the biggest portion of food! Fatigue and hunger fuelled our dissension. But now any need to argue dissolved away, as we huddled together eating our milky oats and sipping sweet roasted barley under a latticework of branches. This theme repeated itself again and again on the run: whenever we encountered a beautiful wild place or were close up to a wild animal, our emotional woes faded.

The perpetrator of the paw-prints trotted into view: a *culpeo* fox, a large grizzled version of our English species. Unaware that we had awoken, he passed down to the stream, sat by it for a while and then disappeared into the trees. He had made our day. Such glorious wildlife encounters laced those first physically-painful weeks of the run with gold. They were the moments we yearned for, that charged our thoughts and spurred our feet forward. That morning was spun with even more spell-binding encounters. A small flock of Austral parakeets scratched for seeds in the snow. Snowflakes gently settled on their feathers. Their plumage was an exquisite collection of leaf, emerald and olive greens, sea and sky blues, with a scarlet tail and belly-patch, all fluffed up into a feather-duvet. When most people picture parakeets, they're cackling through steaming forests, not grubbing about in a freezing steppe. It was amazing to see these birds here, *in the snow*.

And so we ran, with snow under foot and parakeets filling the air. Over the coming days we saw flocks of over 50 *chimango caracaras* (mottled-brown, hawk-like birds) huddled together for warmth in the skeletal branches of a tree; we heard Austral blackbirds' fluty song and were dazzled by the scarlet chest of the long-tailed meadow lark, which looked as if it was bleeding into the snow.

An odour that was a mix of fruits, spices and musk wafted through our steps and flooded our nostrils, signalling the passing of one of Patagonia's more nocturnal residents. There could never be a question of mistaking the owner, because nothing could emulate the distinctive, pungent blend of the pied Humbolt's hog-nosed skunk. Even when flattened under the wheels of a passing car, the black-and-white, bog-brush envelope that remained continued to overwhelm our noses. I wondered whether the passing powerful smell of two sweaty runners had a similar impact on a skunk?

Running through southern Patagonia in winter meant we met very little traffic. The back roads we chose, with their pot-holes and unconsolidated gravel, allowed us to run for hours on end alone with our thoughts, the birds and the landscapes stretching to a distant horizon. The sighting of a reptile, anphibian or mammal was rare, they being either nocturnal or camouflaged. Birds, in contrast, are much more visible and became our companions on the long, winding road.

One morning we dived into a bus-shelter by a cluster of houses barely clinging to the earth, battered by the winds that raced over the plains. A young mother and her smiling son joined us with their miniature pooch whose nose appeared just above the precipice of her handbag. We relished speaking to someone, anyone – and it gave us the chance to air our Spanish. '¿De dónde vienen?' she asked. (Where are you from?) Followed by, '¿Tienen hijos?' (Do you have children?) And, '¿A dónde van?' (Where are you going?) We soon realized that these three little questions were designed to elicit the most important details from an odd pair of *gringos* bowling down their road.

She further added, '¡¿Y cómo se bañan y cómo van al baño?!' (And how do you wash and how do you go to the loo?). Our response of, 'Well, we don't, really,' to the first, followed by a vague sweep into the distance for the second, was met by peals of laughter, then a look of real concern. The truth was, we stank. We had been on the road for over a week. At the end of a long day the thought of washing a pair of socks or a top was about as far away from our priority list as the idea of plunging our pink and goose-pimpled flesh into an ice-covered river. At least our scent was natural, like the wild and rugged world we were running through.

One morning two policemen stopped by the side of the road to check how we were coping in the blizzard. They chatted amiably, sealing their departure with a fat kiss on my cheek, as we had come to expect in Chile. For the remainder of the day my nostrils were swamped by the cloying stench of aftershave. It felt alien and intrusive. Consider your average pooch; it thinks nothing is better than smothering itself in the heady aroma of badger or fox droppings. We wondered whether our rich fragrance, considered abhorrent by your average *Homo sapiens*, allowed us to merge into the landscape, so that passing foxes were oblivious to the two figures crouched by their tent.

We achieved 200 miles; a huge victory in our crusade of mini running-hurdles, and for the first time since leaving Punta Arenas there wasn't a roaring in our ears from an incessant gale – just us and the snow softly compressing under our footfall. The landscape, with its hollows, rolling hills, lakes, streams and forests, was plaited into an enchanting winter painting. As the late afternoon sun flooded the frozen fields with gold, a flock of upland geese grazed on a plain. A speckled teal flew from under my feet, and a long-tailed meadow lark's crimson breast glowed in the sun as it scratched for larvae in the snow.

Horses were fascinated by us: they snorted and galloped into the distance, before they returned in high-kicking, extended trot to investigate the weird apparition. Cattle were similarly spooked, but generally stampeded far away, more startled than intrigued. A gaucho passed, wearing a woollen beret and a long, thick, sheep's-wool smock, with a shaggy dog at his horse's heels. Otherwise we were alone, with only the birds and the odd fox for company.

David had heard of a hotel that could provide us with a warm meal. This being winter in Patagonia, our hopes of it being open were pretty muted. Nevertheless, we concocted sumptuous imaginary menus, to fill our gurgling stomachs. To our astonishment, 'Ruben's' was open. Stepping into the warmth of the bar was utter bliss, with our limbs tingling as the blood flowed back into them. We chose a table pressed against the open fire and steamed.

A woman chuckled at our inane expressions and delivered two hot chocolates, two tinned chickpea-and-meat soups, followed by peaches in syrup, with tinned cream. It wasn't exactly the feast we had imagined, but not having to cook, coupled with the chance to roast our extremities by the fire, elevated its status to that of a culinary extravaganza.

Then something extraordinary happened. A girl with tousled blonde hair escaping from under her woollen hat bobbed into the hotel. Two large, blue eyes scanned the room, ran over the pair of *Chileno* workers hunched over the bar chatting to the landlady, to the digger- drivers sipping Nescafé through toothless, moustached mouths, and, having exhausted options, alighted upon us. She grinned and bustled over to our table. 'Hello! Hello! I'm Vicky. I've heard all about you and I've come to rescue you!'

We sat stunned, completely gormless. Finally I mustered, 'Oh gosh!'

'I've come from Puerto Natales, and I have all sorts of things for you. You know, the stuff I imagine I might yearn for if I was running so many miles every day. You do realize you're mad, by the way? I have Snickers and Milky Ways, loo-rolls, batteries for your head torches, water, blister-plasters, bananas – I'm sure there's more. Oh, and I've baked a cake, and I've some warm coffee back in the car for you. I'm training for the new *Torres del Paine* marathon. I know it's nothing compared to what you're doing, but it's made me think about you guys and imagine the essentials, the things you'll be dreaming about and also the things you need to function day-to-day'.

'I can't believe you've driven all the way to see us,' I said. 'Over 35 miles through thick snow to find two complete strangers!'

'I didn't want to miss you! Claudia said she had seen you two days ago. I worked out that, based on your 20 or so miles a day, I shouldn't have to drive too far. I was just worried you would be in your tent. Then I saw this place and thought I'd better check it out. Thank goodness I found you!'

It was lovely to hear her dulcet English tones. She was the first foreigner we had met, and we thanked her again. 'So, what are you doing out here?' I asked.

'I moved to southern Chile six years ago. Why? The old favourite: I fell in love with a gaucho! Yeh, I know, but it was everything: him, the horses, this incredible country; so wild and wonderful. I had to move out here. England held nothing for me. We're all independent: my Mum, my Dad, my brother and I. So I just started again.' She gulped, 'My life has changed irreversibly. I can't imagine ever returning home.' We listened fascinated and agreed to meet her later in the day, once we had achieved a decent mileage. She drove away into the snow and we ran off, our heads ringing with her words and our hearts awe-struck by her generosity.

Stray dog

Trotting by our side was the dog

4 Cracks in Our Relationship

A sheet of brilliant blue sky spread far into the distance, and snow shimmered in the bright sun, but we ran apart, with a good 60 metres separating us. We were annoyed with one another. Arguments had become regular daily events, as we grappled to adjust to the extreme physical demands of the expedition and our different ways of approaching tasks.

There was the nightly alarm-clock dispute. 'What time are we going to get up tomorrow?' David would ask, his eyes glinting, 'Oh, I don't know,' I would shrug. Then I would start to prickle at the injustice of it all and retort, 'Do we have to get up so damned early? Why can't we allow our bodies to recuperate?' To which he would snap, 'What's wrong with you? Am I the only one in this team who has an eye on the future? We have to get running early; get the day done. If we spend all our time in this pit, we'll NEVER get there.'

When crawling out to do a wee in the night I would invariably trip over the guidelines, twanging the tent, which infuriated David. 'Why can't you be more careful?' he would growl. 'The tent has to last all year.' 'I know!' I would snarl, and soon we would be cursing and screaming at one another.

Then there was the trailer. After its initial break and subsequent collapses, David was twitchy about its fragility. Whenever I was in harness, I felt I was doing a fantastic job, avoiding the minefield of rocks and potholes that lay in wait, but regular barks from behind suggested otherwise. 'Mind the trailer! For god's sake, CAREFUL!' So when I saw David mounting a kerb or dragging the trailer over a hefty boulder, I couldn't resist shrieking at his hypocrisy, to which he would retort sanctimoniously, 'I'm the one who'll be mending it.'

The GPS watch, which we swapped every five miles with the trailer, became an unlikely bone of contention. David meticulously planned every part of his trailer-stint by it, correlating it to the figures on signposts, endlessly summing-up and revising distances in his head. I didn't. I would glimpse at it every now and then. Sometimes towards the end of a day's run I would have my eye pinned to it. Other times, I would sink into repose and forget the watch entirely, running over my allotted five miles. This infuriated David, who needed the clear divisions that our shifts provided. My attitude was more fluid, based on the landscape, wildlife, weather and my emotions.

Ultimately, there was feeding-time. Two predatory runners would eye the contents of the saucepan menacingly. The battle-line would be drawn down the centre of the gruel, and we would take turns shovelling out our allotted portions. But a fracas would invariably break out when a sausage or lump of potato strayed (probably pushed) into enemy lines, or the spoon lingered too long with the other. Such prodigious appetites necessitated careful monitoring of food-supplies.

This time it was the first glimpse of Puerto Natales, squatting below us by a glistening streak of sea that expunged our disagreements. Elation swept over us; we had run 238 miles, and our belief in our ability soared. Luckily we knew the name of a place to stay. This was a huge relief, as trawling around towns after a long day on the road was never conducive to marital bliss. We sank hazily into our beds. And that's where we should have stayed. But after days of running, we had built up a stockpile of ideas and tasks. Our bodies were screaming for rest and yet our minds were whirring. So we took turns tapping on the laptop late into the night, battling with flaky internet and one another.

> I have never been this miserable (I wrote in my diary, as tears rolled down my face and splashed onto the page in front of me). We have such different ways of doing things. David needs order and precision, I need the opposite. We lived and worked within fifteen metres of one another on the boat, yet somehow now, in the vast open expanses of South America, we feel more trapped. We've been together for seven years and I have never felt as wretched as I do now.

David's first diary has disappeared; bearing in mind our state of mind in those first weeks, it may be for the best that I never read it! We are both strong characters, and we were arguing over even miniscule tasks. Yet each battle seemed crucially important for laying down rules for the entire expedition. We were exhausted by the new regime, sleep-deprived and hungry. The expedition was paring away the conventions of modern living, with its success depending on our answering basic animal needs. We had to work out how these could be balanced amicably.

In Puerto Natales we met Vicky again, together with Claudia (a friend of a friend). They had arranged press interviews and presentations for us. Forty-five students sat before us. We had no props, no translators, just ten minutes to explain what we were doing in a language we had barely spoken. They stared. I swallowed. Silence. Then I stepped into the fire, leaping into the air, explaining where we were from, that we adored running: the freedom of it, the feeling of our bodies firing on all cylinders, the amazing wildernesses it carried us through and the glimpses of wildlife it revealed. David added facts about the distances, the trailer, the equipment we were carrying and the species we had seen. We survived. Of course, what exactly we said we will never know. David called it Tarzan Spanish, and no doubt our tenses swung wildly and I got my endings all muddled-up, but the audience comprehended something – if only that two crazy *gringos* had a passion for running and wildlife, and that if you are determined, you can fulfil your dreams.

Before leaving Puerto Natales we bought two plastic containers as bowls. Extra weight was viewed gravely, but efforts to save our marriage outweighed the concern! Like all our kit items, the bowls would double-up as water-collectors, storage-containers and wash- basins. We were yearning for fresh food, as an extract from my diary reveals:

> Salted scrambled egg sandwiches followed by jam sandwiches today for breakfast. For lunch we ate more sandwiches, but this time with processed cheese, followed by empanadas (similar to a pasty). Tonight David cooked Viennese sausages and mash. The result tasted awful, but at least there was lots of it. Then we ate a whole pack of biscuits, followed by a milky drink. I'm craving salad, vegetables and fruit; something vaguely associated with the earth.

And so we returned from the shops with dried nuts and fruits, a cabbage, carrots, onions, garlic, apples, bananas and split-peas. I also wanted to create an energy-torpedo factor in our diet – so 'rocket-fuel' was launched. It was more a case of assembling than cooking: melting chocolate, crushing and chopping biscuits and nuts. The said dark-brown gloop is sensational, and should be spooned into a container and refrigerated. A provision we could easily accomodate for, as we were running through Patagonia in winter and were effectively living and running in a fridge.

We hit the road fully-provisioned for the next, nine-day stretch to Argentina. The fresh food was due to last us for the first three days, with garlic and onions seeing us through for the rest of the period, in addition to our other travelling stores. The only problem with our improved rations was their weight, with the trailer clocking-in at 95 kilograms. The other problem was the temperature, which regularly dropped well below freezing. But although this made life tough, it was perfect for running, and great for food- preservation, while the world we were passing through crystallised into magical forms.

> We are so very, very, cold (I wrote in my diary). Patagonia gives a new meaning to the icy word. The wind whipped through my bones as I surveyed birds this morning. There's no cover, it's been grazed away by swarms of sheep, cattle and horses. Last night we camped behind a boulder, the only barrier we could find against the mocking wind. Our shoe-laces

are frozen solid each night. A fine layer of frost forms over the inside of the tent. I thought I saw a flock of terns, but it was shards of ice, set free from the river by the screaming wind to pierce the sky. The lake beneath where we ran today splintered and cracked into a vast jigsaw of glistening polygons. Beautiful. My breath is condensing and I'm losing the feeling in my hand as I write. A million stars glitter in the velvet blackness above us. Time to turn off my head-torch, hunker down and sleep.

David's feet are singular; his arches high and his toes long and claw-like. The smallest toe is hardly there; perhaps it is receding into his heel? He says he is at the pinnacle of *Homo sapiens* evolution, blazing forward while we lesser, plate-footed specimens die out! Either way, his odd appendages were functioning remarkably well. He hadn't had a single blister since we started, whereas my perfectly-formed 'foot fingers' had already suffered three. The miraculous thing about this cold weather was that it acted like a giant, all-round ice-pack, because when we arrived in the warm hostel, his feet blew up like balloons.

A couple of days out from Puerto Natales, Vicky joined us for the first seventeen miles of the day. It was lovely having someone else to chatter with. The day was bright and blue and we headed skyward, spiralling up hills and dropping into a beautiful river valley on the *Ruta 9*. Long after she had left us, as the day was gloaming, something rushed across the road. Our minds took a second to register,. 'It's an armadillo!' I hissed.

I had dreamed of seeing so many creatures in South America – pumas, jaguars, macaws, tree-frogs, *vizcachas* (rodents that look similar to rabbits) and *guanacos* (the wild relative of the llama) – but somehow had failed to register that this scuttling, sixty-million-year-old, armour-plated guy was also part of the glorious stitchwork of the continent. This was one of the immense benefits of spending our lives outside, and something to which most of the people we encountered were oblivious. Just like the rest of the world, they spent their lives looking into or sitting within the turbid world of a box: whether they were driving to work, stuck in an office or at home, staring at the TV or a computer, life beyond had blurred into a fog, without meaning or interest, bereaving them of the spell-binding, ever-changing, awe-inspiring complexity of the natural world.

Next morning an Austral thrush and two southern *caracaras* flew over my survey circles, and a pair of *thorn-tailed rayaditos* (pretty little titmouse-like birds) shouted from the branches of a ñirre beech tree. This next survey involved clambering up a near-vertical hill. At the required distance, I turned around and couldn't believe my eyes. Far below, beyond our camp-site wood was a lake, and on it tens of hundreds of Chilean flamingos. Almost one kilometre away, they were no more than marshmallows on the horizon, but through my binoculars they transformed into the most serene dancing birds in their surreal pink livery. If it wasn't for that early morning survey, we would have been totally oblivious to our neighbours.

Millions of people charge through life without ever truly seeing the world: without seeing a kestrel hanging as if by a wire, motionless in the air, as it searches a tussock for a vole; without seeing a hummingbird's back sparkling like jewels as the light plays on its plumage; without seeing the individual scales of a coral snake as it pushes through the bush in its red, yellow and black warning cloak. Seeing the world through binoculars is like looking with a peregrine falcon's eyes, which have eight times the magnification of our own vision, and finding the world afresh, multi-coloured and precise. The dot high in the sky or far on the horizon springs into life. Binoculars reveal life. Ever since buying my first pair as a young girl, I have been transfixed by the beauty of the world through their lenses.

I listened to the regular rhythm of my foot-falls, crunching in the loose rubble road. David was running tall and free up ahead. The trailer pulled at my hips, my calves and thighs strained and my back leaned into the hill. The fabric of my balaclava was damp where my breath condensed and rasped with the incline. We were 280 miles into the challenge, and I felt strong, but still had a long way to go before I would feel truly 'elite' fit. Blubber still coated my bones, serving to ward off the cold, but increasing the bulk I had to propel forward. Then the GPS watch chimed 15 miles, time for our third load-swap of the day. A small wooden hut appeared on the crest of the hill, providing us with shelter from the wind. We had been carrying eggs in a bottle; orange yolks perfectly preserved in a cold white sea of albumen. That morning David had converted them into scrambled eggs, laced with butter, thick with salt and pepper, dispatched on hard, white, little rolls (the mainstay of a southern *Chileno* diet). They were delicious, and followed by rocket fuel and water.

As we sat ruminating on the miles that lay ahead, a gaucho clipped past on his large bay mare, with two old dogs padding heavily in his wake. From below his bottle-green beret his glance brushed over our huddled figures. We were clearly that weird traveller breed, not worthy of contemplation, save that it had migrated to his cold Patagonian shores far too early in the season. I relished these rare refuelling breaks as a time to rest my legs and enjoy eating. David viewed them as traps; robbing us of daylight hours and compromising our running rhythm.

I was beginning to realize that David's need for process made sense. We were developing systems for packing the trailer, assembling the tent, cooking and running. With each layer of process grew a layer of tranquillity in our relationship. Routine bred certainty and order into our day, eschewing the need to argue over daily tasks. Considering what a vast area of South America lay ahead of us, it was vital that we had finally worked this out!

We ran across Paso Rio Don Guillermo, into Argentina. It was a fantastic feeling to have arrived in our second country on foot. The soon-to-be-familiar turquoise-and-white striped national flag marked our entry, but apart from scattered sheep grazing the steppe, we were alone. The gravel track undulated through a stark, open landscape. In two hours one car passed us, leaving us in a cloud of dust. A hut appeared on the horizon, marking the end of no-man's land. Slightly concerned about our uncustomary mode of travel, we ditched the trailer and bustled into the office with large smiles. The official was friendly and was soon quizzing us about the run and laughing at our *tracción a sangre* (human powered) mode of travel.

After the initial euphoria of crossing into our second country, my mood had descended with the brown desolate plains, criss-crossed by rows of new electricity pylons that stretched into infinity. We were running down a tarmacked road in the dark. Cars streamed past, blinding us in their headlights. No one hooted or wished us well; there was none of the contact to which we'd grown accustomed. That night we slept in a layby, deep in snow. We dug out snow with our hands and hunkered the tent below its yellow walls. A freezing tent peg stuck to David's hand like super glue.

The next morning was bright and clear. As we jogged down a hill chatting, a huge trunk of a man hailed us from the side of the road. He stood near a couple of clapped-out lorry containers and a large metal barn. An intense smell of barbequed meat wafted through the air. He invited us to breakfast. I was in the middle of explaining that we had already eaten and needed to keep running, when David dug me in the ribs. He was craving meat; there was no way he was going to miss the opportunity.

Huge hunks of mutton smouldered in the fire, overlooked by the enormous, overalled man whose width was out-competed only by his height. A younger guy, whose Spanish was indecipherable, pushed wine and bread towards us. Perhaps they were lonely or intrigued by the sight of us? Either way, it was astounding generosity to two absolute strangers. We chatted as best we could. 'The *estancias* we're running past are enormous.' I ventured.

'Aye, they're big enough all right,' Mr Trunk nodded, 'Farms are merging into mega-estancias down here and throughout Argentina. It's more economical that way.'

'And guanacos: I'm curious. We haven't seen many. I thought we would be running past great herds. What do you think of . . .' He didn't let me finish.

'Flaming things!' A large globule of phlegm hit the mud as he spat in condemnation. 'They're a plague, robbing our sheep of pasture and water. They're much bigger than sheep and consume ten times the water of a single ewe. There's hardly enough water down here anyway, let alone for those things.'

I wanted to point out that the guanacos were here first; that only ten percent of their original thirty to fifty million-strong population remains, in less than forty percent of their former range; that they evolved in harmony with the steppe; that it was the non-native new grazers (the sheep, cattle and horses) that were causing the problems. But there was no point discussing it with him - and anyway, my Spanish wasn't up to it.

'The only good guanaco,' he chuckled, 'is a dead one! They taste good on a barbeque.'

'What about ñandú (rheas)?' David ventured, 'Do farmers feel the same way about them?'

'Aye, they're a plague an' all. Wouldn't eat them myself, mind. Poor man's meat, you know. Dogs'll have them, though.'

'Do you ever see pumas?' I asked.

'A friend of mine shot one the other day. But they're rare now. Haven't seen one for a while. They're no longer in the lowlands. They're still up there.' He motioned with a sweep of his great arm towards a range of rugged hills climbing into the sky. As we departed, I realized that the mound of soft, silvery mattress-stuffing left out to rot in the rain was in fact the hair-like feathers of a rhea.

The Argentine's words rung in my ears as we swept along. I imagined the grasslands surrounding us shimmering with vast herds of guanacos and rheas. And in their wake? Postcards of quintessential Patagonia depict a sea of fluffy sheep guarded by the stalwart, romantic gaucho. On first impressions such a vision looks beautiful and natural. But these non-native grazers, introduced by European settlers, have stripped away the tapestry of wildflowers and grasses that once emblazoned the steppes, leaving clumps of unpalatable grasses in a dust-bowl of fragile, trampled, soil. The earth is unable to hold water or nutrients, and takes to the air. Without soil and water, even those postcard sheep are leaving Patagonia, driven out by their own voracious, unsustainable appetite.

Soon, as we ran, the sheep and their stripped landscape were dissolving. A wall of snow was mounting before us, and the wind that sliced into our sides was intent on whipping it into a blizzard. As snowflakes filled my eyes, I could barely see. A car appeared from nowhere; the first of the day. It stopped. David talked, while I winced in the cold, my lips turning purple, as I steadily lost the extremities of my body. We had to run to maintain our warmth.

Suddenly, the leaden clouds parted, the wind lulled and the snow gently spiralled around us, as if someone had tipped us upside down in a snow-scene model. All was tranquil. A condor soared above us, his long primary feathers divided like great fingers, black-and-white on the mountain updraft. His ermine scarf warmed his turkey neck and his dinosaur comb crowned his bare head. This is a goliath of the mountains, with a wingspan of up to three metres; rivalled only by the wandering albatrosses, the mighty juggernauts of the Southern Ocean.

Andean condors roam the mountain spine of South America, drifting on thermals up to 5,000 metres high and travelling up to 300 kilometres in a day. We would explain to schools along our route how important this iconic species is in nature and to humankind in its role as the 'undertaker', cleaning carrion from the earth, like the black vultures and turkey vultures that share its range. But the Andean condor is declining, threatened by poaching, poisoning and habitat loss. Nor is it helped by its slow reproductive rate, with only one chick produced on a mountain ledge every two years and adults only starting to breed from six to eight years.

That day we reached Tapi Aike; a cluster of flea-bitten shacks grimly clinging to the scorched earth. It was as if we had run into the wind-torn pages of Bruce Chatwin's 'In Patagonia'. A dead guanaco hung in a barbed wire fence. Further corpses lay in a pile in the field. Tapi Aike lies at the junction of the *Ruta* 40, a magnet for motorcyclists and drivers, as one of the longest roads in the world. It follows the backbone of the Andes from the south to the north of Argentina's vast landmass. Mindful of this pedigree, we had assumed that we would be able to re-provision in a shop, but the shop was in fact a shed, attached to a small garage and upon its door was pinned a scrap of paper with, 'Gone walkabout.'

Considering that we hadn't seen another human being in tens of miles, it didn't look as if we were going to discover the meaning of this statement. Then I noticed a small hut with a black jet of smoke shooting out at right angles from a chimney. I knocked on the metal door. '¡*Hola!*' Just as I was about to give up, a stocky, corkscrew-haired lass appeared with a grubby baby perched on her waist. 'Have you any idea when the owner of the shop will be back?' I ventured. 'Don't know,' she grunted. 'Could be any time between now and next week.'

We slumped by the trailer, uncertain where we would make home for the night. A gaunt dog joined us. Then a clapped out Volkswagen Beetle careered around the corner and screeched to a halt. In it, miraculously, was the owner. Bundling ourselves into the shed and out of the wind was magical. Our tired bodies collapsed, grateful even for the hard school- chair embrace. Gradually, but perceptively, we began to seize-up in the gas-fired haze. I scanned the single dusty shelf behind the man's head. A small collection of: biscuits (sweet and savoury), powdered milk, sugar, instant coffee, packet soup sachets, pasta, potato mash, tins of sardines and fire lighters appeared to represent the necessities of existence down here, at the bottom of the world – although it didn't look as if anything had moved from the shelf in several decades.

As the man boiled water on a primus gas stove and carefully presented us with a bowl of sugar and instant coffee granules, the folly of our desire to sit in the warmth was exposed. We were carrying biscuits, powdered milk, instant coffee and tea bags and had our own stove, yet here we were using up our diminishing cash supply. But our will was weak and our need to recharge out of the wind too strong.

Galletas (crackers) or *galletitas* – using the Argentinian's favoured diminutive *ita* – (little) would soon become our daily bread, being a mainstay across South America, often the sole stock in tiny far flung stores. On the front of the packet it would say, '*Crocante*' (crunchy), which they were not. They had an unpleasant taste of cleaning fluids, which also permeated into cheese, ham, and biscuits. We decided their popularity was largely due to their indestructible nature; being unreactive to extreme temperatures and capable of lasting for decades, crossed with being as dry as a desert on one's tongue and the fact that nothing could possibly survive on their tasteless surface. No other reason explained why such a thin slice of sawdust could be so hugely popular.

In the fug of the shed we quizzed the shopkeeper about the dead *guanacos*. He claimed that it had been a hard year, with insufficient rain, leading to their natural die-off. This didn't ring true. Guanacos are members of the camelid family, able to inhabit the dry and harsh climates of the Patagonian Steppe and Andean range running north into Bolivia and Peru. Like camels, they are able to store water and extract moisture from the grasses and shrubs they graze. Although they can suffer from drought, the dead animals we had seen looked in good condition, suggesting that something more sinister had caused their demise.

Our next question voiced our daily preoccupation about where to camp. He unreassuringly scratched his head, ruminated for five minutes or so, then finally gestured towards a large building across the road, 'Perhaps the police might let you stay?' He didn't seem convinced. We certainly weren't, but we had no other option. So David pulled the trailer by one arm and we made for the building. I knocked. No one appeared. I wasn't keen to snoop around the back of a police station, but matters were becoming urgent.

A pile of metallic rhea feathers greeted me. Geese and hens pecked at the ground. Wires stretched at head-garrotting height from the station to a radio mast. A washing line waved its cargo of white shirts, and a bin lay on its side, litter shimmering in the grass. From behind a half-recumbent corrugated iron shed a bright-eyed guy popped up. I explained our predicament and he nodded, flashing a smile. 'This is a good place to camp,' he said. 'It's quite flat and there's plenty of room.' The only difficulty of sleeping in someone's garden (especially the police's) was the need to relieve one's self. I was quite happy darting behind his hedge in a well-timed wee manoeuvre, but leaving a number two was trickier. Unfortunately, this was now becoming a pressing certainty, and so I hopped over to the station to plead. The policeman ushered me into a warm television room where two other officers were ogling a football match.

'Here is the loo,' he said with a flourish of his hand, 'and here's the shower, and we have plenty of hot water for you to cook with. Help yourselves!' he grinned. This was the stuff of dreams. I plunged into the steaming shower, a mere trickle, but as amazing as if it had been the thunderous Victoria Falls. I marvelled at a thin slice of soap and a small bottle of shampoo, revelling in the novelty of cleanliness. Drying myself on my T-shirt, I hung my damp clothes on the police station radiator and trotted out to David.

There was no place for being backward at coming forward on our expedition. If we were going to survive and keep nibbling away at the mighty mileage, we had to have the pluck to ask favours and accept kindness. This was an altogether un-British attitude, but as the miles increased, we found that people appeared to gain great pleasure from helping us. We saw it as a goodwill debt which we would need to pay back in the future, even if it was on the other side of the world.

That evening we were joined by the dog from the garage. It wasn't clear whether he had a home, but he had a kind face and his barely-fleshed skeleton yanked at our sympathy chords. He had an endearing habit of emitting a low, guttural, grumbling chatter, as if he was trying to communicate. He certainly wasn't impressed when we zipped up the tent, boxing the fabric in protest at leaving him in the cold. '¡Callate!' (Shut up) we shouted. But he wasn't going to be dissuaded so easily. A wet nose pushed through the gap at the bottom of the tent, appearing at the bottom of our sleeping bag. That night we slept under the lights of the police station, with our guard dog's silhouette traced against our tent.

In the morning, David asked the policeman whether there was much crime in the area. 'No, no. It's very safe here,' he said. 'All we have to worry about are sheep and cattle changing hands when they aren't meant to! And of course road accidents; in the summertime tourists arrive, they don't understand how to drive down here, so they crash . . . a lot!' he laughed.

We set off on the *Ruta 40*, bound for a rugged, 43- mile gravel track into no-man's land. Trotting by our side was the dog. He was such a character, offering us companionship and heat, while we could provide unrelenting exercise. But we couldn't offer him a secure home, nor pull the extra food he would require. Most importantly, we couldn't allow him to hunt the wildlife we adored. '¡Para la casa!' (Go home) we shouted half-heartedly. But he wouldn't listen. So we shouted louder, repeating the warnings, each time more sternly. At which he would stop for a minute or two, cocking his head in disbelief at our betrayal, before trotting after us again. It was heart-wrenching. We were probably the only people who had showed him any warmth in his entire life. He stood staring at us. Finally, he turned for wherever was home, stealing the odd surreptitious look back as he plodded away.

One truck passed us that day, with a great, bearded man grinning from its cab. I was always glad when people saw us sprinting: there was nothing more disappointing, after racing furiously up a hill or against the wind all day, than having a passer-by stop just as we were changing our shoes. There was also the issue of who was seen pulling the trailer. David imagined people thought he was either a sadist, running free while his wife lugged the home and office behind her, or a pansy incapable of grafting. I, on the other hand, felt I was fulfilling stereotypes when I didn't have the trailer, especially in a continent where sportswomen are rare – but I felt empowered when I did.

A herd of guanacos appeared on a hilltop, but galloped into the distance on scenting us. Their extended necks gave them a lolloping, comical appearance, especially in combination with their horse-like, braying whinny. Yet they moved over the rugged terrain with a ballerina's ease, their soft, padded feet absorbing sound and their sandy coats creating the perfect camouflage for their disappearing act. Their passage was preserved in the road by a series of two-toed prints. Later, lines of three-toed tracks marked the passing of Darwin's rheas. Running always felt so much easier when we were in the presence of these amazing wild animals.

The road was bleak, the land disintegrating into gravel and sand, but we were alone and we loved it. That night, at the twenty mile mark, a cluster of white buildings and an old wooden corral rose just below the road, with a wisp of silvery smoke confirming that someone was at home. The gauchos were happy with us camping, so David started frying garlic in one of the outhouses and I wandered over to the farmstead for water and some meat. A calendar with a rodeo scene was fastened to the wall alongside a magazine cutting of a stallion and some prize bulls. Cast-iron pans were stacked on a shelf near the coal-burning stove, and a large table with six white bread rolls and a few wooden chairs filled the room. The gaucho sieved water running from the well and placed an enormous slab of beef in my arms.

Wild and domestic geese honked, cockerels crowed, the dogs howled and the horses neighed. It was lovely being so close to animals, just difficult to sleep! We ate beef and cheesy mash with a long, hot toasted-barley drink. In the night David heard an engine; someone had come to check the horses in a little old Triumph. We woke to the birds singing, and I cooked raisin and cinnamon bread with *manjar* (a South American speciality of cooked condensed milk) and jam for breakfast.

Now we were running through a beautifully rugged and remote area. It was what I imagined Kansas must look like. Photo opportunities presented themselves round every corner. Golden tussock and fescue grasses glowed in shades that shifted subtly from minute to minute in the ever-changing light. We played cat-and-mouse with a group of birds who scuttled between the vegetation and our path. They were least seedsnipes, the first we had ever seen. The male wears a dapper, dark-grey bib, separated by a jet-black line from his pure white belly. On his back and the crown of his head are feathers like petals of gold. It was this colouration that helped this jewelled 'dove' and his mate disappear, as if by magic, from in front of our feet into the ochres, rusts and steely greys of the pampas.

By the time the sun bled from the sky, the seedsnipes had found their home for the night, but we were still running. We scanned the steppe for boulders, a ditch; anything that would provide cover from the fierce local winds that could easily overwhelm our tent, but its flatness was complete. Eventually we realized that some distant, flickering lights were passing cars, and that we only had to keep running for another half hour to claim the white light of El Cerrito.

I groped around in the shadows, finally locating a supervisor who showed us towards a shed. It was made of corrugated iron and bricks and was enormous. He pulled back the colossal metal sliding doors. They were over ten metres high and I could barely move them. 'These,' he motioned, 'were ripped off last summer by a gale and sent bouncing across the yard like new-born lambs!' Our mouths dropped. We had run through strong wind, but nothing as fierce as that.

David's hip was plaguing him, and pain seemed to delight in jumping randomly around my body. To ease the discomfort we were routinely taking

Ibuprofen and often Diclofenac first thing in the morning. After the first sharp miles, the pain would seep away. The landscape provided another drug; it was awe-inspiring, with the jagged spires of Torres del Paine sending our thoughts spiralling into clouds of exhilaration. We chatted of plans and of nonsense, of people and wildlife and running revelations. The hours ticked past until, before we knew it, we had completed another twenty miles and were pegging the tent into a wall of crusty snow.

That evening we saw two small grey foxes and a *culpeo* fox (much larger, redder coloured fox) meandering by the ice sheets. The hardship of winter and the difficulty of finding food in the snow were driving them to behave more boldly than usual. A slow string of *guanacos* meandered across the sinking sun as it was disappearing behind a barbed chain of mountains that swept down to a glacier-mint landscape. As those mountains are believed to be the haunt of the puma, I willed one to appear.

The tent glistened with frost on the inside and outside. My breath was condensing. Everything had frozen: the pans to our clothes, our gloves to the pegs, the laces to our shoes. We couldn't even open the water-bottles, as their tops were set in place. But we were deeply content, sinking into a blissful cloud of down and thoughts, contemplating the stark, icy beauty of this incredible land through which our run was propelling us.

In the morning a long, slow incline finally levelled off. We stopped, awestruck, on the precipice of our mountain plateau. Way below lay a craggy plain stretching into infinity. To the west rose up a mighty chain of snow-covered mountains, and somewhere at their feet lay El Calafate.

Before we reached the town, we had to run past guanacos rotting by the side of the road, speared by fences and piled up in fields. Neither of us had considered the impact that fences would have on our daily lives, or on the wildlife and wild places for which we'd be running. For us, fences were merely a hindrance, on which we hitched our clothes and bags as we ducked under them to make a camp. But for wildlife the story was very different. Fences prevented dispersal and the long-distance migration of herds witnessed by early explorers, and also produced barricades into which landowners could pursue them.

We counted 152 guanaco carcasses in a ten-mile stretch, strung up and mangled in the roadside fences. Then we watched a family of four each clear a fence, but when it came to the turn of the *chulengo*, it proved impossible, with the youngster repeatedly dashing itself against the barrier. Heartbroken, we watched the herd move on, leaving their baby behind to a probable death without its protection.

Male & Female Torrent Ducks
Merganetta armata

Breathless, we watched as they hurled
themselves into a raging whirlpool

5 To the End of the Road?

The full horror of how we were going to cope in Argentina's arid zones hit us on a remote stretch of road north of El Calafate. I swallowed. My mouth felt gritty. All my saliva appeared to have drained away, and my urine turned a burnt orange. We spent the first miles of the day searching for moisture: ditches, streams, lakes, ponds; but nothing appeared. Finally, we found a cow-pat-ridden pond and had a minor row about whether or not to drink the fetid brown soup. Eventually we pumped a little through our Lifesaver bottle, desperately pouring it down our throats. A few miles later we found a well powered by wind, with good clean water. We drank and drank until our tummies turned into tight drums and felt as if they might actually pop.

The river we had been making for offered the tent some holding in its loose sandy banks, but any water it once owned had long since seeped away. We had one litre of brown puddle water for cooking, and only a litre of clear water to share during the long, parched hours of darkness.

We became infatuated by the need for water and where we would next find it, collecting anything we stumbled across, no matter how shitty. Finding accurate information about what lay ahead was extremely difficult and plagued our route-planning. David would scour google-maps for signs of water, but the reality on the road was very different, with stream beds turned to dust and communities abandoned. We talked to local people wherever we could, but as they lived their lives behind the wheel of a car, to them the minutiae of landscape were irrelevant and distorted; ten miles disappeared in the matter of minutes.

We started running without shoes for a couple of miles a day during our trailer-free sessions. Often the surface of the tarmac was too rough, but the painted white lines provided a haven for our feet, and we ran free with wide smiles. It also appeared that a smooth road improved our running style, triggering a lovely, light gait which our bodies remembered in the next miles with the trailer.

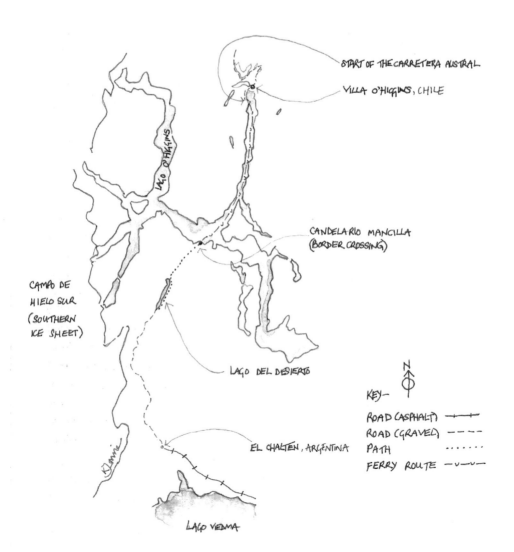

START OF THE CARRETERA AUSTRAL

VILLA O'HIGGINS, CHILE

LAGO O'HIGGINS

CANDELARIO MANCILLA
(BORDER CROSSING)

CAMPO DE
HIELO SUR
(SOUTHERN
ICE SHEET)

LAGO DEL DESIERTO

EL CHALTEN, ARGENTINA

LAGO VIEDMA

N

KEY -
ROAD (ASPHALT) ┼┼┼
ROAD (GRAVEL) ─ ─ ─
PATH ⋯⋯⋯
FERRY ROUTE ─ᴜ─ᴜ─

Map 4 – Andean Border Crossing
between Chile & Argentina

One night we found somewhere to camp with an old table. Such a simple luxury, yet for David it was magical, allowing him to unfurl from his bent-over, preparing-meal squat. That night the sausages, courgettes and pasta were delivered and consumed with even greater relish upon the four wooden (somewhat rickety) legs.

We wanted to cross the border into Chile at El Chaltén (See Map 4). The plan was to run north from there to Lago Desierto, follow a narrow path skirting the lake with the trailer, kit and provisions strapped to our backs. When the path ran out, we would wait for a boat to cross Lago San Martín to reach Villa O'Higgins; the start of Chile's Carretera Austral (a stunning track that weaves for nearly one thousand miles through mountains, fjords and temperate rainforest to Puerto Montt). We were assured the ferry operated in winter, as it had to service the *gendarmería* (Argentinian policemen). Chilean *carabineros* (policemen) and Argentinian *gendarmería* hold remote border posts to stave off any clandestine advances from the opposition in still-disputed territory.

Running allowed us to avoid reality, as our bodies followed the daily simple rhythm of putting one foot in front of another. But now we were plagued by the uncertainty of whether the Chilean and Argentinian officials would agree to our plan. Luckily we had María, a friend from Puerto Montt, who organises holidays via her firm Patagonia Trails. She knew people in El Chaltén, and, being Argentinian and fluent in Spanish and English, was able to investigate the possibilities for us. When we spoke to her on the satellite phone, she confirmed that as it was still winter time, the border was closed. But during her investigations, she had stumbled across a bylaw, one that hadn't been implemented for the past couple of years; nevertheless, it stated that a special permit could be granted for pedestrians to cross the border. The permits depended upon the discretion of the *gendarmería* and *aduana* (customs) and we would need to wait a couple of days to secure them. Waiting for permits from officious police smelt risky. Nevertheless, we decided to run to El Chaltén and confront the border guards in person.

That evening, a Patagonian armadillo bustled across the road. It then ran back again, summing up in a flash why we had seen so many of his friends flattened. The poor little guy, with his armour plating, perfectly designed to see off his natural wild foes, is no match for the three-tonne hulks of steel that plough through his territory at terrorising speeds. He bustled into a bush a few metres away from us. David slipped forward with the camera. I hung back, hardly breathing. Slowly I approached, my eyes running over the long bristly hairs that sprouted from his back, his scaly tail, surprisingly large 'Shrek' like ears, piggy nose and raking claws. He sat motionless, playing dead, with only his blinking eyes breaking his camouflage. We couldn't believe our luck, being so close to such an extraordinary wild mammal.

Suddenly he shot off through the scrub. A spray of sand flew up as he furiously dug a hole with his formidable front claws. Within minutes he had submerged his head like the proverbial ostrich, as if to say, 'If I can't see you, you can't see me!' But we could see him! Thus another of the strategies this ancient mammal had acquired over millennia to fox his predators, had been rendered obsolete in the eyes of his greatest enemy of all, *Seres humanos*.

We ate an amazing supper of fried salami, with dried tomatoes and mushrooms, herbs, tomato-puree and pasta, followed by porridge and figs, watching the sun solemnly sink in a flaming ball over the jagged mountains of the Fitzroy range.

During the first two days of running into the lap of the ice-shrouded mountains which guarded the small town of El Chaltén, we were extraordinarily lucky with the weather. Blue sky marked our passage, with a flock of pirouetting Chilean flamingos dancing in a steaming lake. But on the last day the wind wrought its fury upon us and the true reality of life under the Andes' southern ice sheet was revealed. It tore at our bodies and the trailer. Great swirls of debris and dust flew into our eyes. All sound, other than our screaming, invisible foe, was obliterated. Running became nearly impossible, as our bodies were pushed backwards by the force of the wind. We resorted to running in single file, with the trailer-less runner ahead; so somewhat blocking the wind from the one behind who traced his footsteps a couple of paces back. In this fashion we continued to make slow but steady process against the element.

That night we lay awake listening, from a small bunk-bed in a dilapidated hostel in El Chaltén. Windows and doors crashed, dustbins took to the air and dogs howled. Like a frenzied inmate just escaped from prison, the wind wrought its revenge on the ugly town, which soils the astounding beauty of its birth place. A mind-boggling beauty, where slate-coloured rocks skewered dizzyingly through a mantle of snow into the heavens, like the razor teeth of dinosaurs. Glaciers carved into their heart, shearing rock faces, grinding boulders to pulp, cascading into turquoise lakes. Native beech forest groped for a foothold in their mighty shadows, flecked by chalk-blue ponds and lagoons teeming with wildlife.

The following morning we arrived at the *gendarmería* to ask for consent to cross the border. A neat little man greeted us, with black hair carefully smeared to his scalp. He was impeccably turned out, as was his rehearsed smile, 'Have a seat', he cooed. David explained that we wished to follow a low-level path to the border and that what we were proposing was much safer than the trails the tourists walked daily to the glaciers. 'Ah, I see, yes', he nodded. 'But these tourists are with guides on set routes. It is permitted, it has been for many years. It is a very different proposal from what you are suggesting.'

We explained how we had been running for weeks through Patagonia, that we had all the kit we needed to make the crossing, and that the Chileans were happy to receive us at the border post. We showed him María's letters, which highlighted the bylaw that would allow special permits to be granted at the discretion of the *gendarmería* and *aduano*. He appeared interested, 'Very good. Well, I will need to write to Rio Gallegos for approval and they will need to write to Buenos Aires for their approval', he said. 'How long will all that take?' David asked, unable to supress his frustration. 'Perhaps a week?' He didn't seem convinced, we certainly weren't.

We rushed back to the hostel for the satellite phone, to explain the situation to María. 'I'll ring Rio Gallegos straight away', she said. An hour later we heard back from her. 'Well, it seems there is no point in your waiting for a permit, as the woman your *gendarmería* told us to contact (his boss) is in fact dead!'

Our lifeline had dissolved and we were forced to accept we had reached the end of the road. The next morning, with heavy hearts, we began running towards Lago Desierto, the furthest point that we could reach with the trailer. Running there and back would ensure we covered the miles that we would have taken to meet the ferry. We would then begin a detour overland on buses and ferries via Rio Gallego and Chile Chico to reach the Chilean side of the lake.

We trotted under our first trees in weeks through spectacular scenery, yet we moved over the vertiginous, cobbled hills in a torpor of exhaustion. It wasn't until we caught sight of a pair of torrent ducks, diving into the furious rapids of a meltwater stream, that we forgot our woes and refocused on the extraordinary place through which we were threading. These stunning ducks are endemic to the Andes, with their range exactly mirroring their course up the western spine of South America. They are specialists of such high altitude cold streams, to which only three other ducks in the world have been able to adapt.

We scrutinised the striking couple through our binoculars: the female in her livery of oranges and the male streaked black and white, with his impeccably rouged beak. Breathless, we watched as they hurled themselves into a raging whirlpool, convinced they had dropped to their deaths. But within minutes, these most unlikely of high-octane swimmers had resurfaced and were battling upstream against the waves, before jumping, undeterred, onto another boulder. How they managed to catch their prey in such seething mayhem was mind-boggling, but perhaps their secret is the fact that they are highly sedentary and loyal in pair- bonding, so that both individuals must know every cranny and crook of their hunting ground.

We clocked twenty-three miles on the GPS watch and pressed the binoculars against our noses to catch a glimpse of the end of the lake and the distant hills which marked the start of Chilean territory. We camped under the trees and cooked. Williwaws screamed down the mountainside, through the woodland, walloping the tent. Thankfully it stood firm, and soon even the howling wind couldn't prevent our spent bodies from collapsing into a deep slumber.

Water poured from the sky all night and all the next day. But I felt like a new woman, fuelled by the slightly-charred and rain-damp cinnamon and raisin bread I made for breakfast. By mile 17 I began to wane, as the cold took hold of my muscles and seeped deep into the core of my body. Even David, who is like a furnace, was shivering in his saturated clothes and barely able to see out beyond the hood wobbling around his face.

Back in El Chaltén, we began the heart-wrenching work-around, from one side of Lago Desierto to Lago O'Higgins, via the world. Jostled from place to place, waiting for buses that didn't turn up, shunted into ferries, refused lifts, banned from summer-only camp-sites and enduring torturous nights in flea-bitten hostels in the company of landladies from hell! Oh for the simplicity of running, determining our own schedule, our own route and our own resting places; of our world in a trailer, beholden to no man, landlady or four wheels.

But in the depths of winter, in the abyss of southern Chile, nothing was going to happen quickly. It wasn't until a whole mis-spent, mis-adventurous week later, that we finally found ourselves back on our feet, after a protracted mini-bus ride with a cargo of Chilean *campesinos* (country folk). They comprised a bunch of rotund vagrants, who had been lured to the south through government incentives geared to tame the 'unproductive' rainforests by logging, fire and grazing. They came with their sundry plastic goods, a kitten on a string and a puppy in a box, whose nose was shoved down whenever it stuck it out for air.

We resurrected the trailer in the square of Villa O'Higgins, in front of an audience of inquisitive toddlers, grandparents and the mayor. This was the southernmost town of Chile's Carretera Austral. We strapped all our kit aboard and headed south, to the official start of as the Carretera Austral on the shores of Lago O'Higgins, where we would have been deposited by ferry.

You might think that after a week's break our bodies would be honed and coiled for action. Unfortunately, the contrary proved true, with old injuries, long lulled into submission, re-awoken. The bones in the arches of my feet were painful, and I was developing a tender spot in the sole of my foot that would send me reeling every-time I landed on a sharp stone. But we ran in a cloud of happiness, elated to be on the road again, sleeping under canvas and moving through such an extraordinarily beautiful land.

We awoke early to bird song. Serendipity had guided us through the darkness to a dry, flat area of woodland, where we hadn't been discovered by cattle or people. We wound along a gravel track through a corridor of forest, beyond which reared a Tolkienesque range of snow-capped mountains and forgotten lands. The sun shone warm on our backs, our white legs dazzled the day and not a single car passed us. We were euphoric to be here, and praising the day we had decided to forgo the treeless dry Argentinian side of the Andes for this mossy splendour.

There have been numerous studies into how nature affects human psychology. That hospital patients who gaze over trees and natural landscapes get well quicker than those who peer at concrete jungles. That people who travel to work through rolling hills and woodlands are calmer than their urban counterparts. It's pretty simple when you think about it: we are made up of the same basic elements of carbon and oxygen as all the living plants and animals with which we share our ecosystem. We will return to the soil, just like them, to feed that ecosystem and create more plants and animals.

The relatively new concept of *mindfulness* draws on what people have been doing for generations; taking time to be in tune with one's self, but most importantly to be in tune with nature. Tapping into our innate connection to the natural world and our animal roots allows us to relax, refresh our minds and counter illnesses. For me, it's straightforward; my mood soars when I run through wild and pristine environments, but plummets in built-up areas or destroyed natural lands. When I'm happy, I run better, and vice versa.

In South America running provided us with the medium to see wildlife, as we trotted along for hours at a pace that revealed the detail and complexity of the world around us, while at night we slept within a millimetre of nature. That pared-down, raw existence on the wild tracks and roads was the essence of life.

One day we ran twenty miles, at the end of which a gaucho's hut appeared at the perfect moment. It was built into the side of a massive fallen tree, with half a barrel providing a fireplace, dry wood stacked by its side, a table cut from a trunk and a bed of four planks. With hot water on the stove, a little ochre *huet-huet* bird calling outside and a waterfall nearby, we knew it was going to be hard to prise ourselves away from it next morning. We slept contented, our bellies bulging with sausages and lentils, reflecting on how little we needed to make us happy, and that the gaucho's hut was pretty much it.

Rain poured down during the night, but luckily it didn't find its way through the gaps in the roof on to our faces. Rain was still sluicing down in the morning, and within minutes of running we were soaked, but the warmth from the hut and the dripping forest festooned in lichens and mosses buoyed us onwards. Our euphoria didn't last long. After we'd gone barely a third of a mile, the trailer struck a boulder, veered to the right and flipped over, smashing the axle in half and depositing its bearings all over the road.

David rapidly repaired it with a spare axle and wire and after a quick succession of star jumps, we stripped off our feather jackets and ran off again. But the reliability of the trailer was seriously vexing him. He constantly fettled with it; tightening the bearing locking nuts that perpetually worked loose and plotting how he could improve it. Our fundamental problem was weight; we were still carrying too much, with the load constantly exceeding eighty kilograms. We couldn't eat less, forego our Spanish book and dictionary, nor the wildlife guides. So we settled on sending some of our solar kit forward at the next town.

As we watched a family of adult condors and their young circling us, we nearly ran off a cliff, spell-bound by the birds' graceful flight. A female with a turkey-gobbler neck perched within arm's reach, sizing us up with her beady eyes from within grey, leathery folds. Perhaps she was willing us to die so she could strip our flesh? The valley had been incised by a gorge with a river gurgling deep inside it. Lakes gave way to precipitous wooded hillside. It was mesmerising. No amount of exhausting hills could detract our attention from it. We were happy beyond words.

We found a dreamy camp-site, in a gravelly layby, on top of the world. David stuffed rolls with cheese, butter and mayonnaise for the next day's lunch, fired up the MSR and stewed dried mushrooms, garlic, bran, milk powder, spaghetti and four fat sausages. As the sun finally dropped behind the mountains, it spun the valley into gold. Stars soon began to prick the black velvet expanse above our heads. I pulled out my camping mat and we stretched into our yoga routine, watching the stars light years away from us. There were no artificial lights for mile upon mile, just the southern sky shimmering in a vast, arching milky-way way above our heads. I snuggled into our sleeping bag, imagining what would happen if the world decided to flick off the lights.

We awoke to no pumas or *huemuls*. We were desperate to see both species; puma because it is the essence of wilderness, power and freedom and an emblem for the pristine landscapes we were running for; *huemul* deer because it is endemic to Chile and Argentina, and represents the struggle between man and wilderness. Its population has declined by ninety-nine per cent and its distribution by over fifty per cent, due to habitat loss, competition for grazing and increased exposure to disease from livestock, and hunting by man and feral dogs. An estimated 2,000 individuals remain, the same number as the giant panda – so our chances of seeing one were low, but we were running through some of the most isolated wooded mountain terrain, exactly where the *huemul* should be.

Next morning a horse rider appeared around the corner of the mountain. His bristly, grey-flecked beard nestled into the neck of his woollen poncho; a purple cloth cap sat atop his nest of coarse hair, and thigh-high sheep-skin chaps protected his legs. Two old sheepdogs sloped behind. The coat of his chestnut mare formed lathery peaks. Her eyes grew as large as saucers at the apparition (us) in front of her. She stuck her heels into the gravel, snorted and pounded a front hoof in protest.

'Have you seen my cows?' he asked.

'There was a group chewing the cud in the centre of the road near Villa O'Higgins yesterday,' we told him. 'But we've seen nothing today. Have you come far?'

'From down there.' He stabbed his thumb down the mountainside. 'And you?' he asked.

'Villa O'Higgins,' I said.

He nodded. 'Where are you going?'

'The Caribbean,' I grinned.

He looked down at his great, bony hands, nodded again, kicked his horse in the ribs and trotted off. Although a man of few words, he had seemed content to sit and pass the time with us. We wished he had dallied longer, that we had asked about his life. There was something beguiling about him, as with the other gauchos we had met. It was as if he had walked out of the pages of a dusty novel and would evaporate as quickly as the smoky fragrance that accompanied him. He would know the hills' secrets and their every knot, ridge and furrow, as he wandered them night and day in search of his livestock. It was a simple, honest and hugely appealing way of life.

David had been dying to do a trick he had learnt from a David Attenborough documentary. That day the opportunity arose. Two black Magellanic woodpeckers flew by. They were joined by a third and celebrated with a squeaky, 'daffy-duck' chortle. The setting was an open, boggy cypress woodland, with plenty of dead standing wood. Magellanic *carpinteros* are impressive birds. They are large, about 40 centimetres long, with the male distinguished by his flashy, brick-red head and the female by her Essex-girl, black top-knot. They pirouetted around quite close to us and then dived off into a tree, with the familiar looping flight of woodpeckers around the world. This was David's chance. He stood ankle-deep in bog by a dead tree, grabbed two hand-sized stones and rapped the trunk in quick succession. Then again. Nothing happened. He tried again.

Suddenly, the female burst towards him in a direct line of flight, banking only at the very last minute, leaving David ducking for cover as she landed on his tree. He continued tapping in quick succession and then . . . she tapped back! She kept rolling her head from side to side, scampering around the tree, her top-knot trembling and her claws grating the bark eight inches above his head, as she strained to get a better view of him. David was being chatted up by a woodpecker! His coat was the perfect colour-match of a male's head-feathers; in her eyes he had become a giant woodpecker. The males had absolutely no interest in the scene that was unfolding; being too obsessed by the fat grubs they were excavating. Then suddenly the female flew off, her spiralling flight knitting a path through the branches, leaving us in stunned silence.

Long-tailed pygmy Rice Rat
Oligoryzomys longicaudatus

Suspect number one

6 A Close Shave with Death

Six-hundred and forty three miles into the expedition, I suddenly felt a stabbing pain in the side of my right ankle. I knew it was of a different magnification from the twinges I had grown used to, and it seriously troubled me. It was probably due to my sprinting up a 14,000- foot pass with the trailer. David took the trailer early, to see if running unencumbered might reduce the pain. It didn't. I hobbled on, unable to repress the odd sob of anger, but only managed thirteen miles before we agreed to find a camp.

Anxiety engulfed us. What would this mean of the expedition? David began to list possible options, 'First, we're only 60-odd miles from Cochrane: we could easily bale out and rest for a couple of days there. If rest doesn't work, I guess it's a mountain bike or horse…' he tailed off. I felt nauseous. The options were rotten.

An ancient tree caught my eye. It was twisted and bent, its roots nosing through the undergrowth and its limbs draped in pendulous mosses. It stood like the old man of the woods, having spent century after century watching over those who passed by. We dumped the trailer and I squirmed into its huge hollow centre. The thick odour of dank, rotten wood filled my nostrils. Beyond was a small patch of lawn grazed by goats and cattle. It was a perfect hiding place; our tent would be invisible from the road.

Rotund beetles bombed through the air, their four fine wings buzzing frenetically, legs splayed, antennae pointing the way, bee-lining for our tent, bouncing onto it, then sliding to the ground. After a few minutes spent righting themselves, they would take to the air again, all cylinders cranked, before crash-landing into the shrubs at our side. They reminded us of a pilot friend who was slightly accident-prone: we always giggled at the thought of him announcing over the tannoy, 'This is your pilot . . .', and how we would dive out of the plane onto the runway before he had a chance to take to the air.

Next day my ankle felt fine, but after the second mile the piercing pain returned. After limping, jogging and shuffling my way to mile eight, we decided to stop. David had read about a 48-hour remedy used by the U.S. military when on exercise to combat strains and minor ailments. It was called *RICE*: Rest, Ibuprofen, Cold compress and Elevation. We had bucket loads of Ibuprofen; the ambient temperature was zero, and we could easily elevate my ankle. So we found a spot next to a river and set up camp. I crawled inside and began 36 hours of unplanned, enforced rest.

The only hitch was that our food supplies hadn't been calculated for two extra days on the road, and they were woefully low. We had to ration our intake, which, considering that we were constantly hungry, laid the foundations for a pretty acrimonious rest.

David made a huge fire to brew constant cups of tea, and began fishing. Every four hours I religiously downed the anti-inflammatory pills and rubbed Ibuprofen gel on my ankle. The tent entrance was wide open. I watched the river and the clouds threading through the mountains. Condors occasionally soared way overhead. A hummingbird hurtled past, in hot pursuit of something, I couldn't work out what. Two men with a dog floated past in a small wooden boat, but otherwise we saw no one.

I hardly slept that first night, dreaming of David charging out in front while I wheeled along in his footsteps, morose, on a mountain bike. I am fairly competitive. I remembered a cycling jaunt during which I abandoned a would-be boyfriend, as he gasped pathetically up a hill while I belted to the top. He told his mate afterwards that he felt emasculated! Needless to say, we didn't get together. David's different. He comes from a large family, with strong, independent and successful females. On our first cycling trips or fell-runs together he didn't worry that I could beat him up the hills. Unfortunately, he soon started beating me, so I had to train even harder.

The enforced rest worked. I could still feel a dull ache in my ankle, but nothing more. We ran two full-20-mile days and on the third day stormed into Cochrane. A huge sense of relief and fulfilment swept over us as we arrived in the small town. Chickens pecked in the streets and apples hung over the walls, but the place featured large on our map, in an otherwise pretty-much-unoccupied part of the world. We organised presentations at the local school and felt the familiar rush of warmth and purpose, chatting about wildlife and running to tens of upturned, inquisitive faces.

Only 11 miles north of Cochrane lay one of the chief foci of the run, Valle Chacabuco, a huge, former over-grazed *estancia*. It was hard to imagine that sheep and cows alone could have destroyed this 56-mile-wide chunk of Chile, but that's exactly what had happened. What was amazing was that very quickly, with a little help from the charity *Conservación Patagonica*, nature was returning the land to functioning steppe. We planned to stay a couple of days there, to tell its story first-hand.

We walked out of our guest quarters into a herd of *guanacos*. Our previous sightings had been of distant specks galloping away from us, or of dead bodies. In Valle Chacabuco something remarkable had happened: the guanacos had lost their fear of man. After only seven years without hunting, these graceful camelids had come down from the mountain slopes and begun grazing the plains of the valley, as generations had before. Nor was it only *guanacos* that had been tempted from their mountain hideaways; their natural predators, pumas, were also prospering. But although we saw fresh puma tracks and placed a camera motion-sensor along a puma trail, the huge cats once again evaded us.

What we did find were *guanaco* latrines: enormous mounds of large, black raisin poos, a bit like sheep droppings – but sheep on steroids. These fruity-smelling piles serve to mark territorial boundaries, and help to avoid energy-sapping disputes between young rival suitors and the patriarch, who protects his harem of females and young.

We disturbed an Austral pygmy-owl, napping in a thicket of ñirre beech trees. A perfect, speckled owl in miniature, it calmly assessed us through its enormous bright-yellow eyes. There is something imperialistic about an owl's gaze, making you feel insignificant and futile. If you consider that it is a bird that has mastered hunting in darkness, and is able to detect the mere rustle of its prey with pin-point accuracy, it's little wonder it should gaze down at us, with our paltry senses and disconnect from our natural world with utter disdain.

There was another species we hoped to see: the mountain *vizcacha*. An odd-looking rabbit with a fox's tail, it's a large rodent belonging to the chinchilla family that hangs about in rocky outcrops. It's incredibly agile and can scamper at full pelt down vertical cliffs, darting into its warren of tunnels. It forms huge colonies in these rock galleries, whose extent is critical to its survival, allowing it to seek refuge from predators such as eagles and small cats. One of the beguiling aspects of its nature is its propensity for napping. Being 100 per cent herbivorous, it has no need to rush about finding prey. With grass and shrubs at 360 degrees, all nicely recuperating thanks to the new landlords, we thought our chances of catching sight of one were high. We were wrong; the *vizcacha* become another of our disappointments, and another reason for returning to Patagonia.

The accommodation on the *estancia* was beautiful, and for three nights we slept non-stop. This was one of the best features of the expedition: that one night we would sleep under a blanket of stars, a hair's breadth away from a hunting wild cat; the next on a bed of straw, surrounded by snoozing chickens, but just once in a while we would be invited into complete luxury. The contrast was delicious and made us appreciate the extremes of our lives, from rags to riches, even more.

Patagonia's wild landscapes haunt the imagination and infuse one's dreams. It is said that anyone who eats the wild *calafate* berry is bound to return to this enchanted land. We ate plenty of these smoky blue berries of the *Berberis* plant, but even before popping the first in our mouths it was too late: we had already been long smitten, with a part of our hearts already stolen by this haunting region.

Among the natural features that amaze the eye are Patagonia's ultramarine snow-melt rivers. Their colour is so surreal it seems fake; as if a band of painters had tipped the contents of their tins into their waters. We camped and ran alongside one of these misfits, the Rio Baker, that roared along the Carretera Australa from near Cochrane to Puerto Bertrand. It is said to be one of the earth's wildest rivers, meandering through temperate rainforest, canyons, snow-capped mountains and grasslands, fed by the world's largest ice-fields outside Antarctica and Greenland.

But the Chilean government had its eye on it. And the bureaucrats weren't focusing on its astounding beauty, its symbol as a bastion of wilderness, its immense biological diversity or economic importance for tourism and rural jobs. No: what they had in their sights was energy and a plot to gag the river forever to provide electricity for the copper-mines of northern Chile and the kettles, washing-machines and lights of the Chilean capital of Santiago, some 1,600 miles to the north. Wherever we ran, hoardings and graffiti berated the plans. *'Patagonia Sin Represas'* (Patagonia Without Dams) they shouted from the roadside, with montages of mighty dams and enormous power lines slicing up the country. People were defiant, furious that the land should be destroyed by greed from the over-populated north.

The proposed dams would drown 6,000 hectares of wilderness, leading to increases in methane, which, over a 100-year period, has 20 times greater impact than carbon dioxide. Construction of transmission lines would necessitate the clear-felling of 1,000 miles of endangered forest and intersect fourteen of Chile's most spectacular national parks.

But for the moment we had a more immediate problem: rain – something for which southern Chile is notorious. We were running through a rainforest, and rain was falling in bucket-loads. Every morning we would squeeze our cold bodies into sodden clothes. Our useless garments would cling to us, fingering icily into our muscles, sapping any meagre warmth that our twenty-mile runs attempted to produce. We were convinced it could get no wetter, but then the next day a monsoon would arrive; with water cascading from the sky in relentless torrents. Changing-over the trailer became unbearable, with our muscles seizing up instantly. A brutal contrary wind, beating on the hoods that covered our ears, meant we couldn't hear anything, so traffic became potentially lethal, especially around hairpin corners and on precipitous mountain undulations.

The highlight of one day arrived at the 16-mile mark, when a jeep ground to a halt. A family of Israelis were on holiday and seemed fascinated by us. We chatted, forgetting about our own predicament, as rain slanted through the car windows and the occupants shuffled to avoid it. After about 20 minutes they said, 'Do you need anything?' We were saturated, cold, hungry and thirsty, absolutely dying for a hot drink to revive us. Being British, we stoically and stupidly replied, 'Oh, no, no, we're fine. Thank you very much, but we'll be on our way.' And with that they accelerated off in their warm cocoon, leaving us in the cold.

The encounter raised our spirits, but it depleted any warmth our sorry bodies could muster. We ran on in a wretched state, until a *puesto* (a wooden hut used by shepherds and cattle-herders) miraculously appeared, and we gave up on reaching 20 miles, having no idea whether we would find shelter in the next three or 30 miles. That decision nearly cost David's life, although we would not know this until two weeks later.

The hut was filthy, with a mountain of rubbish accumulated from past occupants. We cleared old newspapers, rusted tins, plastic bottles and mouse droppings to the side, to make room for hanging our sodden clothes and erecting our tent, which we had decided to sleep in for extra warmth. Thus began the night of hell.

'David, are you awake?' I hissed.

'Of course I am.'

'What's the time?'

'It's midnight, and there's no way we're sleeping with that bastard rodent rampaging about.'

For the last hour we had been tormented by the scratching on our saucepan and plates and the rustling and grinding through our belongings, centimetres from our heads. 'I presume it's a mouse, not a rat?' I said. 'There's at least one more out there.'

'I know, I heard the bugger scampering past. How the hell are we going to sleep? I can't carry on like this, I'm utterly shattered.' He began rummaging around.

'What are you doing?' I grunted.

'Trying to find my shoe.'

'What the….?' But he didn't have time to reply before I heard an almighty BANG!

'Got the bastard! David screamed. 'I don't believe it! I got it!'

Ten minutes later the scratching started all over again. By the morning we were ragged, but the only remainder of our night's ordeal was one mouse lying stone-cold on David's shoe. He picked it up, examined our long-tailed foe and hurled it into the bushes.

For many people, especially women, there is one question that needs answering about our expedition, 'How did you relieve your bowels when there wasn't a loo for hundreds of miles?' The answer: you select a loo with a view. This I would choose over a million indoor thrones. To pull down your pants, crouch down and look out over a beautiful mountain range, to peer at a column of ants or a woodpecker excavating a dead branch, made the act, in the great outdoors, so much more relaxing and natural than the indoor equivalent.

As for wiping our bums – well, we became connoisseurs of the natural *brilo*. Moss, grass tussocks, fuchsia bark or a handful of dandelion-leaves became the firm favourites in the south. If we did use tissue, we would bury or burn it, because it is not faeces which are the problem in the wild (they are quickly attacked by hordes of decomposers and turned into soil) but the paper. This hangs about for a remarkably long time, as we can testify, from the large amount of papier-mâché we ran past.

Our next camp was beautiful and a huge relief after the mouse encounter. It also answered the second-most popular question we've been asked: 'How did you wash?' Although we generally smelt, washing really wasn't a concern in the cold Austral south. I would occasionally sit or dunk my head in an ice-melt stream, but that was about it. David is pretty much allergic to water, so he did even less. A rest day on the other hand meant we could properly cleanse ourselves.

A rushing stream babbled down the hillside, weaving through trees and shrubs. We sited the tent so that the entrance faced it, and David made a fire. I collected some water, propping the saucepan up on boulders above the flames. We poured the hot water into our water bags, hung them from a tree, part-opened the nozzle and showered. It was magical. Nothing quite compares with standing stark naked in the wilds, with warm water trickling over your body, gently removing accumulated grime, after days of working your muscles remorselessly and existing on as little as you can stuff in your rucksack (or trailer). The contrast of washing, sitting by a fire and eating a hearty meal is exquisite; as if it was the first time you had ever tried it.

Over the following days we watched eagerly as spring encouraged enormous *nalca* (gunnera) leaves to begin their mighty growth-spurt. These gigantic leaves can often be found in formal gardens in the UK: they resemble rhubarb on speed, and by the time they have reached their summer growth, you can happily shelter under their virtual umbrellas. In Chile gunnera is collected from the countryside and sold in markets, generally being eaten raw with salt. We cut up the thick stems and lobbed them into stews as a passable crunchy vegetable. I also gathered common sorrel and dandelion leaves. Both plants were introduced to Chile from Europe in grass-seed mixes and have since spread as weeds. Sorrel – related to the dock family – has a bitter taste, but together with dandelions is good in salads, and it added a few vitamins and iron to our diets. We also found wild celery near the seashore, which gave a lovely kick to stews. Unfortunately, we never tasted the small, knobbly fungi that grow on the branches of *coihüe* beech trees as they ripen in autumn. They're said to be delicious and were eaten by the *Chonos* and other indigenous groups that once roamed the shores and lands of Patagonia.

Cerro Castillo awaited us; another snowy pass, with a series of impressive switchbacks. It marked the end of the *ripio* (unconsolidated road surface) which we had been seriously looking forward to, as a break from the 'brakes' of the gravel. Along the way we met a red Ford Fiesta caked in mud. It had passed us once already, but this time the driver stamped on his brakes and emptied its contents: a Uruguayan with dark, greased-back hair, an Argentinian also with dark, greased-back hair, but also with aviator glasses, and an enormous roly-poly Bolivian with no hair.

They passed us a two-litre, three-quarter-drunk bottle of fizzy orange and two and a half sandwiches (with a bite taken out of one) filled with raw bacon, other sundry squished meat products and cheese. The Argentinian had just completed an ironman and was keen to hear what we were up to, as were the others. The only tricky moment in the encounter arose when we said goodbye. David put his hand out to shake the Uruguayan's, but the fellow leapt straight in for a kiss! Wow! I could see that David was flustered, but trying to remain calm. Regaining his cool, he stretched out his hand again, this time to the young Argentinian, but once again the guy out-foxed him, springing around David's paw and smacking him royally on his cheek. David eyed the Bolivian mountain. He was clearly feeling more confident about the process. After a slight hesitation, in which he appeared to be sizing up the best spot to mount his offensive, he bent towards him with his lips puckered. Can you believe it? The Bolivian recoiled backwards, nearly tripping over in his flight! 'What are you doing man?! We don't do that in Bolivia!'

'Poor bugger was as unaccustomed to it as I was,' David wrote. 'Bloody greetings!'

That evening we finally saw the animals we had been searching for: three *huemul* quietly grazing the slopes of the pass. The young buck scented the air, twitching his nose, but he appeared completely at ease with us watching him. We slept under their hillside, with a languid peach sunset filling the valley, melting the deer's forms into the night. The next morning they were, amazingly, still there, so David crawled up the slope and stalked them while I did a bird survey. I watched David and his quarry from the valley floor, as he shuffled within four metres of the male, wishing I had another camera to photograph him in such close proximity. Suddenly I sneezed, and all three deer looked up, wet noses scenting the air. It seemed they reacted only to scent and sound, rarely to vision.

We were sorry to leave the *huemul*s, especially as the land either side of the road to Coyhaique was a moonscape of the charred remnants of the mighty forests that had once cloaked the hillsides. I couldn't hold back tears at the devastation. During the fifties and sixties vast sections of the south had smouldered. Water-logged forests, their soils and wildlife, had gradually charred into the earth in a drive for order and agriculture. The depressing thing was that many of the areas that went up in flames were later abandoned, as they were found too swampy for cultivation or grazing. A huge rainforest by Puerto Montt, of ancient *alerce*, the largest and oldest tree in South America, was one such victim.

We were all too familiar with this kind of destruction in the UK, where mighty forests once cloaked 80 per cent of the land and were home to animals such as lynxes, brown bears, beavers and wolves. Our original ancient woodland now covers about two per cent of the country, replaced by agriculturally-manicured and largely lifeless fields. In Chile, it was because the destruction was so recent that it affected me so deeply. The contrast with the pristine areas we had just run through was staggering. Enormous black trunks were stacked in fields. Newly-ploughed and seeded fields were already washing away in the torrential downpours that were once intercepted by rainforests, so that they percolated slowly into the soil, replenishing life-giving ground water and preventing floods.

To compound it all, flotillas of trucks shuttled backwards and forwards like swarms of ants, frenetically pulling down the remaining forest to fuel the people of Coyhaique. As long as the forests stood, leña (firewood) was considered abundant and so primary forests were packaged into neat little piles to be stacked into incredibly inefficient log-burning stoves. These were stoked all day and night, heating up houses and the world, as the front doors were left open to control the oppressive temperature inside.

We slowly wove our way north, pulling 'mark-three trailer' which David had re-invented in Coyhaique from the cut-out rear sections of two gifted scrapped bike frames. It was a huge improvement, sailing much higher off the ground and would see us all the way to the Caribbean. It was flexible and light, but stronger, with wheels angled slightly inwards like a paralympic wheelchair, and better set up to withstand the thousands of miles of corrugated dirt roads that lay ahead. We had also given up carrying anything on our backs, strapping the small Inov8 rucksack to the top of the trailer and removing all but the belt from the trailer rucksack harness. We felt light and reinvigorated as we sprinted onwards.

Spring accompanied us, unfurling her new leaves and blossoms and emptying her dizzying fragrances into the valleys, forests and mountains. My mood soared. Night arrived later and later as the sun refused to set. So the bustle in the woods and rivers continued: the local frog quartet clattered and tapped, a South American snipe rose high in its courtship display, shuddering notes through reverberating tail feathers in great arcs above our tent. While one side of the world awoke, we gently fell asleep.

We were intrigued by the rainforest frogs, whose high-pitched yapping resonated from deep inside the cathedral of trees. Trying to see them, we scrambled through dripping undergrowth, delving under ferns and nosing into caves and hollow trunks. The sound seemed so close, and yet its origin was impossible to pin-point. David was particularly smitten by these beguiling creatures, and was elated to discover fat tadpoles in a roadside ditch. He mused on how incredible the frogs were to have mastered both land and water, and began pondering the logistics of posting himself into the tropical rainforest canopy, where this remarkable group are so abundant and diverse.

There was one species we were particularly keen to find: Darwin's frog. This beautiful, emerald-green or brown creature has a long, proboscis of a snout and looks like a leaf. It seamlessly merges into the forest leaf-litter, disguising itself from would-be predators. Such a feat is nothing, however, compared to its reproductive tricks. The female deposits her eggs in the leaf-litter. Her phlegmatic partner then watches over them for up to three weeks, until the young offspring begin to move within their egg sacs. Then something extraordinary happens: one, by one, he pops them into his mouth.

'Infanticide!' you cry. But no, this is the act of one of the most devoted fathers on the planet. Each of his little young is held lovingly in his vocal sacs. There, after about three days, they begin to hatch and continue to live within their protected confinement, feeding off their egg yolks and their father's secretions. Only once the metamorphosis is complete and they have become tiny, identical images of their father, will he trust them to the perils of his mossy world. And so with an almighty belch he begins to deliver his little army, froglet by froglet, onto the forest floor.

It was on one of these enchanting spring days that we ran 20 miles and then found a river gushing across our path. We thrashed into the tangle of forest and found a relatively flat spot; unstrapped the trailer and carried our kit in relays. As soon as we pitched our tent, a hummingbird zoomed in to see who had intruded into its territory. Momentarily contented, it burst high over the tree tops like an overgrown bee, issuing its soprano looping call. Hummingbirds live a high-octane life, with their tiny size and frenetic lifestyle that demands continuous refuelling. They dash to their nectar sources with unique, 180-degree wing rotation, allowing them to fly backwards, up and down and hover, at up to eighty beats per minute. Blink and you miss it. There's no peace for this little tornado when life is run at such pace; nectar is gold dust, rivals must be driven out.

David started preparing supper while I put up the tent. He was cutting onions and garlic on a plastic disk when something tickled his forehead. He wiped his hand across his face and looked up. Millimetres from his nose was the tiny, emerald-backed, fire-crown hummingbird, eyeballing him. It seems that over millennia, hummingbirds have developed a particular association with red flowers, and that David's pal believed an enormous new nectar source had just sprouted in his patch.

The next visitor to arrive was a *chucao* – a bird very similar to the European robin, but with a black-and-white striped undercarriage. It hopped over a mossy branch and scuttled around the tent in a mousy sort of a way, cocking its head to the side as my feet moved, before stabbing a beetle larvae. It hung around for ten minutes or so and then bustled under a bush, twitched its tail, threw back its head and shrieked, '*Chucao!*' nearly deafening the pair of us. I suppose it's no wonder that it has developed such a strident call, bearing in mind that it lives in the dense thickets of a rainforest, with creaking trees, thundering waterfalls and rushing rivers to out-compete.

The *chucao* became my favourite Chilean bird; popping up from nowhere to keep me company as I did an early-morning survey or collected water from a stream. It would usually stay for a few minutes, hopping over my feet or shouting its emphatic gun-shot call, before scurrying off for more promising foraging.

I lay on my back doing yoga, with annoyed hummingbirds whizzing through the canopy and shooing one another away. Soon the stars sent them to roost, and we washed and cooked by the river. I had never seen such angry, savage rivers as there were in Patagonia: huge, green conveyor belts surging through the mountains, reflecting the olive forests they piled past. We ate chicken with half a litre of wine. It was a rare treat and really appreciated. In those forests – astounding, pristine and verdant – I felt elated, my mood a mirror of them and the exceptional weather we were having. It reminded me of a couple of lines from one of my favourite poems, 'Sally', by Phoebe Hesketh:

> *But when the sun called*
> *She was gone, running the blue day down*
> *Till the warm hedgerows prickled the dust*
> *And moths flickered out.*

I was entranced by southern Chile, willing it to remain untouched forever, without a new road or mega-dam. There are few places left in the world like it. We brand change as 'progress', but I knew that none of our progress could make me feel as rich and happy as I felt then, surrounded by such breath-taking beauty.

Next morning we awoke to sunshine speckling our tent. I collected the binoculars and took off for a bird survey. The sun burst through the azure sky, its rays sparkling in a trillion dew-drops that shone from the trees. Slivers of clouds filtered through branches and hung in the bowels of the rubble road. It was one of those utterly sublime days in that rain-shrouded world. I bashed through dense thickets of *colihue*, crawled under *arrayán* trees, stepped across silver streams and finally arrived at my spot. Almost immediately a *chucao* arrived to investigate who had created the disturbance and what creatures may have been flushed. She looked at me quizzically, before snapping a spider and hopping away.

I heard a thin, rollicking *rickity-rickity-rickity* call, accompanied by a rustling in the bamboo. Something tiny flitted past and disappeared into the foliage. I could hear the newcomer moving within, but couldn't set eyes on it. Then suddenly she flicked into view: a buff, bauble-bodied little bird, with a thin beak and six fine, long tail feathers – a Des Murs wiretail, and utterly charming. Next came a powerful, resonating *whoo-whoo-whoo–whoo*. Within minutes the perpetrator had appeared and was hopping from branch to branch glowering down at me through his enormous black eyes, outlined in white – a black-throated *huet huet*, clearly fascinated by me. When I called back to him, he couldn't contain himself, puffing out his chest and reeling-off an enormous, amorous, *whoo-whoo-whoo–whoo,* centimetres from my ear.

The climb up through Queulat National Park, on an almost-vertical rubble road, was exhausting. A yellow warning sign on the ascent depicted a picture of a car on an 80- degree incline. But the woodlands, canyons and mountains blew our minds away. It is possibly the most beautiful national park in the world. The air was soaked with sound, as bird-song echoed through the mountains, waterfalls tumbled from snow-covered heights and streams thundered.

There were also caterpillars. Hundreds of the little orange-and black spiky fellows were making an excruciatingly slow, kamikaze bid to cross the road. I'm not sure what urge was filling them to make the manoeuvre; they were leaving what looked like a perfectly adequate wall of vegetation for what appeared to be the exact mirror on the opposite side. Nevertheless, they were moving in their droves. I couldn't stop the urge to help them along their way, picking them up and launching them across the road. No doubt this confused matters horribly, and had them about-turning to re-cross the road, but at least a few would avoid the inevitable annihilation that awaited many from the ten vehicles that passed us that day.

One morning, past Puyuhuapi, a cyclist came piling down the hill towards us – only the fourth traveller we had seen since starting the expedition three months earlier. 'G'day!' he grinned, 'You must be David and Katharine! I was getting worried there that I'd miss you! How's it going?!'

'Good, good,' said David. 'But how do you know us?'

'I'm David, Ozzie David. I contacted you a while back, about meeting up. Remember? I've come down from Mexico.'

The penny dropped. Ozzie David was bursting with high spirits and enthusiasm, which was just the tonic we needed. We chatted about the run and his cycling trip. 'So, how's your Spanish after all those miles?' I asked. The question usually evoked a response of, 'Ah pretty good,' when actually the said person was dire and could barely buy a beer. But this David didn't have an ego. 'Shit-house!!' he roared, laughing.

Before he left he pressed a packet of Milo in our arms. 'I bloody love the stuff, reminds me of home! Been lugging it across Patagonia; reckoned you could do with it. It'll up your calorie count per day!' And with that he swept away, leaving us in a haze of his happiness.

Ahead lay La Junta, the town in which (a pair of cyclists had told us) lived an interesting couple, Paul and Konomi, who would have us to stay. No road led to their doorway, no car lurked under the eaves. In fact, nothing was altogether as it should be. We squeezed through a wire fence, following cattle trails, climbing past tall, flowering shrubs buzzing with fire-coloured bees. Then we spotted the peak of a roof cresting the hill and entered their earth kingdom. Two figures were bent over rows of vegetables. The woman, had a delicate frame. Her long jet black hair was flecked with an occasional silver strand and was tied neatly into a pony-tail. The man by her side wore a thick knitted jumper, upon which hung a long grey plait, giving him the air of a magician. He looked up and grinned.

We stowed our bags under a cherry tree and followed Paul down the maze of paths they had created to the front door. The fragrance of herbs and incense wafted through the warm air of their home. Caramel-coloured Hessian rugs carpeted the walls. 'We found our slice of hillside three years ago,' Paul explained. 'Ever since, we've been sculpting it by hand. In place of wood or corrugated iron, the preferred building materials here in Patagonia, we chose earth. Slowly our Hobbit Hole grew from the hilltop, as we filled sack after sack with a mix of volcanic earth dug from our plot. The network of holes and gullies created for the house are now filled with greenhouses, a composting loo and pools of water to feed our organic vegetables and the hundreds of native trees and shrubs sprouting from the hillside.'

It was very simple, very beautiful; but most striking was its warmth. The thick earth walls provided perfect insulation in winter, but in summer they create a pool of shade, similar to the centuries-old, thick cob cottage-walls of home. The locals, Paul said, had at first been wary of their new neighbours and their odd house. 'People couldn't understand us. Who were these *gringos*, walking for miles backwards and forwards from the village with heavy rucksacks full of provisions, through driving rain and biting cold? Why didn't they have a car? Are they so very poor that they must build with earth?'

Konomi giggled, 'They said we were too thin, that we wouldn't survive the first Patagonian winter. But we kept walking; heaving the supplies we needed up the hill on our backs. Slowly, step-by-step, our house grew and we shaped the permaculture gardens of our hillside. Now, three years on, we're still alive!'

I gazed out over the mountains and chalky-green river through a window framed with long grass, sipping green tea, while David sat hunched and unusually quiet. It wasn't until we returned to our tent, that he admitted to feeling rotten, and as the evening drew on he grew progressively worse. He writhed on his sweat-soaked mat, millimetres from the hard floor, his nose running as he groaned, complaining of a fierce chill, yet he was flaming hot to the touch. Then he said he couldn't breathe properly, that his chest hurt. I became increasingly alarmed, at which point it dawned on me that all his symptoms pointed to the Hantavirus, a deadly pulmonary syndrome. The two-to-three-week incubation period fitted perfectly with the night of hell in the mouse-infested *puesto* – and the long-tailed mouse that David had whacked with his shoe was the exact *Doppelgänger* of the creature we were seeing with 'Danger' emblazoned all over it on billboards alongside the road..

Hanta was introduced to Chile from the Far East a couple of decades ago. The virus is spread by mice and their faeces. Sun and fresh air are supposed to kill it, but if you are unlucky enough to contract it, there is a 38 per cent chance you will die. Country people sporadically succumb to it in rural Chile, but every decade or so, when the bamboo blooms and subsequently seeds, food becomes abundant for the mice and their populations explode (known as *ratadas*) and many people die. We researched what we could via a slow internet link, and found that there is no specific treatment, cure, or vaccine for Hanta virus. So bailing out from the expedition on an expensive medevac (the nearest hospital was over 200 miles away on rough back roads) merely to take a test didn't seem like a sensible plan. We chose rest and hoped that David's super fit body would fight the condition.

Next day he still felt hideous, yet doggedly insisted on running, so I pulled the trailer. He managed only ten miles before sweats and the tightness in his breathing made the idea of further progress farcical. Amazingly, we knew of friends of friends who owned a fishing lodge only three miles down the road and so we limped on in the hope that they would have us and David's virus to stay.

Carolina answered the door, a tall, beautiful Chilean from Santiago. She and her Dutch husband, Marcel, had created their home and business on the magical River Palena. I stood at the doorstep, explaining our tenuous link. She looked blank. Suddenly, a flicker of recognition chanced across her face and she invited us in, explaining that Marcel was away fishing for the day with some friends from Holland.

She appeared unsure as to where she could put us. We felt awkward and suggested we could camp in the garden (though desperately hoping a bed might be free). We looked dreadful; David half alive, both of us sweaty and dishevelled, with a filthy, clapped-out trailer and muddy bags: not exactly the most desirable of guests. But she wouldn't hear of us camping in the garden and instead showed us into a lovely bedroom, overlooking the banks of the river. David immediately collapsed into the soft mattress.

Marcel and Carolina injected a shot of serenity into our madness. For David it was essential, allowing him to eat sumptuous food, rest in a warm, dry, comfortable home and rebuild his strength. It also served as one of those rare times in our perpetual motion when we were able to stop and be with friends.

On the day we left them, we ran 20 miles, fuelled by Carolina's steak and quinoa lunch and stops for the homemade bread and little chocolates which she packed for us. I had no aches or pains and David had emerged out of the hanta virus fog with only a slightly restricted chest.

It calmly assessed us through its enormous bright yellow eyes

Bonnie.

Austral Pygmy-owl
Glaucidium nana

7 The End of the Carretera Austral

As we rounded the corner, something large was rustling the roadside vegetation. Out of the shrubs emerged two massive brown-and-white heads. Bulls! A plank of rough-hewn wood was strapped behind their curved horns, and in the middle of the yoke was a chain with which they were pulling an enormous tree trunk. They stared at us in a non-plussed, placid sort of a way. We stared back: four beasts-of-burden eyeing one another's cargo.

Our next meeting was far less congenial, being with a proprietor at Villa Santa Lucia. We had been running all day through torrents of rain and pounced on a café in an effort to warm up. Well – it was less a café, more the front room of a small, mean-mouthed woman's home. She eventually served us a small cup of instant coffee and a dishevelled white sandwich, with a thin slice of processed ham trapped inside. The miserable morsels barely bounced around the cavities of our stomachs, while her cold house only deepened the chill that was gripping our bodies. Our saturated clothes stuck to our legs as we dejectedly walked down the road, in search of somewhere to stay. Two hostels were closed; the third was open, although in retrospect it shouldn't have been: it should have been condemned.

It was a large house, which meant there were powerful drafts thundering through its walls and windows. Rain hammered on its tin roof and dripped through the sheets of plastic wavering in the windows. The hot water we were promised dribbled out of the shower in warm trickles, trending to freezing cold. We shared it with the landlady and her hairy family – although whether between them they had any hair remaining seemed debatable, considering the amount stuck to the shower and choking the plug holes. Wall sockets were to be used with the full realization that they could mark the end of one's life.

Our miserable stay was topped off by finding that a dog had stolen the meat from our trailer. But at least we did manage to dry some clothes around a meagre fire, while virtually standing inside it, much to the landlady's chagrin, and David repaired his threadbare shoes with a bicycle tyre in the hope that they might hold out for the next 200 miles to Puerto Montt, where new pairs were meant to be awaiting us.

The next settlement we ran through was Chaitén, 61 miles to the north of the hostel. Four years earlier the town had been engulfed by ash from a catastrophic eruption when a volcano came to life after 9,500 years of dormancy. Ash still cascaded from chimneys and windows, and the forests surrounding the three-kilometre diameter caldera were charred and coated in powdered white embers.

We found a café with wifi and watched a stream of *campesinos* (country folk) making a day of coming to town for the local elections. The café owner was frantically assembling one of the nation's favourites – white bread slices holding a sliver of reconstituted ham and processed cheese. It soon became clear from the length of the queue that one of the election candidates had bought a clutch of 1,000-*peso* tokens, giving one to each *campesino* in return for a vote. An assortment of thick-set, largely toothless voters were wielding their tokens, along with plastic bags bulging with household cleaners. Soon flushed, smiling faces were smacking their lips around sandwiches and slurping down instant coffee.

We asked about camping, at which people would poke their heads out of the door, then peer at us as if we were crackers for not being able to see that the whole place was a camp site! So we put up the tent in an abandoned garden at No. 311. It turned out we couldn't have been the first, as David stood in a human turd. The smell chased him about all the next day.

A little girl came and weed in our garden, receiving the shock of her life when she saw me tapping an article on my computer with my head torch within a metre of her bum. Aghast, she ran out screaming to her Mum, '¡*Mamá, hay una señora que está viviendo en el jardín!*' (Mum, there's a lady living in the garden!). Her Mother chided her, saying that of course there was no such thing, that she was imagining it. Luckily her daughter didn't persuade her to check.

David did his incredible trick of falling asleep within seconds of his head touching his mat. In the morning we awoke to a sound of a man in the garden mumbling something. When we finally crawled out, David discovered that he had been hacking the tap off, leaving the pipe gushing with water to flood the area.

The chaos and unpredictability of Chaitén didn't end there. After running eight miles from the town, we found that our road had turned into a runway. Lorries were bustling backwards and forwards in storms of dust, full of material for building a new airport. It all seemed rather fishy, like something from a James Bond set that we weren't supposed to have witnessed. Why on earth were they building an airport here, in the middle of nowhere? Perhaps it was linked to the expansion of the salmon-farm industry, the creation of the mega- dam project, or for other extraction imperatives aimed at developing the wild south. The dust troubled David: after the Hanta episode he was still finding it hard to breathe.

Running through Parque Pumalin, on the other hand, was blissful. This extraordinary protected area covers 715,000 acres of pristine, protected, Valdivian temperate rainforest and stretches from the heart of the Andes to the fjords of the Pacific Coast) It was a perfect evening, with a warm, golden light washing over the trees. Forest blossoms drenched the air with heady fragrances, and a dreamy sunset was spilling into the sky. We found an icy stream to dip in, and a *chucao* found us, her beak full of fat grubs. It felt like we had stepped into fairy land, as we dried our bodies with our running tops under a stand of gigantic gunnera leaves.

For me, this was paradise, and a stunning contrast with things at the other end of the continent. I thought of that clichéd greeting, 'Welcome to paradise,' which we often heard in the Caribbean at the sight of a cream-coloured beach and blue sea. What the person forgot to mention was that the sea had been over-fished, the coral was bleached and crumbling, the bay polluted and the beach stripped of its mangroves for the concrete hotels that now lined it.

To our paradise came a flotilla of visitors. As David made a spiced chicken-and- quinoa concoction in honour of Carolina, and boiled eggs for the next day's lunch, a small, caterpillar-like creature reared its head – a leech lured into our tent by our warmth and carbon dioxide breath. Three more followed, but unfortunately for them, each was hurled unceremoniously into the bushes, sparing our blood from their unconditional attention.

The next day saw the onset of rain and our arrival at the 15-mile marker we had been instructed to investigate by two cyclists we had met. A thin wisp of steam was the only sign of something lurking in the thick vegetation; but as we parted the leaves, a stench of sulphur filled the air and we came on a small, slightly-bubbling pool. We stripped off and sneaked in, perfectly hidden from the road, as we wallowed in the hot(ish) water under drips of rain and a ceiling of foliage in which a spider was knitting her web. It was lovely, especially when my turn came to push my buttocks into the hole we had excavated with our hands that was the main source of warmth.

Running through Parque Pumalin also heralded our impending rendezvous with two amazing people, Doug and Kris Tompkins, whom we had met when sailing south round Chile bound for Uruguay. Over the last twenty years they had conserved over two million acres of wilderness (more than any other private individuals in the world) in Chile and Argentina through their respective organisations, Conservation Land Trust and *Conservación Patagonica*. Their motive, they said, was simply 'To pay our rent for living on this planet.'

Buying land for the sole purpose of conserving it had never been heard of in Chile. Conspiracy theories abounded. There were claims that the Tompkins were setting up a new Zionist state, that they would claim Chilean border-land or steal Chile's water to sell it to Africa. The media revelled in the hype: they couldn't believe that someone would buy land to keep it wild, not build on it, not burn it for farmland, not chop down its trees for timber or extract its minerals. But we believed it, and before we started our run we had been determined to meet the couple again to find out more. What they had achieved through their trusts for conservation, as well as providing employment for local Chilean and Argentinian people, was monumental, and so we had decided to select *Conservación Patagonica* as one of the charities for which we would raise money

We were chuffed at arriving in the Park on foot, this time, and couldn't wait to catch up with the couple again. We settled deep into cushioned sofas and began asking Kris about her life, as plump raindrops burst against the windows,

'I've always loved grasslands,' she said. 'I grew up on a ranch in southern California and spent long days outside, exploring. The loss of the great grasslands of North America deeply troubled me. They were once home to tens of millions of bison, which shaped the vast floral and wildlife-rich ecosystems. That biodiversity-rich habitat and its enormous potential for carbon sequestration have been replaced by intensively-grazed, biodiversity-dead pasture and croplands. Only about one per cent of the former prairies remain.'

When I asked her about her greatest wildlife moments, she replied in her easy, unassuming manner, 'Sitting on a hill, looking over the Chacabuco Valley and watching guanacos from up on high. It was like a whole story in a snapshot: that the grasslands had never been in better shape (since modern man arrived) and that there, at that moment: guanacos, armadillos, pumas, rheas, and mountain vizcachas were all thriving.'

'What about those pumas?' I asked. 'Have you ever seen one?'

'I guess they're like boyfriends,' she said. 'When you look, you just can't find one. So I stopped looking, stopped concentrating on seeing them – but I still haven't caught sight of one!'

A ferry deposited us in the town of Hornopiren. It linked the road from Parque Pumalin that dropped into the sea 20 miles earlier. We decided this was an unfair advantage and that we should run the missed miles. In retrospect this was a good decision: allowing us to claim a first for running the entire Carretera Austral of Chile, it also meant running through the stunning foothills of the Hornopiren National Park and meeting with a new animal.

We didn't need the trailer, so instead took turns carrying a rucksack stuffed with a water bottle, food, camera and binoculars. We often discussed the limitations of running with the trailer. How much further would we be able to run per day if we didn't have to pull it? How much was it impeding our running style and sapping our energy? How much would our physical and mental wellbeing improve if we had a support crew looking after us, providing food, drink, showers, massages and a bed each night?

We hoped to be the first in the world to run the continent unsupported – *i.e.* without all the above, but we knew that Pat Farmer had run South America *with* the above, and this intrigued us. He ran up to fifty miles each day. Could we manage that with a team caring for our wellbeing, without the daily battle of sourcing and preparing food and finding a place to sleep? We thought this 20-miler might give us an idea. Our conclusion: running 20 miles is always tough, with or without a trailer, and our admiration for Pat Farmer remained unabated.

A miniature deer, similar in size to a badger, stepped into the middle of the track. We were downwind of the little guy, and we froze. Its wet nose sniffed the air and its oval ears twitched. Its dark eyes bore into us. It was a Chilean *pudu* which had miraculously decided to forsake its shelter at the instant we rounded the corner into its world. We watched for over ten minutes, transfixed, as it quietly snuffled the gravel, trotted down the track and threaded in and out of the undergrowth. Then it snuck off into the forest, leaving us alone, clinging to the whisper of its memory.

As we ran the last miles into Puerto Montt, we once again connected with the sea. A man was collecting pitchforks-full of seaweed from a grey mud flat, overlooked by two dogs. His horse stood patiently, attached to a home-made wooden cart into which he threw his treasure. Great, rubbery fronds of seaweed (*pelillo* or *gracilaria*) are knotted together and hung in the markets and open-fronted shops stretching from Chiloe to Valdivia. Apparently it's a delicacy, full of nutrients and great in soups and stews or as *nori* for ceviche. It's also industrially exported for soaps and shampoos.

Puerto Montt marked the end of the Carretera Austral. A CNN Chilean reporter had got wind of the expedition and a camera reeled millimetres from my nose. 'We're the first in the world to have run the magnificent Carretera Austral,' I beamed. 'We didn't think we would ever make it. What a place, what wildlife! One of the most magical lands in the world! We shall miss it.' What we didn't say was how sad we thought it was that the road was being *improved*. Across copious billboards was written, '*Mejoramientos*' (improvements). We looked at the overhanging trees, the scarlet and purple fuchsia blooms, the hummingbirds zipping across, and wondered how the government really thought it could improve this.

Puerto Montt also marked our meeting with a special group of friends whom we had met when living there on our boat. It brought our first major kit change: swapping cold-weather gear for the warm-weather kit we had left with them and meant the arrival of our desperately-needed new shoes. Leaving our friends was tough. Once again we were about to be on our own, vagabonds on the long, winding road north. But charging through town soon concentrated my mind, as I powered forward, adrenalin surging, rocketing past cars in my bid to outrun them.

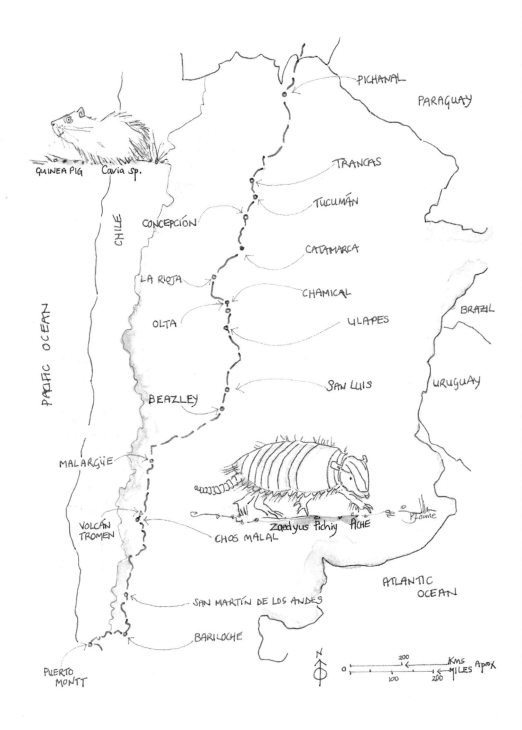

PICHANAL

PARAGUAY

QUINEA PIG   Cavia sp.

CHILE

CONCEPCIÓN

TRANCAS

TUCUMÁN

CATAMARCA

PACIFIC OCEAN

LA RIOJA

CHAMICAL

BRAZIL

OLTA

ULAPES

URUGUAY

BEAZLEY

SAN LUIS

MALARGÜE

Zaedyus Pichiy   Áche

P. Towne

VOLCÁN
TROMEN

CHOS MALAL

ATLANTIC
OCEAN

SAN MARTÍN DE LOS ANDES

BARILOCHE

N

0   200   Kms   Aprox
100   200   Miles

PUERTO
MONTT

Map 5 – Our Running Route through Argentina

A Male Californian quail, peered out of a bush at us

8 Running Blind

Enormous gardens, opulent 'piles' and towering electric fences surrounded us on every side. We were running through the wealthy suburbs of Bariloche in Argentina, (see Map 5) and the residents had done a fine job of preventing vagrants, such as ourselves, from infiltrating their territory. Finding a place to camp was going to be tricky. As the evening drew in we got more and more crotchety with one another. Then I noticed a field behind a bus stop, with a gap in the fence and a well-used path. In the fading light it looked like a park of sorts, so we plumped for it, putting the tent up under a hedge.

Just as we placed the first steaming morsels of mashed potato and sausage in our mouths, we were blinded by searchlights and shouts. We couldn't decipher what exactly was being said, but there was definitely mention of police, guns and criminals and it appeared to be directed as us. I shouted from the tent, *'Hola, disculpeme, ¿está todo bien?'* (Hello, sorry, but I hope everything is ok?) Predictably, this didn't work: a renewed volley of verbal abuse was launched, and I scrambled out to face the fireworks.

An irate woman was straddling the fence, with steam shooting from her ears. 'What the hell do you think you're doing on my land, my *private* land?' she screamed. 'You have no right. How many are you? I have a gun and I will use it! The police are coming.'

I was horrified. How was I going to calm down this fuming witch?

'You're lucky I didn't shoot you,' she went on. 'You must get off my land right away.'

I desperately tried to placate her. 'I'm so sorry. We thought we were camping on public land. It's just my husband and me here; we're running the length of South America for charity. It's so very hard to find places to camp. We're exhausted. We had no idea this was your land, otherwise we would have asked you.'

I went on. She was still annoyed, but her fire was dying. Finally, after many apologies from me, she said we could stay, but that we must leave as soon as it was light. 'What a bloody miserable woman,' I growled when at last she had gone. 'How ridiculous! What was she thinking? Murderers would hardly begin an attack by sitting in someone's garden in a tent and waving lights around! Welcome to Argentina!'

We woke up as a thread of light was creeping over the horizon. I peered out of the tent. A man was hauling a frog-eyed Jersey cow on a lead down to the grass. I shoved on my leggings and top and ventured out to speak to him. He was the partner of the demonic woman, and so I repeated our apologies and explained our situation. He was very amiable and to my amazement offered us water and a shower, catapulting us from criminals to guests in one night! The thought of warm water was too good a temptation to eschew, so David and I walked up to the house, wondering if breakfast might be added to the invitation!

The husband was an interesting guy, with a collection of whittled wooden chairs that appeared to have been made for a council of wizards. We spoke in hushed voices, as *La Señora* was still sleeping, thank goodness. But by the time I padded down from my fabulous de-lousing, she had surfaced and was constructing breakfast with a poker-faced intensity that suggested she did *not* feel the same way as her husband. We didn't dally for offers of food, but hot-footed away, before she had time to chase us down with her gun!

We had always hoped we would be able to run with people along the route, but the practicalities of organising and achieving this on the hoof in remote areas, without internet or phone access, meant that it very rarely happened. Our first major town in Argentina seemed like a perfect place to try. So we contacted a friend to see whether she knew of any running groups who might be interested. We never imagined how deeply this would affect us.

We waited at the bus station for three running partners. Soon after Kari arrived so did Hector and Negro, each holding one end of a short length of black elastic. Kari casually mentioned Hector's lack of sight, but made no big deal of it. It somehow felt normal that we should be embarking on a ten-mile run along the busiest road in the area, peppered with large stones, broken drains and a rough verge, with a blind athlete and a heavily-laden trailer. After some last minute logistics (giving Hector a chance to try out the trailer) we sped off, with an incredible sunset forming over the mountains.

After 1,400 miles, David and I had some fairly significant twinges, but as we loosened up the stiffness that had formed since the morning's 12-mile stint, the significance of the evening bore in upon us. We ran as a group, each with a little something different in his or her closet. Never did Hector complain about his lack of sight, and his companions, the ultra-marathoners Negro and Kari, scarcely mentioned their own feats as they guided him through various hazards. That evening we learned something about overcoming huge hurdles; of thinking not of the barriers, but only of the attitude that allows one to surpass them. I felt sure there would be reason to remember that further down the track.

One of the first camp-sites we found north of Bariloche was hidden among weeping willows and broom on the banks of a river, 300 metres from the road. I waded through beds of mint and sat mid-current, naked and slightly blue, feeling the water swirl around my stomach. Birds flicked through the foliage above my head and tiny fish darted past my toes. It was beautiful; finding a camp by a river was and would always be the ultimate in terms of relaxation, ease of cooking, drinking and washing; but also for the wildlife that was drawn, just like we were, to this most fundamental of life forces.

A fine dust of *ceniza* (ash) was falling on us. A volcano in Chile's Puyehue-Cordon Caulle chain had erupted the previous year, cloaking the border pass and the town of Angostura in drifts of noxious pumice. Unfortunately for Argentinians, prevailing winds are from the west, so that the inhabitants have to deal with the consequence of the explosions. I hadn't imagined we would be living in the ash some 17 months later. Our problem was that it was so fine that it found its way into the keys of our laptop, settled in the zip of the tent, coated our belongings and food and filled our orifices. I couldn't wait to run out of it.

Our road north through Argentina was by no means straightforward. Originally we had planned to run in the foothills of the cordillera, where freshwater springs should theoretically abound. But now dreams of running on the flat were tempting us inland. The settlement of Confluencia was one of the points at which we could start making our bid for higher speeds, by taking a sharp north-east turn to Neuquén, before heading north to 25 de Mayo, Santa Isabel and San Luis. But local people, and the satellite images we checked, forecast days of water-shortages in a land of salt-pans and seasonal rivers. The area is extremely remote, so we couldn't rely on finding houses either.

So, instead of striding out flat and fast, we elected to run slow and steep, on a thick gravel track, spiralling up into the heavens of Parque Nacional Lanin over Paso Cordoba. Luckily the petrol station of Confluencia (there was no settlement) had a few shelves of biscuits we could add to our provisions, but more importantly a coffee and a custard-tart flan that fuelled the day's ascent. Even luckier, the guy behind the counter was lovely, and after a long chat plied us with biscuits smothered in *manjar* (think the topping on a banoffee pie) and chocolate.

We set off on a series of switchbacks through a stunning, sun-blistered land-scape reminiscent of Syria or Spain. Xerophytic (drought-resistant) vegetation prickled through the dry earth; lines of willow and navy lupins marked the course of a few tinkling streams, and conifers needled from the mountain slopes. The ground was fragile, with the plants only just anchoring it in place. Most spectacular of all were the jagged peaks, like fingers probing the sky, looking as though they might tumble to the earth after the next night's episode of freeze-thawing. I marvelled at the mystical castles conjured by the rock extrusions, and imagined the hillsides wrenching themselves to their knees and shakily taking their first steps. In one seam of rock a small cave had become a home, which, along with a number of other cavities we spied, was used by passing shepherds.

Having somehow notched 22 miles, we found a patch of grass tucked away from the track, under a cluster of wizened ñirre trees, with a little stream weaving through boulders 50 metres below. It was three o'clock, and we were exhausted, so we unrolled our mats and lay comatose in the blissful shade. I imagined scorpions scuttling into our ears, as I have read they are wont to do in similarly-parched southern European landscapes. But luckily no one visited our eardrums. Instead, I found a puma footprint in the ash at the entrance to our camp, and then a male Californian quail, which, although on the wrong continent, was extraordinary to behold, with its black feather plume jutting out from its forehead like an old-fashioned railway signalling mechanism.

After a short slumber, we clawed ourselves from the grip of lethargy and scrambled down to the stream to drink, wash and wake up. We filled our pans with water and soon had them boiling, to fill our bellies with as much food as possible. As we cooked, a condor soared over the peak that guarded our camp-site like a sentinel. House wrens chortled, rufous-necked sparrows, black-chinned siskins and Austral blackbirds flittered through the bushes. The setting was perfect, and we wished that every night could be like this, under the eye of a mountain, remote and silent, save for the whisper of wild animals and plants. An enormous full moon climbed into the sky, and twinkling stars joined it in this 360-degree wilderness.

We awoke to a frost and a coolness we had only dreamed of during the past sun-baked days. Delighted by its fresh embrace, we meandered through conifer plantations, around lakes and along rivers. The next major settlement, San Martín de los Andes, was 45 miles away, at the bottom of a mountain, below a series of snaking curves. When David mentioned to a couple of Germans staying in the hostel that we intended running through the Amazon, they replied by slowly drawing their fingers across their throats.

The next two long days saw us running through gravel and dust over a continuous chain of hills, as we headed for the Aluminé valley. The heat was becoming oppressive. We made gloves to protect our hands from the sun and wore spare T-shirts over our caps, creating odd, nun-on-the-run apparitions. The arrangement was great for avoiding the rays of the sun, but not so great for oxygen or air movement, steadily flooding our faces a beetroot hue.

Luckily a brief reprieve lay ahead. Fiona (David's sister) and Octavio (her friend) were on their way to meet us. Now with lesser mortals the vague arrangements we made for a rendezvous might be considered ill-conceived, but Fiona has a rare instinct that has allowed her to find us in the most obscure and remote places, using all manner of transport methods to get there.

And so it was that three days after leaving San Martin we were trotting down the road with a huge herd of cattle galloping in a cloud of dust, when the first car of the day came hurtling up behind us and skidded to a halt. Out jumped Fiona and Octavio. A mixture of pleasure and gratitude swamped us. Having decided to meet again in a few miles by a river, they steamed off for food, ice and cold drinks.

We took a whole day off, chatting, eating and swimming under the willow trees by a turquoise river. The only event happened when, across the river, a southern lapwing chick make a bid for adulthood, much to the distress of its screaming mother. Octavio plunged in, rescued the squeaking, waterlogged chick and returned it to its parent. Meanwhile, a steamer duck eyed us from the cradle of a nearby willow tree, where she was steadfastly warming four fluffy chicks under ample feathered skirts.

Next day Fiona and Octavio disappeared back over the pass to Chile. We were alone once again – just us, and a sinking feeling about the thousands of miles that stretched out in front. The following days were filled with more dust, heat, punishing wind and an explosion of earwigs which swarmed through our tent. We stopped to speak to a smart old man digging a ditch. Folds of leathery skin hung from a smiling face, punctured by two sparkling eyes. He shook our hands firmly and motioned towards the black-faced ibis that were probing the field, 'Comen bichos muy feos!' (They eat nasty/ugly animals). 'Bichos muy feos' was a phrase we heard throughout South America in relation to just about anything that moved. Luckily for the black-faced ibis, they were the only creatures we had come across that weren't good for the pot, largely due to the fact that they ate the 'ugly ones'.

We failed to find any source of water along the tracks we were running. This had a knock-on effect on our psychology, but more pressingly on our physiology. Water is necessary for all bodily functions, especially when you're running nearly a marathon every day in an oven. Our difficulties were compounded by our inability to plan for top-ups, as the only maps and satellite images we could source were woefully lacking in detail. This forced us to filter water from a pool in which a donkey had just shat.

Luckily our water-pump was amazing, with its ability to filter-out not only dirt, but also amoebas and metal contaminates. Apparently it's also able to convert urine into water. So we were confident in having the means to create drinkable water: it was just a question of finding something that vaguely resembled it and then bracing ourselves for the hours of pumping that would provide the 20 litres we needed per day (not including the extra water we would need for cooking). Washing ourselves and our clothes was out of the question.

On the road out of the small town of Aluminé we ran past dusty slopes peppered with monkey-puzzle trees. We had been hoping to see these extraordinary fossil trees, that can live for over a millennium, in their native home. Firm favourites of Victorian plant hunters, they are familiar in gardens and stately homes in the UK. We heard a lot about them in Chile and their importance to the *Pehuenche* people, whose entire society was formed around them and their edible seeds. But for us, it was the notion that dinosaurs would have roamed around then, over two hundred million years ago, that really sent shivers down our spines.

Jagged, spiked vegetation straddled the roadsides, showing what measures life had to take to survive in this inferno. A string of lorries passed on their conveyor belt of a route, bringing propane to Chile from Argentina's southern gas fields and ferrying empty lorries back from Chile. This provided the clue as to why gas was so cheap in Argentinian Patagonia – why households burned gas ovens all day and night and heaters were left on for days on end. It seemed extraordinary that this transport of gas was worthwhile, considering the fuel expended by the lorries. Why weren't they returning with *palta* (avocado) or something to make the transaction more efficient?

Chile's *palta* is amazing. Nowhere else have we found it as delicious or eaten as much. It's a long-distance runner's delight, packed full of calories, dietary fibre, vitamins C and B, potassium and magnesium. We would squish it on bread or crackers or squeeze it straight into our mouths. The *Hass* variety, a small, dark-skinned cultivar, is the king, and miraculously it would turn up even in the most sparsely-supplied and least-expected remote Chilean corner stores. As a boost to our trailer's provisions, we missed it sorely in Argentina.

Butter gave us another medium for calorie-boosting. It transformed even the most cardboard-tasting bread into something luxurious, especially with a sprinkling of salt – something our bodies were craving. But our ability to transport it was now floored by the soaring temperatures. This didn't stop us from trying to find it, but a transition to olive oil was inevitable. This led to another problem. No sooner had we laced a cracker (these were our mainstay, being ubiquitous in grocery stores across Argentina) than the golden liquid was lost through the holes. The only response was to swig some oil back, allowing a small pool to form in the reservoir of our mouths, and follow it with a good bite of cracker, so that the mixing went on within, rather than without.

Our Patagonian freezer was sorely missed. No longer could we store five shelled eggs in our water bottle for an undetermined period of time. Now we had to create serious strategies for food consumption, or, as was often the case, eat something just before it upped and walked out of our bags of its own accord.

A flash of green pulsed in the desert. Sand blasted our legs and arms. The heat-haze morphed that green spot of hope into nothingness. At times it seemed it couldn't possibly be 15 miles away, but the asphalt road was unbelievably straight. That green spot, which flickered and wilted in the mirage, was Las Lajas; our next town and refuelling stop. But first we had to descend 1,844 metres from Paso Pino Hachado.

We had been working our way up to its heights since Aluminé, but now the road was asphalt, and we were coming down fast, for 24 miles to be exact, before we found a ditch to crawl into. The descent was excruciatingly uncomfortable. This is the reality of running long-distances: the up-hills are a breeze compared with the pain of drumming knees and hips on the descents. Add to this the strain of holding-back a heavily laden trailer, and the pain would become audible – at which point we would begin the cyclical discussion as to whether we should fit brakes to the trailer. This would help our joints, but would add weight to the already-groaning beast we hauled behind us. Anyway, we were destined for flat lands, which would render the addition pointless. That night my knees burned, and neither of us slept. A ditch offered zero protection from the wind that grew ever fiercer, and by one o'clock in the morning, as the gale ripped at the tent, we were ready to take off.

Somehow we survived and sleep-walked our way through packing up our gear. As we checked the camp-site a last time for anything we had missed, our three roll-top waterproof bags were standing by the edge of the road. Suddenly a pick-up appeared from nowhere and stopped. The driver jumped out and heaved the bags into the back of his truck. We couldn't believe our eyes, it was happening so quickly: in 30 seconds all our belongings would be lost forever and the expedition finished. We sprinted across to the pick-up shouting.

The poor man looked up, shocked at the *gringos* bursting from the thorns. He had clearly thought the baggage had dropped off a lorry, and hadn't dreamt that someone would have intentionally put it there. '¡*Disculpe, disculpe!*' (Sorry!) he spluttered, his ruddy cheeks flushing to an even deeper hue as he practically propelled the bags back into the air and scrambled back into his jeep, roaring off into the dust.

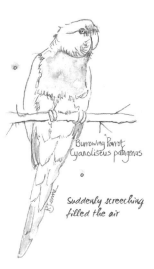

Burrowing Parrot
Cyanoliseus patagonus

Suddenly screeching
filled the air

9 Into No-Man's Land

A shiver of fear flickered through my senses as we left the safety of Las Lajas. Ahead lay a forbidding expanse of desert. We were following a road, but traffic was infrequent and in contrast, the expanse of nothingness felt all-pervading, stretching for mile-upon-windswept-mile. The few vehicles that passed did so at breakneck speed, leaving us in their scorched wake, as if they too desperately desired to rid themselves of this hellish no-man's land.

The steppe-land had, like Patagonia to its south, been grazed to destruction. The dry earth, liberated from the millions of roots that had once tethered it, was now eddying into the air and dancing across the road, joined by endlessly vaulting and spiralling tumbleweed. A dried-up carcass of a cow reminded us of what would happen if we strayed off the road. A broken plastic stool had been propped upside down among a stack of boulders. Further down the road, an old tyre was held in place by a cairn of stones, with a plastic bag tethered to it, rippling in the breeze. A set of tyre tracks marked the entrance to an *estancia,* lurking far off in the indiscernible distance. That was it: for the next 20 miles we saw nothing save discarded bottles, plastic bags and used nappies chucked out by passing motorists and flung into the bushes by the wind.

When we first opened the South American pages of our atlas and traced endless possible routes down its long spine, we had marvelled at the romantic-sounding place names such as *Pozo del tala, La Buitrera, Cabra Muerte.* They seemed full of intrigue and excitement. It was only now, with our grasp of Spanish improved, that we could fully appreciate the significance of the pedigree of the places we would be passing through: *Pozo del tala,* literally means 'well of the fellings' (dread to think what might have been felled). *La Buitrera* means 'vulture colony,' and *Cabra Muerte* 'dead goat'! Not exactly cosy inviting places to be aiming for!

Sudden screeching filled the air as an unexpected flock of birds bombed into view. Parrots! Their plumage was olive, with grey breast and yellow belly, blotched scarlet. Their eyes seemed huge, with white hallows and upward streaks, as if they had been at the eyeliner and painted their tummies with lipstick. How on earth could they live here in such a barren world? Evidently they had eaten whatever it was they had found to feed on, and now they were streaming back to a colony of nests excavated in an unconsolidated limestone cliff by the side of the road. Burrowing parrots construct the largest colonies of any parrots, with zig-zag-shaped nests interconnecting to form elaborate labyrinths. Heads poked out of the Swiss cheese rock, scrutinising us; others preened, some shrieked, but all within their tight pair bonds.

My knees still throbbed from the mountain descent into Las Lajas, and as the elation of seeing the parrots wore off, the running became tough. It was also hampered by the wind that was back with a vengeance. But there was no option for making this a short day; we had three days' worth of water strapped to the trailer, before (we were told, and prayed) there would be a house at which to replenish. Our mission was set and impossible to change.

As we wore down the day's miles, so the sun sank, and the desolate, rocky hillside turned yellow. Then something remarkable happened: the sky exploded. The thin layers of mare's tails went on fire, red blazed against indigo, before turning into peach and mauve. It was extraordinary, we had never seen anything like it, and it seemed to go on for mile upon mile in this land of the sky.

Night was rapidly descending and our desert bedroom was becoming shrouded in grey. We had managed to reach the 20-mile mark, and now we had to find somewhere to camp before the last of the light was extinguished. As we were ditching the trailer to prospect in the thorns, a mini-tornado swept down the road towards us, swirling earth dust and thorns in its vortex. First came a howling wind, then the debris tearing at our bodies, and suddenly the 100-kilo trailer was lurching down the road on its own.

We ran after it, shouting at it, one another and the wind. Eye-scorching lights bore down upon us, then were gone, with only two red spots marking their passage. We looked back, trembling. In the gloom we could just make out our life-line, the trailer. Somehow the jeep had swerved out of its way, somehow it was still in one piece and our provisions were intact. This land was not to be taken lightly. I felt it was watching us, that it could easily swallow us if we made a wrong move.

Desperate to sleep, and with few options in the dark, we decided to string the tarp up under a thorn bush. It was a bad decision; sleep evaded us as we tossed and turned on the hard, bumpy surface, five-centimetre thorns skewered us, the tarp flapped and insects crawled over us. The wind wouldn't abate, and all the next day we ran uphill against its infuriating force.

People must think we are crazy, battling against our invisible foe through an empty land (David wrote). We can't hear or speak to one another because it roars in our ears and carries our voices away. The grit pelts us in the legs, arms and face. Dust fills my nose, eyes and ears. Katharine is miserable. She says she would rather run up a mountain than against the wind.

Everyone advised us that there would be no water for three days so we loaded up with extra supplies. We couldn't trust people's advice, or our basic maps and satellite images, which meant we always had to run heavy, with extra water, just in case. But even with that safety net, we still weren't drinking enough. We were hardly peeing, and when we did, it was a thick orange syrup. I felt faint. We vowed to drink more and started taking rehydration salts.

Black vultures circled the road, picking the carcasses of leathery horses, goats and cattle. I have a reverence for these royal birds, with their acute eyesight and honed sense of smell, allowing them to detect a fallen animal from thousands of metres away. But I was convinced we were a tumble away from their coming for us. I scrawled in my diary that night:

> Bottles are strewn by the side of the road, many half full. Is it water? Perhaps some left-over orangeade? I'm desperate to grab them, to pour the liquid down my throat. But I suspect that it's urine, so I run on. David makes supper; spaghetti and salami. He says he'll sprout a curly tail, the amount of pig we're consuming, and that he'll never eat salami again (I know he will). I yearn for home food, dream of making scones, oat cakes and jam; of salads, vegetables and fruit. It's a good job we have vitamins, because I think we would start falling apart without them. I imagine writing my book in Spanish. David elucidates how it would go in a thick Geordie accent: 'Well, erm, *mucho frío* (very cold) to start with, then, *mucho viento* (very windy) for a long time, descending to *mucho calor* (very hot)…' It's going to be a huge success!

After 80 miles and four days of running from Las Lajas, we reached Naunauco. Burrowing parrots were regularly shooting across our path, and we found some clues as to what they forage upon, watching them picking seeds from shrubs near the road and from herbs on the ground. We had also entered the world of the guinea pig, with sand-coloured, hairy rodents dashing into scrub and hurtling down burrows as soon as they caught a glimpse of us. Even when we stealthily slipped into the bushes to observe them, they would be gone in a flick of sand.

We ended up staying for three nights in Chos Malal, the next town on the map, while David administered the same treatment (RICE) that had cured me in southern Chile upon his own ankle. But he found it difficult to sleep, with sore, restless legs and an out-of-kilter body-clock. We quickly learnt that, to avoid the heat of the day, the town slumbered between midday and six in the evening; but we found a local source of the sweetest, freshly-picked cherries. I had an encounter with an Argentinian's daily meat quota, witnessing the carcase of an entire cow sailing down the conveyor belt of a small local shop for the price of a couple of pounds.

With the RICE remedy once again winning, we struck north out of town, straight into the teeth of a fierce wind, which pelted us with stones and grit as we ran up the mountainside. We were making for Tromen Volcano, but the conditions were dreadful and we had no idea where we could find shelter. When a small farmstead surrounded by trees appeared half-way up the mountain, it seemed our only hope that night.

No one answered our calls, but the emaciated, brindled greyhounds that snapped and growled slunk into the shadows when we hauled the trailer through the gate. I walked towards a brick shed and peered into the windows. An old wooden table, a large cleaver, a few rusting chairs and bags of animal feed filled it. Various leather reins and harnesses hung from the joists that held up its corrugated iron roof. An enormous flock of speckled hens, ducks, turkeys, geese and chicks of various ages rushed after me. They were flapping their wings, squawking and chirping in a frenzy of expectant feeding, while trying to remain earth-bound in the furious gusts.

A hay barn had been constructed with walls of boulders. The roof was made of criss-crossed wooden planks, topped with corrugated iron. A couple of roughly-hewn poles acted as pillar supports. It sounds sturdy, but it was sagging dramatically in the centre. Turrets of square hay bales reached to the roof. House sparrows were nesting in cracks in the walls, and their chicks sat with yellow mouths agape, calling for food.

We had found our home for the night and began to arrange the softest of hay mattresses to sleep on. A red-and-white Hereford calf wandered into the barn and licked our trailer as we ate salami and cheese sandwiches, while the feather-duster hens scurried about in an effort to line up their chicks for bed. This was one of the most perfect homes we would ever find: we just hoped everyone would behave themselves and settle down to bed and that the owner wouldn't appear. 'In the top row, that's enough talking for one night!' David warned the chickens squeaking in the hay loft. A marmalade hen fluffed herself out to extraordinary dimensions and attempted to keep the five chicks nestled within her plumes from wandering off. Despite her attempts, startled heads kept peeking over her parapet.

The stars began popping out; I mused about which one we should be following. The owner still hadn't appeared. The dogs were tightly curled into the hay. I had lost the blood in the end of my finger, even though we had sipped steaming hot chocolate; incredible when you think how brutally hot it had been in Chos Malal – but then we had climbed to 1,400 metres.

A fine layer of sand and grit covered us. We imagined being unable to open our eyes in the morning. The wind was insane and must have been gusting over

50 knots as it hurled itself at the barn; it had bent us double as we ran. Everything creaked and clattered. The trees screamed, their leaves cascading to the ground and their branches violently shaking. Inanimate objects were coming alive and taking to the air. We stared at the wildly-contorting roof, praying it wouldn't come down.

We awoke to find our orifices filled with sand. At least we woke up and weren't found dead beneath a collapsed barn! The owner arrived in a clapped out old Ford with sacks of grain and proceeded to feed all his clamouring livestock, without the slightest concern about the two battered runners emerging from his dusty barn. The wind hadn't abated, but we ran on. On the pass between Volcano Tromin and Cerro Wayle we reached 2,400 metres. Black, crusted larva flows watched us unblinking from a menacing moonscape. The wind was squeezed between the hills until it raged like a furious animal. We could barely stand up. David crashed to the ground. We gave up speaking. We tried filming, but the roar of the wind was too great. I had no control when I peed; the wind sprayed it all over my legs.

A gaucho came riding through the thorns, herding his goats. A kid broke away and hurtled, bleating, towards us. The pleading ball of wool was difficult to resist and fortuitously attracted the gaucho. 'You'll find a cluster of trees and a hut in about four miles,' he shouted. 'There's water, too.' Relieved at the prospect of escaping from the hurricane, we ran on, gradually beginning the descent from the plateau. Seven miles later, with heads and shoes full of grit, there was still no sign of a shelter or a stream. 'What the hell was he thinking?' David snorted, furious with the man and his false forecast. We had long since drained our water supplies and were desperate for moisture.

A sweet and unexpected smell of jasmine filled the air. The desert was blooming yellow and blue, but all we could think about was our bodies screaming for water. We had run 22 miles, and needed to stop. At which point we noticed that the road was descending into a canyon. There was no way we could camp until we found water, even if it meant running all night. We were fools not to have filled up in a stream on the other side of the pass. We had wanted to avoid heaving extra weight in the atrocious conditions . . . Then I noticed an Andean gull wheeling in the air. Could this be the sign we had been dreaming of? We ran on, and just as our watch bleeped 24 miles, we saw it. 'Water! It's water!' I shrieked.

David was already scrambling out of the trailer harness. Together we ran to the stream, gulping the freezing liquid from our hands. If people passed fizzy drinks to us when they saw us galloping along the road, the combination of 'sugar, cold and wet' was fantastic, filling us with energy and cooling us. But nothing could ever quench our thirst so well, or rival the taste of this pure, gurgling, living mountain water.

After waterlogging our innards and filling our saucepans, bottles and sacks, we stripped off and wallowed in the icy torrent, watching swallows flitting over our heads. Patagonian sierra finches, *canasteros* and earth creepers were singing and stabbing insects in the boulders. A speckled lizard, almost indistinguishable from the rock he was sunbathing on, bobbed his head, while clenching a bright-yellow flower between his lips. An astounding cloud formed overhead, filling the sky as it layered up into a giant meringue. It looked other-worldly, burning with the colours of the dying sun, as though at any stage Martians would file out of its crust.

The days that followed were hellish, as we pulled the trailer like a pair of oxen ploughing along the gravel and sand road. The wind tormented us and dust storms pelted us. A heat-haze shimmered over a hostile, barren landscape, littered with bones and carcases cremated by the sun. I couldn't conjure any kind of love towards it, with its spikes and destitution, its parched vegetation and stripped earth. We were both feeling low and sore.

> I'm not enjoying running (David wrote). I'm not even enjoying the camping! At least in Chile there was beautiful camping, protection and abundant water. Here the wind pummels us by day and by night we battle to prevent it from casting us into the air or ripping our tent to pieces. Water is a constant concern in this barren world.

I too was starting to hate Argentina and its nothingness. I understand how someone might want to journey through it by car, even by bicycle, but on foot, in 20-mile chunks, it was insufferable. Nothing changed, nothing fed the soul: just a slight bend in the road if you were lucky. The funny thing was that when one of those rare bends appeared, it was often accompanied by 300 metres of signage, preparing the motorist for the monumental occasion. We imagined finding fallen Argentinian road engineers floundering by the road, overwhelmed by its relentless curves.

Then one afternoon we had an encounter which brought our mood to a record low. We had already run 20 miles and were desperate to end the day, but nothing, not an iota of camping opportunity revealed itself – just that scorched, windswept, treeless land, smirking at us. Then on rounding a corner we saw, perhaps three miles away, a cluster of poplars; the first of the day. Hope filled us.

A sandy track, over half a mile long, wound towards a collection of decaying buildings. We crossed two small streams which would allow us to drink and cook. A dog barked and I noticed a man working in one of the buildings. I practised my best Spanish phrases in my head. It took a while to summon his attention, but finally he came towards me. His mouth was set in a snarl and his eyes were black. I tried to be jovial as I explained our predicament, but he stood expressionless, studying me. A good two minutes passed.

Finally he grunted, '¿De dónde eres?' (Where are you from?) 'Chile,' I replied. This was my stock answer, as we had started the expedition in Chile and it allowed us to avoid mentioning the UK, which is not the greatest of bed-fellows with Argentina. He shook his head, a flicker of disgust travelling across his face, 'No, ¿qué país?' (No, what country?) There was no avoiding it, 'Reino Unido' (the UK), I blurted. 'You mean England?' he eyeballed me, his teeth grinding and his head shaking. I pleaded, 'We won't bother you; you won't even know we're here. We just need some cover to camp in far down there under the trees.'

'Madre de Dios,' (Mother of gods) he spat. 'But you are bothering me, because you're English.'

A mixture of anger and indignation surged through my body. He started muttering something, but it was barely audible. He cast his eyes around the buildings and growled, 'If you must stay, you stay close, where I can see you.' I could feel a lump forming in my throat. 'This man's a pariah,' I thought. His land was the only possible shelter we had found in twenty miles, and yet he was happy to cast us out, because of our nationality. Tears were welling in my eyes; I couldn't bear to be near him. I scrambled back to David. 'We're leaving.'

I was inconsolable, and outraged at his inhuman behaviour. I had been discriminated against only once before. The one consolation was that both incidents provided a tiny glimpse of what others go through, often daily, through absolutely no fault of their own; just dealing with the brutal face of ignorance. We searched for hours for a place to camp; annoyed, exhausted and exasperated with the man, Argentina and ourselves. Eventually we found a small goat corral. The shepherd had created the fencing out of thorns, weaving them into a wind-break. It would have to do. It proved scant cover from the raging wind and we awoke to the inside of our tent carpeted in dust and goats' droppings, with ants scurrying all over the detritus and us. Then we noticed the trailer. Its tyres were skewered by a thousand thorns that we must have run over when reaching the corral in the dark.

Forty-four miles down the road, after two more days, we found ourselves eyeing another stand of poplars. How would my question be received this time? I wandered towards the cluster of buildings. No one answered my calls. I turned away, but suddenly noticed a woman. As I drew closer I saw she was stoking an enormous clay oven. Her long, black, glossy hair was combed into a centre parting and swept back into a pony tail. I approached smiling and to my relief she smiled back, insisting we camp wherever we liked.

Three children came skipping towards us in order of height, with the smallest, who couldn't have been more than three, trailing behind his bigger sisters. They were bashful, with huge chestnut eyes, but determined to help us with our load. We passed them a water bottle, my jumper and a pair of trainers. They trotted in front of us with their prizes, showing the way. Most of the land had been reduced to dust, but the family had planted a couple of hedgerows and so we pitched the tent in the lee of one. The children were fascinated, and we soon learned their ages and names: Diana (seven), Suyana (five) and Juan (three). 'And what age do you think I am?' I grinned at the three upturned faces. 'Eighty, seventy-five, ninety!' they chimed.

They insisted on ferrying our chattels from the trailer into our tent. We had laminated a map of South America, so we showed them our route through it and described the landscapes and animals we had seen; what the weather was like and what the people grew in their fields. They asked us what *our* country was like, and we told them, adding that in the past many Britons had migrated to Argentina to farm and construct railways. We were shattered and needed to sleep. They whispered outside our tent for a few minutes, then scurried off.

Perhaps 40 hot minutes passed before our zip was pulled open and three little faces appeared grinning at us. 'It's lunch time!' I looked at David, 'I'm sure they mean it's their lunch time. They can't be inviting us?' I hesitated. The faces looked expectant. We decided I should go first and suss out the situation. Two little hands latched onto mine and we trotted over to a rectangular building. Inside, their father and mum stood beaming, welcoming us into their home. I ran back to David, hissing for him to hurry. He rummaged through our bags for a present, luckily finding a large bar of nut brittle that we hadn't broken into yet.

A bent, wizened figure was shuffling towards the house. This was granny, who joined the family for meals. Mum had man-handled the *chivito* (young goat) out of the oven with a colossal iron spade, and the father was carving it on the table. We had been searching for goat meat for days, but none of the herders would sell us the much-prized delicacy. We were so delighted that we cooed at the feast, devouring the sumptuous flesh and crispy fat. More was offered and then with a flourish the father presented us both with the *glándulas* (glands); apparently the richest, most tasty part of the goat. I couldn't detect why they were considered so superior, but happily chomped on them.

We were also passed lettuce coated in oil and glasses of red wine. Everything was from their land, except the wine which they traded for goat meat. The 40-year-old father was charming and talked freely, while his 29- year-old wife sat quietly, shy but smiling. The grandmother barely uttered a word, but then she was fairly caught up with sucking meat through her toothless gums. The children were impeccably behaved, with Diana asking to get down from the table, but not before wishing us *'!Buen provecho!'* (Have a nice meal!).

We asked the father what he knew of the land ahead, as we were still trying to decide which road to follow north. We pulled out our map and he pawed over it, telling us he had family inland and had travelled between San Rafael and San Luis and that it was high pampa full of *bichos muy feos* like enormous snakes and spiders.

We waddled back to the tent with wonderfully full bellies. Soon we had a visitor, this time just Diana. She sat at the entrance chatting, gradually inching into the vestibule. I invited her in. She leapt at the opportunity and bounced in on-top of us. I showed her our bird book. She loved it, carefully leafing through the pages and gazing at the pictures, exclaiming whenever she recognized a species. I pulled out a little child's ecology book we'd been given in Chos Malal, and she read it to us in the most immaculate and sweetest of Spanish voices, trilling the rrrrs like a little bird. Soon she was squirming into our sleeping bag and crawling all over us, giggling and imbuing the tent with a lovely goaty aroma, until we posted her out and sunk into a peaceful sleep.

It felt as if our heads had barely settled when the zip was once again pulled down and Diana's little head popped in, 'It's six o'clock!' We had visualised slinking out before the family got up, but of course they were all already working: it was only us rotting in our beds. We kissed and hugged the parents. The children helped us ferry our belongings to the road, and then we turned to give them all a hug. For once Diana wasn't smiling. I looked at this gorgeous, intelligent girl and wondered what life would hold for her. Perhaps she could be a teacher? Or if she became a goat herder's wife, I hoped she would find someone as thoughtful and bright as her father. I didn't want to leave her. She and her siblings were so full of fun, running in the wilds, helping their parents and playing. With a heavy heart we turned away. I hope I will see her again.

As we ran north towards Bardas Blancas the *ripio* transitioned to asphalt. This made the upward pull much more manageable. We camped for the last time in the Andes, below a line of poplars by the side of the road. That night it snowed, even though it was nearly mid-summer in the southern hemisphere. We relished the cold and snuggled together in our feather sleeping bag, in a deep and wonderful sleep.

Next morning we summited the 2,000-metre pass through cacti and scrub. The view was incredible – of an enormous basin opening out to infinity below us. It rippled in the heat-haze and looked to all intents as if we were about to plunge into a giant sea. Of course the sea was nothing but an inferno of heat, and its waves thorns.

We descended for the last time; leaving the jagged, snow-capped mountains of the Andes behind us forever. We found a site beside a thorn bush to camp, and used only the inner skin of the tent, as the heat was so oppressive. As we ate our pasta we watched leaf-cutter ants file past with carefully-selected shreds of foliage. Why did they wander so far? What was so delicious about the far-off leaves they sought, versus the leaves they passed *en route,* which looked exactly the same as the ones they collected? I find ants fascinating, which was a good job, as in the coming months they would infest our lives.

As the stars pricked the heavens above us, we pondered the date: the 21st of December 2012 – the day the Mayans predicted the world would end. All we could hope was that the wind would end, and that we would enter a new world, tranquil and flat.

Beaked Toad species
Rhinella sp.

Pest Control Services par excellence

10 Into the Oven

An enormous, portentous, cloud brewed in the sky above Malargüe. We eyed it suspiciously. It could only spell destruction. Was it harbouring the dreaded *granizos* (hail stones) the size of boulders that flatten crops, shatter car windscreens and obliterate roofs? David was becoming obsessed by this terrifying phenomenon and was constructing plans of defence, should we be attacked.

What the cloud marked was wind; more demonic wind. Wind that would sweep through the camp-site, extinguishing *asados* (BBQs), hurling soil into a maelstrom, carrying tents into the sky and trees to the ground. It screeched through the streets, pulling tiles from roofs and sending signs and bins clattering through the air. Christmas celebrations (marked on the 24th of December in Argentina) were put on hold, with part-charcoaled flippers and sides of animals abandoned.

Our tent was half-pitched in a hedge under the trunk of a tree. After months of running through roaring wind, we had become adept at clamping it to the ground. We had bought our provisions and now just needed Christmas day to dawn, so we could gallop off into the wilds again.

Christmas day proved tough. The wind didn't abate. Tear-streaked and exasperated, I howled back at it. 'When will it stop?' I asked everyone we met. To which the farmers and country folk would shake their heads with a wry look of hard-worn acceptance. The wind starts in the ice of the Cordillera, descending the mountain sides with increasing ferocity to the plains, across which it scorches until an obstacle gets in its way. But there were no obstacles where we were running.

We ran 19 miles before we found a small farm. The owner appeared with a large family of various ages and seemed quite happy for us to pitch our tent beside his corral. In Malargüe David had bought a small bottle of champagne, and we feasted on chicken casserole with fresh vegetables. A turkey was very interested in the proceedings, walking gamely towards our little pan, but unfortunately going short of plucking itself and diving in. Piglets snorted nearby, a horse hung its head over the fence, and three skeletal puppies peered at us dolefully. I had forgotten the wind, and at least for a while it had forgotten us. David gave me a ten-centimetre black comb he had found by the roadside. It was a perfect present, light and useful, I still use it today. I can't remember what I gave him. Perhaps nothing? We sat blissfully eating and chatting, happy to be free of another town and relaxing in the *campo* (countryside), aware that no other Christmas in the past or the future would ever mirror this.

We began our date with the 'oven' just after the town of San Rafael, with eight days of food and three days of water strapped to the trailer. We had been given plenty of warning of what lay ahead. 'No one lives on the road between San Rafael and San Luis,' they said, eyes narrowing. 'It's full of enormous *bichos,* with devilish pampa and thorny bush stretching as far as the eye can see.' In hushed voices they went on, 'It's a furnace; you'll never survive.' We had no choice. The trailer was groaning; we were armed and ready for war.

I lay on my side, pencilling thoughts in my diary under the boiling afternoon sun. We were 58 miles and three days into the oven. Tiny bees swarmed in my eyes and over my body. They were after moisture and salt. They didn't sting. I didn't mind them, even quite enjoyed their light pattering, but David couldn't abide them, flailing wildly to be rid of them. There was nowhere to hide, and after a couple of hours even I grew twitchy. We tried diving into our sleeping bag and then into our silk liners, but suffocation threatened. David stood up defiantly, 'I can't live like this.' He grabbed the tent and within minutes had it erected under a nearby tree. I was too lazy to move, resigned to lie with my ranks of insects and close my eyes. After what can only have been ten minutes, I heard a yelp. David exploded from the tent howling, 'I'm on fire!' It appeared the tent, zipped up to deter intruders, was cooking the poor boy alive.

We desperately needed a new sleeping strategy: something that would allow greater ventilation, but deter insects. Over the coming weeks we began stitching a new tent made from fine mosquito-netting, and attached it to the existing ground sheet, with some old tent poles for support. It was light to carry, and allowed air but not insects to pass through, with the bonus of permitting us to see out in case any interesting wildlife was in the vicinity.

Luckily there was a precious window of coolness in the very early morning. It felt like running through water, being free from the stranglehold of the sun. Otherwise life followed a ritual of furnace and thirst, apart from one night, when it rained for two whole hours. The fragrance that oozed from the earth next morning was sublime. It reminded me of southern Africa and the smell of damp soil after the first rains. Swarms of creatures emerged, triggered by the long-awaited, life-giving moisture. Dense clouds of tiny flies danced above the road, filling our eyes and noses. Termites took to the air in their one and only nuptial flight, and tens and hundreds of tiny froglets began their annual migration to newly-filled ponds.

> The alarm clock dragged us from bed at five o'clock this morning (I wrote). It's now two o'clock and we're nearly through our water. I'm desperately thirsty, so I'm focusing on the *tuco tuco* that I can hear calling. It's as if the earth has a heartbeat. The 'tuc-tuc' sound resonates deep into the ground, through his maze of galleries to my belly. I wonder why he's calling.

These subterranean rodents do the equivalent job of our European mole, aerating and mixing soil and assisting water infiltration through their network of tunnels – except that our mole isn't a rodent or a vegetarian with the enormous, yellow incisor teeth that the *tuco tuco* has for chomping through grasses. It's carnivorous, preferring to dine upon ants, beetle larvae and moth pupae.

It was as if we had fallen down the rabbit hole in *Alice in Wonderland* and were living in a miniature world: little red and black ants and black and grey-bummed ones hurried over us and the earth; leaf bugs leapt onto my diary; two praying mantises appeared and slowly swayed, with their front legs poised to impart a lethal punch to any passing insect; tarantulas scuttled in the vegetation by our feet; a battalion of crickets, hundreds and thousands strong, hopped and fell while crossing the road; lizards practically flew through the air, super-charged by the heat, and an enormous stick insect leapt at David. I hadn't realized stick-insects were acrobats.

The running was hard. The thermometer regularly clocked 39 degrees Celsius, with only the hours between two and five in the morning offering a reprieve. The long, cold days of the south, when we had time to watch wildlife on the hoof, were a distant memory. Now it was all about speed; getting out of camp quickly, running fast and bolting for cover before we baked alive. Even the corn flakes failed to go soft, with zero humidity to make them soggy. We didn't sweat when running; water was wicked from our body and our mouths. This was great for avoiding rashes and rubs, but terrible for maintaining hydration. We ran earlier and earlier to avoid the branding iron of the sun. I started to question how long I could maintain the pace; the lack of sleep was killing me.

But we were ticking off the miles, and despite the hardship, we were having fun, chatting nonsense, inventing idiotic radio interviews and quizzes and discovering huge quantities of wildlife. When we finished the day's run, we would punch the air elated and dance like Zulu warriors.

David wrote little during those eight days, summing up his experience in seven bullet points:

- Bloody hot – 39 degrees C.
- No sleep.
- Not enough water.

- Dreaming of sitting on a bus.
- Amazing bottle of Sprite at the provincial border.
- Watching out for *granizos* (hail stones).
- *Bichos muy feos.*

On Day Six we ran 20 miles to Beazley. We had been told it was a former British settlement and railway station. The railway, or *ferrocarril*, was built by the Brits and was still functioning, trains with commercial cargo rumbling through the village at a snail's pace. Beazley was made up of a few brick houses and their earth-baked backyards full of washing, with chickens pecking in the street. The only real feature was *Parador 183*, a café advertising '*Minutas, T.V. satelital, sandwichs y bebidas*' (fizzy drinks). The sign was like manna from heaven. We dumped the trailer and crawled in, salivating at the prospect of a fizzy drink and food other than our own. A rotund, rather sour-faced woman slouched behind the counter. The *minutas* comprised *milanesas* – a favourite in South America, made by pummelling a piece of meat to within an inch of its life, before dipping it in breadcrumbs and frying it. Our craving for salt meant that this salt-fat-fest went down a dream.

What we hadn't expected was our meeting with a dancing waiter in the form of Roni, the long-suffering husband of the slouching *señora*. He tap-danced his way to our table and performed a beautifully-executed pirouette by our chairs. He had lustrous dark hair, great bushy eyebrows and a twinkle in his eye.

A glass cabinet with a long shelf perched above the *señora's* piled bun, offering all manner of oddments incongruously nestling together. There was toothpaste, a hat, a shampoo bottle, a handbag, a sandwich-maker, a gold watch and a plastic dolly. It was like an edition of Bruce Forsyth's, '*The Generation Game*' (just missing the scantily-clad assistant in the corner) and I kept expecting him to pop up. I commented on the booty to Roni and his eyes lit up.

'I do a very good trade – yes, very good. Every now and then my wife and I squeeze into the car and head for Chile. They have great electrical goods there – supreme. They're so close to the Pacific, China and Japan, we can pick up televisions for half the price that they're sold here! Then there are Bolivian watches.' He held up his arms. 'We put ten watches – like this – on each of our arms and we're winners! And slippers – espadrilles – there's nowhere better than Uruguay,' he said, grabbing a pair like a trophy.

Hours ticked by. Soon the sun was setting, and a great fat toad arrived. We watched mesmerised as he flopped around the *Parador*. There was now quite a cluster of café diners chatting, eating and ogling the TV. Nobody noticed the toad – or at least nobody seemed at all interested in it. This wild animal was going about his daily business as Pest Control Service *par excellence,* devouring enormous quantities of flying and waddling insects. No need for sprays, sticky traps and coils: it was all being taken care of naturally, quick as a flash, with a slap of his extraordinarily long, sticky, tongue.

A family of burrowing owls watched attentively as we passed

Burrowing Owl
Athene cunicularia

11 Zone of Fire

'David!' I cried, but the words were snatched from my mouth. I counted the space between the cracks of lightning and blasts of thunder. It was seconds, now, and diminishing; the eye of the storm was blisteringly close. My heart was drumming in my ears, drowning my sanity and paralysing my rigid body. This wasn't like the thunderstorms at home, but a brutish animal rampaging through the night and scorching the ground around us. Ever since we were struck by lightning on our boat in Trinidad three years ago, electric storms had terrified me.

Now we had entered a zone of fire. Every day the temperatures would rocket, often surging above 40 degrees Celsius, at which point we would feel like spontaneously combusting, but would be beaten to it by the ballooning dark clouds, which would burst into an explosion of light, noise and water. People are often killed by electric storms in Argentina; in fact, three cows were found electrocuted as we ran to San Luis. One night, a bolt of lightning hit a pylon 50 metres from us. Sleep was impossible; we just cowered under our hammocks.

Suddenly I heard an almighty thud. A violent gust had severed the acacia branch to which David's hammock was tied. He lay sprawled across the ground. Within minutes rain was hammering down. Angry daggers of lightning struck the steaming earth and sheets of light vibrated through the sky. Our tarpaulins flogged centimetres away from the chop-stick thorns of the acacias, threatening to shred themselves. It was three o'clock in the morning, we were in semi-desert, yet I was sodden and my teeth were clattering. We had no option but to run. Our fingers fumbled to untie the tarp and hammock knots. We wrenched all our belongings through the scrub to the glistening road, strapped them to the trailer, secured our head torches and ran, soaked to the bone, into the night.

To avoid the scorching diurnal temperatures, we had often contemplated running at night; but we had conceded that running into human trouble was too high a risk to take. There were also the problems of traffic, of tripping on uneven surfaces, and of snakes, which are more active at night in hot climes. As it was, that dreadful night we ended up walking for three miles, as running proved too difficult through the contrasting oily blackness and blinding headlights.

The north eastern *sierras* of San Luis province speared out of the plain. These sculptured hills are said to have locked-away traditions and forgotten cultures of simple shepherding folk long preserved in their folds. But we couldn't stop; if we were going to finish the expedition, we had to keep ticking off the miles. And as our track slowly stretched northwards, we began to suffer. David developed a rash in his more private zone. He said it felt like a small flame was shooting up his legs at every step. The stretchy scarves we used as: sweat bands, hair ties, blindfolds, supports and balaclavas (you name it; fantastic things) found a new use wedged into the top of his boxers, collecting sweat before it trickled down to his aggravated parts.

On the road to Luján we found a gigantic snake. At first it looked as if a tractor tyre had been shredded on the verge, but as we grew closer, we realized it was a decomposing two-metre boa constrictor. Its scales were a beautiful chocolate brown and cream, with the familiar oval-ring patterning. Peering into its mouth, we found rows of razor-sharp teeth pointing inwards. Its body was inflated by methane gas to gruesome proportions, and death hung in the air long after we had passed.

Luján, turned out to be an unexpectedly charming village, with a faded, antiquated feel, crumbling walls, forgotten gardens and rambling old houses, all beneath the ever- watchful hills that swept into the clouds behind. I followed one tree-lined street down to a main plaza where tens of embryo monks were training. The whitewashed church, with its tolling bell, overlooked the shaded square in which people thronged. It felt as if I had stepped into the pages of E. M. Forster's *A Room with a View*.

I gazed up at an enormous *palo borracho* tree that guarded the church. It was bursting with pink, lily-like flowers that buzzed with insects. What an extraordinary tree, with its great spines, which are said to store water, its profusion of blooms and bulbous, elephant's-foot trunk, a clue to its African relative the baobab.

During the next couple of days we ran through stretches of vast, intensively-farmed land, including large fields of cotton. A small, buttercup-coloured plane bombed around spraying the crops (and us). Enormous rotary irrigation systems watered them. Apparently the contrast between the luscious plants under the circular water-sprayers and the scorched vegetation beyond was visible from orbiting satellites. A family of burrowing owls watched attentively as we passed. Their chances of finding invertebrates or an undisturbed corner to nest in must be tough in such industrial surroundings, but luckily large areas of natural *chaco* still persist.

An abandoned road meandered alongside the one we were running. The concrete had cracked and was barely visible most of the way, with wildflowers and tall seeding grasses having long since moved back in. I love natural succession: it gives me hope. The road gave us an eye into the *chaco* and a rich edge-habitat for wildlife. A telephone line followed its course, and upon it perched a streaked flycatcher and a white *monjita*, which looked like a snowball that had mistakenly landed in the fire, its almost entirely white plumage shining in the heat-haze of the savanna. Its name, *monjita blanca*, means 'little white nun', but its habits are far from saintly, as it butchers caterpillars, grasshoppers and grubs.

The abandoned road allowed us access into the *chaco* to hide for the night. Watching for cars, we waited for a quiet spot, dashed through the line of scrub, crossed the disused road and man-handled the trailer over a barbed wire fence. We then set off to find a cluster of trees which would provide our hammock supports. Our favourite formation was a triangle, with an apex trunk forming the anchor for one end of each hammock, and two other trees forming the other supports. This ensured we were close together, should someone find us in the night.

Hundreds of spiny trees surrounded us, including one that looked as if it had been painted spearmint green. The thorns were stupendous, and the cause of the numerous punctures we had recently been mending on the trailer. But they did serve as useful needles, for which we kept a couple in our repair kit. Our camp-site was seething with life. Cicadas whined; wasps zipped past, transporting cargos of unlucky, woozy invertebrates, pre-stung, to be fed live to their emerging young; great, chunky multi-coloured beetles eloped in pairs, and birds darted in the multiple layers of vegetation.

We counted 36 unique bird species, ranging from scimitar-billed wood-creepers, to masked gnat-catchers and black-crested finches. We saw our first crested *gallito* – a little rust-and-white-flecked bird that hopped on the ground and in the bushes like a miniature chicken. It belongs to the same family as the lovely *chucao* and *huet huet* of the south. We also found a pair of white-fronted woodpeckers drilling the telegraph poles. Our bird guide was essential; it transformed the landscape from merely a backdrop into a multitude of habitats and opportunities for a plethora of birds and other wildlife.

We were also having some great running days. I was full of energy and chasing the watch for under-nine-minute miles while tugging the trailer. Our euphoria was fed by the wildlife we were running with: many-coloured *chaco* finches and spot-backed puffbirds watched as we passed; little, hairy, jumping spiders launched into the air, outdoing any athleticism we might think we possessed in one mind-boggling leap; while trillions of insects and frogs chirred and whistled their nightly serenade. As we sat eating cheese and salami sandwiches in the dark, chewing the cud, clouds of fireflies danced above our heads, flashing their little bums to attract a mate. We felt immensely content and somewhat amazed that after five years of living and working within about 20 metres of one another, we got on so well.

Next morning David practically propelled himself into the treetops as he flew from his hammock to answer the call of nature. This haste appeared to be a definite by-product of running: our systems were charged, but we were rapidly losing control. It meant I often had to leap from the trailer mid-run and scramble for the bushes, where I would collect a handy clutch of leaves to wipe away the evidence, followed by a burial or a covering of stones, if the dung beetles didn't beat me to it. My one foe was a species of grass with hooked seeds like barbed wire. Its clutch was agony and its ability to hang on prodigious, with one encounter often leaving tens of spiky grenades wedged in my legs, socks and feet.

We ran out of the small town of Ulapes with a blood-red sun rising from behind the near hills. Tens of toads had been squashed by passing vehicles, as had a beautiful grey Mexican free-tailed bat, with long white whiskers on its feet and its distinctive flap of skin extending halfway down its tail. Later we found a freshly-killed Darwin's *nothura* (a bird like a partridge). Road-kill gives fantastic chances of securing a protein snack; it's local, carbon-neutral, free-range and organic. No other mammal would pass it by, and even if we were depriving a fox or wild cat, it was better for us to dine on it than on beef fed on Amazon soya and transported hundreds of miles to our plates. So that night we luxuriated in a one-pot wonder of stewed *nothura*, three carrots we had found dropped on the road, and rice, squash and potatoes from Ulapes.

Even when our stomachs were full, we were troubled by an incident which prevented us from sleeping. One night in the *chaco* near San Luis hundreds of bugs had engulfed us, scuttling over our faces and bodies. We thought nothing of them at the time, but a few days later we were concerned to find how alike the critters were to those on a poster which showed vectors of the *chagas* disease. I couldn't stop scratching, drawing blood and peeling skin from my limbs. Could this be the start of the disease, or just the ravages of a flea I had not located before?

Our uncertainty lay in the fact that the initial symptoms of chagas are like many others, and mirrored the feelings we had most days! These included muscle-fatigue, body aches, rashes and headaches. We would have to wait many months to find out if we were infected, because tests are inconclusive, and the chronic symptoms of life-threatening heart and digestive disorders may not appear until ten to thirty years later.

The next day would forever be burnt in our minds as the day we reached 2,500 miles. This was an enormous feat for two runners who'd had no idea if they would be able to survive running 500 miles, let alone over 2,000. But as we chatted in camp that night we acknowledged one blindingly-obvious fact: we had reached the half-way mileage of our run, but we hadn't run half the continent. The 5,000 Mile Project was becoming the 5,000 Plus-a –lot-of-Miles Project.

This was a huge blow to our morale. The fault had occurred because David had logically assumed that measuring the distance in nautical miles, with one degree of latitude on an ocean chart equating to 60 miles, would provide an acceptably rough estimate. To this he added a good deal of fat, to account for the meandering on which our route would inevitably take us. The unforeseen flaw in his method was that nautical and statute land miles are not the same, with one statute mile equating to 1,609 metres and a nautical mile to 1,852 metres.

We hadn't been able to calculate distances using fine-scale maps, because none existed for many of the areas we would run through; nor was there enough detail on satellite images. As it turned out, in Bolivia and Brazil we often had to question local people about large parts of the route, because of seasonal inundations and the questionable existence of roads. I couldn't blame David for his error, in that, had I undertaken the maths, we would no doubt have been in a far greater crisis!

The dizzyingly colossal number of un-run miles that awaited us threatened to engulf us with its sheer magnitude; but the last five months had taught us to focus on smaller daily achievements, and as these amassed, the stupendous, seemingly-unachievable goal became less daunting. And even though at times the running felt more tough and relentless than I could ever have imagined, neither of us lost our lust for this, the simplest, yet most intoxicating of sports. A remark by the American author Joyce Carol Oates describes beautifully how I feel about it:

> Running! If there's any activity happier, more exhilarating, more nourishing to the imagination, I can't think of what it might be. In running the mind flees with the body, the mysterious efflorescence of language seems to pulse in the brain, in rhythm with our feet and the swinging of our arms.

It's not just a feeling. Studies are constantly revealing the multiple benefits of running. One by Cambridge University showed that it stimulates the brain to grow fresh grey matter, having a big impact on mental ability. This may be due to the increased blood-flow, or to the release of high levels of hormones. Exercise has long been linked to physical and mental well-being, with philosophers from Aristotle to Nietzsche extolling the virtues of it on thought-process. Henry David Thoreau, Charles Dickens, William Wordsworth, Erik Satie and Benjamin Britten are just a handful of celebrated artists who gained inspiration from exercise, especially in natural environments. Progressive businesses are leaving the boardrooms and taking to the parks, to thrash out decisions on the hoof in naturally stimulating environments.

Movement has been integral to our evolution. As 99 per cent of human existence on earth has been mobile, whether as hunter-gatherer, pastoralist or agriculturist, it's no wonder that running is so important to our mental and physical well-being. Only in the last 70 years, with the proliferation of cars and desk-bound jobs, have people become so uniquely sedentary, and obesity and mental illnesses have soared, fuelled by inactivity.

One of our pre-occupations when running was the question of how people re-awaken a passion for the great outdoors. We all had it when we were young: crawling in flower-beds after ladybirds and spiders, watching butterfly metamorphosis, climbing trees, making dens in hedgerows and dams in streams. But too often it disappears, and that fascination with a world full of such mind-boggling behaviour, interactions and morphology, is forgotten. Yet every day, even if we don't realize it, we are connected with nature. It's in our food, in the walls and windows of our houses, under our feet, under our bums, gushing through our taps; it's millions of years old in our fuel tanks; each of us is an ecosystem. Nature is everywhere.

Our latest position felt a million miles away from nature. We were lying on the dusty floor of a disused, cylinder-shaped building, opposite a petrol station, in the middle of a split shift, taking a few hours' break from the worst of the heat. The building provided some relief from the sun, but summed up our generally tramp-like existence. There was no doubt that although camping in the wild was more fraught, because we hardly ever knew who the owner of the land might be, we effectively trespassed each night. It was in just about every instance more wholesome than the urban equivalent.

Olta, a pretty, leafy town full of courtyards, mature gardens, old houses and mighty *palo borracho* trees, was on the face of it a lovely haven. And although the family hostel we discovered had oodles of gently-decaying charm, the room reminded us why camping under the stars was preferable to any human-made equivalent. The sink-hole was stuffed full of curly hairs, and the soap was swathed in them. Cockroaches scuttled between the pipes and behind the loo. The light switch was the usual live-wire number, while the sheets covering the sagging bed definitely laid claim to a decent heritage of guests.

I'm not a cleanliness fanatic (what a waste of precious life!) but in a public setting it seems fair to expect at least a cursory brush or wash in exchange for money. We're both delighted to share a room with a bat family (we were lucky enough to have them fluttering over our heads in a hostel in Puyuhuapi) or with a flock of birds, moths, butterflies – you name it. Cockroaches and rats, however, are harder to welcome, considering the places they delight to lurk in. Add to them the used condom we found tucked under our sheets in Olta, and the room lost much of its ageing charm. As we ran north, we watched husband-and-wife teams and gangs of young children armed with wheelbarrows and buckets working on the roadside verges and any forgotten corners. Grass could not go to waste when there were cattle, donkeys and goats to feed. So they scythed and forked the harvest onto wagons or the back of motorbikes. A boy ambled past on his donkey, his cart stacked high with branches. He told us he would be making charcoal. We were astounded by the resilience of people who survive and prosper in such ferocious climates and barren environments. Whether creating thorn baffles collected from the scrub to protect themselves and their livestock from hurricane-force winds, or making adobe houses sculpted from earth and grasses to ward off the heat, the inhabitants seemed extraordinarily resourceful.

Their fight for existence was extraordinary; but it was also clear that it was breaking the very land the people depended upon for their survival. Soon there would be no more branches for the boy to collect for charcoal or firewood. Soon the livestock would be dead stock, having eaten the last of the vegetation, nibbled the last shoots and taken their last lick of water from the putrefying water-hole; the soil is taking to the air, and with it the ability to grow food.

We ran through settlements completely void of water, where wells had dried up and the meagre resources had gone. In Chamical a graphic tragedy had played out as over-population had caused excessive consumption of water, and in the scorching climate salt had permeated the aquifer. The entire town depended upon shipping-in canisters of drinking water. In La Estrella we found a booming village anchored in a sea of scrub, with absolutely no water. The villagers had to rely on tankers that rumbled hundreds of miles to their remote settlement thrice weekly, in a crazy ritual of turning petrol into water. Yet this was one of many of the arid and inappropriate growth-nodes at which the President had decreed that the population should grow. Someone had clearly forgotten to point out to her that no matter how many laptops, i-phones, cars and gold rings symbolise 'success', without water, we die.

The city of La Rioja loomed on our map. It felt like an enormous milestone amid the heat-mirages, cacti and salt-pans of central Argentina. We had been warned that temperatures would soar well above 40 C. It seemed that whenever we spoke to locals, they predicted that the next stretch of our route would be even more furiously hot and inhospitable than the last. Sleeping was becoming almost impossible as temperatures failed to drop until three or four o'clock in the morning, by which time we were lying in pools of our own sweat and our hammocks were starting to resemble living tombs.

A man waved us down. He was very jolly, and like many other motorists passed us drinks and snacks. He asked us our nationality, and didn't wince on hearing it. But it clearly worried him. He pulled up his T-shirt to reveal a large beer-belly and a swathe of bullet-wounds. 'You're entering extremist territory, home to families who lost sons fighting against the English in *las Islas Malvinas* (the Falklands),' he told us. 'They won't think twice about spraying you with bullets, just as they did me. From here northwards you must take care. You must not say you are English. People hate the English. Cristina [the President] is readying planes to attack *Malvinas* again. Feelings are running high. Argentinians want their islands back.'

This came as an almighty blow. No one to date had suggested people would be so hostile. We had seen graffiti on billboards and bus-shelters screaming, '¡*Las Malvinas son Argentina!*' (Falklands belong to Argentina) – to which all the nation's maps testify. The weather in the Falklands was reported every day across the country. On a number of occasions we had been warned about a Swiss cyclist, apparently carrying an English passport, who had been murdered, but none of this seemed relevant to us.

As we travelled further north we heard of more incidents that caused us concern. Clearly, unpleasant occurrences can happen in any country, but the anti-English attitude was troubling. The first question people would ask when they stopped us on the road was, 'Where are you from?' On receiving a true answer they would gulp, thinly veiling a look of horror, but generally chat on and by the end of the conversation we would have won them over, reminding them that we were individuals and not an institution. Argentinians are renowned for their warmth and good nature, but sometimes the disclosure of our nationality was too much to bear, and the car would take off in a cloud of dust.

Lying about our nationality felt uncomfortable; but we were not running the continent to fight a political crusade. We just wanted people to get outside more, to run and enjoy the natural world. So we decided to say we were Scottish. Just about every Argentinian we spoke to had watched *Corazon Valiente* (Braveheart). The war against the English depicted in the film supported their belief that, in the Scottish, they had comrades who detested the English as much as they did (they may be right there!). What they did not know was that large numbers of Scots fought in the Falklands War.

We could justify our nationality claim because of David's Scottish roots (he even has a family tartan) and the fact that he had spent a good tranche of his life in Scotland. Indeed, once we had made the decision, our being Scottish was greeted by smiles and talk of skirted men, bagpipes and whisky. 'Whisky', which has no Hispanic origin as far as I know, has even been adopted in Chile and Argentina instead of 'Cheese' for the taking of photos. It seems England has much to learn from Scotland's tourism branding.

Since crossing into Argentina 1,238 miles ago and meeting our friends in Bariloche, we hadn't seen a single person we knew. La Rioja marked a change. We had contacted the *Club de Rotoract* (Young Rotary Club) in the hope of meeting some interesting young people and finding a floor to sleep on. Miraculously, the Club had agreed to the idea, and as we drew closer to the rendezvous we saw three figures waving. I felt tears welling up, from a combination of exhaustion, the emotional demands of the run and the realisation that three people cared about what we were doing and had come to welcome us to their city. Adriana, Delia and Matias introduced themselves and handed us ice-cold water, saying they would wait for us at Adriana's sister's home, where we would be staying. When we arrived, they ushered us to our room, where a sumptuous bed and shower transported us into heaven. Only at the end of our two-night stay did we find out that Sofia (Adriana's sister) and her husband Claudio had moved out of their room to sleep on their children's floor.

Camping between Punta Arenas
and Puerto Natales, Chile.

David and I running near
El Chaltén, Argentina.

Collecting water near
El Calafate, Argentina.

Watching a Patagonian armadillo near El Chaltén, Argentina.

The lovely feeling of running unshod near El Chaltén, Argentina.

Re-assembling the trailer in Villa O'Higgins, Chile.

A female and male ringed kingfisher. This super-adaptable species
accompanied us the entire length of the continent.

The breathtaking Carretera Austral of Chile.

It was amazing to see the guanacos and other wildlife returning to the Chacabuco valley once the fences were removed and the sheep farming ceased.

The stunning mountain pass through Parque Nacional Lanín, Argentina.

Incredible sunset just north of Las Lajas; we were constantly astounded by Argentina's extraordinary cloud formations and beautiful sky.

Battling the wind north of Volcán Tromen, Argentina.

On the road to San Luis, Argentina. We ran before sunrise to avoid the scorching sun.

School children joined us just before Santa Rosa, south of Tucumán, Argentina.

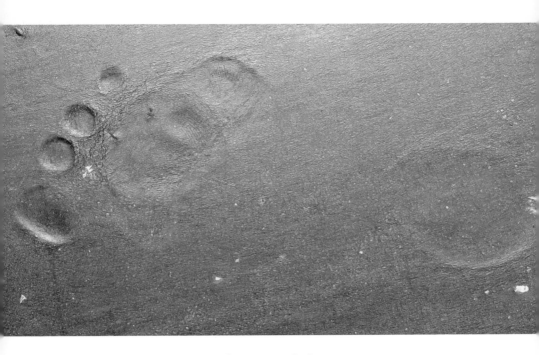

David left his footprint in the tarmac which was softening in the blistering (literally!) heat.

The sight that greeted us when we stopped on the road
from Lumbreras, south east of Salta, Argentina.

Fellow trailer travellers, Tucumán province, Argentina.

A Colla woman and her child whom we chatted to on the road to Boyuibe, Bolivia.

Traffic jam on the road to Santa Cruz, Bolivia.

The snake that shot under my foot, just north of Santa Cruz, Bolivia!

Leaf-cutter ants swarm all over our clothes and kit.

Cocoa chewing rancheros south of Trinidad, Bolivia.

Running north of Trinidad, Bolivia, on a muddy road that had since baked hard.

Crimson-crested woodpecker, north of Trinidad, Bolivia.

Running in the dark towards Casarabe. We were both at our thinnest in Bolivia, being unable to meet our daily calorific demands.

Traffic on the backroad between San Ignacio de Moxos and San Borja.

A caiman eyeballs us by the track in Estancia Nogales, Bolivia.

Four on a bike - a familia sight in Bolivia. This was on the road to Yata.

Collecting water on the road to Yata, Bolivia.

Making a presentation to a tiny village school in Mariposa, Bolivia, about running and wildlife (we painted a game onto our tarp for the sessions).

Traffic coated us and the trailer in clouds of dust, here just south of Riberalta, Bolivia.

Rua do Onces (Jaguar Road) Amazon, Brazil. We both ran with a trailer during this remote three week stretch. Here running on a patch of tarmac that had not yet been reclaimed by the forest.

Cooking beans, garlic and lentils; our staple in Brazil.

The hammocks were essential homes in the tropics.

Coconuts - the most delicious and nutritious food/drink we ate and often for free.

Mud sometimes made the going very difficult.

We reached 5000 miles in less than a year, in the middle of the Brazilian Amazon!

Floating homes near Manaus, Brazil.

Crossing the equator south of Rorainópolis, Brazil

Even in the Brazilian tropics, we would soon become cold after a soaking.

Catching water, Salta Kama, Venezuela.

Buying vegetables
and chatting, on the
road in Venezuela.

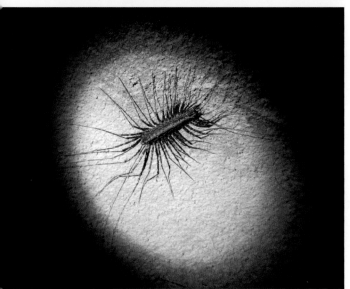

The invertebrate which
shared our shepherd's
hut in the Grand
Sabana, Venezuela.

Running into Ciudad
Guayana, Venezuela.

Our old patched shoes, which we finally replaced in Ciudad Guayana.

Katharine and David, near San Raphael, Argentina.
Photo by Miky Dubrowsky - Thank you.

We passed a point on our map marked Bazán. It turned out to be nothing save a family living in a makeshift outbuilding, with a clutch of scratchy hens and ten hunting dogs. They were selling small armadillos, scaly creatures about 30 centimetres long. We asked for water. The toothless mother seemed reticent. She had barely enough for herself, her husband and her band of dirty boys. But she gave us a few litres of rainwater anyway. No one smiled at the uninvited *gringos*. We asked about how they caught the armadillos. The mum mumbled a few words, saying that they were plentiful, and the boys giggled slyly.

The husband held an armadillo by its tail. It was beautiful, but terrified, its soft, dark eyes gleaming below its carapace and its powerful claws clamped tight. A man stopped in a red Volkswagen. He looked shifty and remained in his car. A transaction was quickly made through the window; a few *pesos* passed to the family and the armadillo was bundled into a bag in the boot. It was probably for his supper. Everyone said how delicious they were. A creature needs to taste bad to escape a similar death.

Two days and 43 miles after leaving La Rioja, we discovered the most repugnant camp-site yet. A policeman had recommended it is a *refugio* to escape the electrical storms, so we ran an extra hour in the scorching heat to reach it. This proved a seriously bad mistake. Three lorries were parked outside, with the drivers in the process of cooking food from the drop-down bellies of their vehicles and setting up tables inside the shelter. The building looked to all intents and purposes like a concrete air-raid bunker and was covered in rubbish and graffiti.

We set up our home on the floor and cooked up our old faithful of mash, herbs and cheese. The shelter stank, which was no great surprise, considering the urine stains adorning the walls and the presence of three crusty piles of excrement. The stench reached a peak as the midday sun registered 42 degrees. Sleep was impossible as we were besieged by mini-tornadoes that swept through the open tunnel, mixing our gear with dead flies, thorns, dust and litter. But we were incapable of moving. The thought of searching outside in the thorny furnace came second to sleeping in a toilet.

During the night lights swished past, and the sound of traffic boomed around our concrete drum. One van stopped and an entire family unloaded to sit and chat around a table, while their radio blared. In their excitement they decided to announce the presence of the two *gringos* over the airwaves, so that the coming hours were full of lonely truckers and bikers hooting their horns and flashing their lights.

At one stage we must have dropped off, but awoke to the squeal of brakes and another lorry pulling up. From around the corner shuffled a squat, pug-faced man, with his flies undone and his jeans draped around his hips. When he found two faces looking up from his favourite toilet spot, his mouth hung open and he rapidly scurried off from whence he had come. We lay with a knife by our sides.

At five o'clock in the morning the boom of thunder marked the start of a storm, and a splatter of raindrops intensified into a full sub-tropical downfall. For two blissful hours we stopped thinking about running, truckers and urine and slept unmolested, wrapped in our green tarpaulin against the delightful chill of the storm.

*We could hear the scrub parting nearby
and then deep, heavy, breathing*

12 Night-time Visitors

The road wound higher and higher into the clouds, and the mountainsides grew ever more fecund in the damp, drizzly air as we left the sleepy village of La Puerta and the city of Catamarca far down below us. We were bound for cloud forest which envelopes a thin slice of mountain, before the Ruta 308 dives down into the hot sticky plains below. We climbed through walnut-groves, apple-orchards and little villages, past grazing donkeys and cattle. Three fat *señoras* engrossed in conversation by the side of the road spotted us. Simultaneously their nine chins wobbled and their chubby paws covered their mouths, before they clapped and shouted support.

'Where are you going? Where have you come from?' they laughed.

'Chile,' we panted. 'We're going to Bolivia,'

'Mother of God!' they squealed.

The road cut into the mountains in a series of switchbacks, each one elevating us further into the sky. Dragonflies and butterflies alternatively zipped and wafted past. A flock of mitred parakeets screamed through the valley below us, gravitating upon a grove of trees groaning with fruit. My mood soared; we were both bubbling with happiness.

The cloud-forest reverberated with wildlife. Lianas hung from the treetops; air-plants threaded and scrambled around every limb, as plants layered upon one another like towering green gateaux in the life-giving mists. Our road teetered on the edge of a precipice. We were a footfall away from plunging into the valley that wound hundreds of metres below us to the plains beyond. For the first time in months water was freely available. We camped by a sparkling stream, delighting in drinking our fill and lying in its freezing water fully-clad and shod, satisfied to be achieving a wash of both our clothes and our bodies.

Back on dry ground, as soon as I expelled a dollop of dung, a two-man dung-beetle team rushed to my assistance, diving head first into the steaming pile. I had never seen such a furious workforce in action. Within minutes the pile had reduced substantially, packed into neat little balls and shoved down into their underground larder. There the female lovingly posted her ranks of glistening eggs, content in the knowledge that her new offspring would grow fat on my soft brown gift. What a perfect recycling service, creating new dung beetles and new nutritious soil.

As we crossed the watershed into Tucumán province, the tarmac gave way to hard-baked earth and gravel. We ran helter-skelter downhill in a soft cloud of rain, with mud flying from the trailer. No one passed us; only occasional wooden dwellings revealed that anyone else existed. A train of pigs dawdled across the road and flopped under a mudstone overhang. They wore triangles of lashed branches round their necks, to stop them from pushing through fences. A tiny, sparrow-sized woodpecker, a white-barred *piculet*, hopped along the underside of a branch, drilling. Beautiful purple-and-emerald scaly-headed parrots crashed out of trees as we passed, while a gang of plush-crested jays clattered in the lower branches by the roadside.

After four days of heaven, we left our cloud forest behind and descended into hell. The contrast was devastating, as if a bomb had landed in our absence. A dark, toxic haze filled the air over the town of J.B.Alberdi from the smouldering rubbish mounds scattered about. Rubbish that wasn't burning formed a stinking slick along the network of roads. Dogs thronged the streets, barking and baring their fangs at us. Gangs loafed on road corners, scrutinising our passage. For the first time in the expedition, people didn't return our smiles or waves. The place felt thoroughly hostile, and the security warnings people had been giving us suddenly seemed substantiated.

The next day, only 12 miles into the run, the sky turned black and with a crack of lightning torrents of rain deluged us. We had nowhere to hide; within minutes the drains by the side of the road turned into raging rivers, the surface of the road into a lake and us into a soup of saturated clothes. Cars and lorries streamed past deluging us in grey, oily water. The world blurred behind a screen of incessant rain. At first it was exhilarating and an enormous relief after the cloying heat, but soon our teeth began to chatter.

We decided to make a bolt for Concepción at mile 17. It was there that we realized that I only had one Vivobarefoot shoe strapped to the trailer: somehow its partner had fallen off. Running completely unshod through towns was generally impossible due to the level of rubbish. The heel-less barefoot shoes gave us protection, while allowing us to run lightly, as if we had no shoes on at all. We believed that the barefoot running style was helping us to avoid injuries, but finding a replacement shoe was impossible in the towns we were running through. We had shoes waiting for us at home from our sponsor: the problem was how to get hold of them, as importing goods was complicated and expensive.

The following morning a man slunk up to us as we were packing up the trailer. 'People have been asking what you're doing. Will you appear on *Canal 5*?'

We eyed one another. We needed to get going, but it was always useful to give a shout about running and wildlife. *Canal 5* turned out to be a live regional news programme. 'Great!' I whispered to David, as we waited for our slot. 'Another chance to humiliate ourselves in front of thousands of Spanish-speaking people!' We were instructed to stand behind an array of microphones. Five cameras stared at us. A cheesy jingle signalled the change of news item and before we knew it, the presenter was upon us, announcing and describing our challenge and ricocheting questions our way, 'So, Katharine and David, why are you doing this run? How far have you run so far? Why are you here in Tucumán?'

I understood the first question, and David chipped in with some more detail. The distance question was easy. Why we were here? That was more difficult. I didn't have the heart to say what a cesspit I thought the town was, so I waxed lyrical about the mountains: well, they were one of the most beautiful places we had run through. We were on a roll and somehow we were surviving. Just as quickly as it had begun, the torment was suddenly over and we were left watching our images fade from the screens in front of us, somewhat shell-shocked.

Miraculously, everyone appeared happy with our performance and so we slipped out to prepare the trailer for off. It was at that point that David came up with the bright idea of my announcing the lost shoe on air. I wasn't keen on going back into the studio, but could see the benefit of reaching a large local audience and so plucked up the courage for Take Two. The story appeared to tickle the presenter's fancy, and within a couple of minutes I was back on, announcing my predicament.

'This,' I said, wielding the partner-less shoe, 'is all I have left. I desperately need to find its companion so that we can carry on running and make our world record. Please, if anyone finds it on the roadside, contact José or us through our 5,000-Mile Project facebook page. I will be eternally grateful.' The presenter closed with one last request for help for *la Cenicienta* (Cinderella) in finding her slipper!

It felt as if we were sinking into a forgotten world of Argentina. It was an outcast region clawing to survive, but barely functioning as it drowned under its own rubbish, addled by the sun and gradually poisoning itself. The riches of Bariloche and Buenos Aires seemed of another universe. Lorries, clapped-out vans, motorbikes and cars funnelled past belching black smoke. Houses bent towards the road, half-built, filthy and sagging.

The despair of the areas we were running through, and our mounting realisation of the needs and priorities for people to survive in this world, severely depressed us. But there was a glimmer of hope. San Miguel de Tucumán was the next city in Argentina's northernmost provinces. We were making real progress on the map: soon we would reach the half-way point of our run and be into Bolivia. At which point, I burnt the sole of my right foot! Usually we ran on the white dashes of the road, but here none had been painted in. It was nine o'clock and already the tarmac was boiling. A range of angry blisters instantly burst from the skin. That I had been able to burn my feet at all without feeling it was testament to how damn hard and insensitive they were. I had a new reverence for the black road.

On the way into town David was again kissed by a man. A pair of middle-aged folk on a motorbike stopped to talk to us. They greeted us grinning heartily.

> And then I saw it (David wrote). The first kiss was on its launching pad, but with swift and decisive action I managed to dodge it with a cultural trump-card of a firm and clear handshake. The difficulty was that once we had talked for a bit they clearly felt friendship and before I know it, a big, stubbly cheek was thrust upon mine to say goodbye. Unpleasant!

In Tucumán we received a message from José at *Canal 5* that he had the shoe. But that's as far as the communications went. No amount of emails and phone calls would elicit the shoe from the man, whom we rapidly branded as a shoe fetishist. Remembering that my sister had once shared a house with a guy who would secretly sniff her shoes, we wondered if José had similar tendencies? Whatever the truth, it was extremely frustrating and meant I could only run barefoot in the early morning in rural areas until we could work out a way of importing a new pair.

Wall-to-wall concrete shimmered around us, and the thermometer measured 43 degrees Celsius. We were running down a dual carriage-way streaming with traffic on our way out of the city. I felt faint, I couldn't breathe. I wrapped my head-scarf around my face so that only my eyes peeped out, in an attempt to spare my flesh from roasting, but this only worked for minutes, as I was soon gasping for breath. Next my thighs erupted into a scarlet rash. They were hot and itchy, as if a thousand needles were stabbing me. All the symptoms pointed to prickly heat. My skin wasn't sweating quickly enough, due to humidity, excessive exercise and sun lotion blocking its pores. I motored up several sharp hills, but felt completely weary and washed out at the summits. It seemed impossible to drink enough fluid. We had entered a new phase of excruciating humidity and severe heat; a potent mix which would draw even deeper on our physical and psychological resolve.

The vegetation was super-charged. Sugar cane reached for the sky and soya sprouted in luscious waves. Even the mosquitos were gigantic. Tropical sun and rain were fuelling the bonanza. But one strand in the landscape remained constant: the face of Cristina de Kirchner, the President, scrutinising us from every bridge, wall and bus-shelter. It was ominous; as if we were running through the pages of George Orwell's *1984*, with Big Sister Cristina's evil eye rooted upon us.

She was there at the entrance to towns, reminding the masses what she had achieved. She was there in the middle of godforsaken-nowhere, insisting, *'Aquí también la nación crece'* (The nation is growing here too). We would eye the surrounding cacti, parched ground, pending dust storm and heat mirage and wonder how that could be. A house-sized hoarding by a new construction site showed a photo of her with the text, 'Cristina de Kirchner is providing more jobs and homes.' We had seen countless similar advertisements along the length of the country and giggled at how she managed to do her day job and lay bricks. It seemed she was modelling herself on Eva Peron, gaining huge popularity with a groundswell of the nation. The country folk and wealthier classes weren't so enamoured. They said she didn't understand their sector, that there wasn't a '*K en el campo*' (no *K* for Kirchner in countryside).

North of Trancas we ran alongside with the thundering traffic of *Ruta* 9, but we found a camp-site in a belt of vegetation 200 metres from the road. Sometime deep in the night we awoke to the sound of sirens. A powerful searchlight swept over our hammocks. I froze, 'They can't be looking for us, can they?' I whispered. David was silent. We waited. The light flashed over us again and then moved on, probing the roadside with its extraordinarily powerful eye. If they didn't want us, who are they after? Ten minutes later, we heard gun-shots. A cold shiver swept down my spine, and I willed the morning to come.

The following day we decided to take a slight detour down a minor road, to escape the traffic (and the police). It was a good decision; a fox crossed our path and birds flocked by the side of the road. Life was tranquil, with only the odd farm vehicle chugging by. We searched the scrubby woodland for a camp-site. We soon found a couple of trees to which we could strap the hammocks, ducked under the fence, hid the trailer and set up camp. We cooked a stew of beetroot, pumpkin, long green beans, popped maize and chia seeds, all of which we had towed from Tucumán.

As I was collecting some gear from the trailer, a gaucho appeared from behind a tree. I waited for the eviction notice. His words reverberated through my head. I winced and then frowned. What had he just said? '¿Están haciendo un camping?' (Are you camping?) 'Sí.' (Yes) '*Bueno no hay drama.*' (Good. No worries). I couldn't believe our luck, and saluted the guy as he rode off through the bush. But although we had been spared our marching orders, we weren't to be spared company. Darkness was falling, and we crawled into our respective hammocks to avoid the mosquitoes.

As we started to drift away, a series of grunts pierced the night, followed by an almighty roar. Was it a puma? My mind raced and my body prickled. Sleep had muffled my senses. Branches were cracking under the feet of a heavy animal. This wasn't the signature of a big cat. We could hear the scrub parting nearby and then deep, heavy, breathing. Of course; it was a bull, who, judging by his behaviour, was in must and looking for a female. I have come across enough aggressive individuals to realize they deserve some respect, especially randy ones! David beamed his head torch in the direction of the intruder. Brown eyes reflected gold, and his pungent breath refracted the light. He was waist-deep in scrub, metres from our hammocks. David yelled, the bull yelled back and then David bashed a stick in defiance. The great hulk snorted and galloped off.

Sleeping outside was one of the great pleasures of our expedition. But instead of viewing it as eight dead hours, it was better to think of it as a whole process of experiences, with small chunks of sleep in between. We curled up in bed once more and tried to drift off again. Sometime later a shriek cleaved the air, followed by two *humphs* and more explosive, blood-curdling yelps. It was a vixen. I yearned to see her in action, something rarely possible when one lives behind stone walls and double glazing. She was so close; I could hear her soft footsteps. I shone my light on her hindquarters; she was just below David's hammock, sniffing the ground where we had eaten. But within a split-second she was gone, with the light bouncing off the mist and nearby grasses as if she had been a figment of my imagination. Aside from one or two retreating yelps I heard nothing more. Some hours or minutes later, a few sleeping stints at least, the high screeching of an owl shattered the still of the night as it glided silently over our heads.

A thin film of light spread across our makeshift home revealing beads of dew glistening from every leaf, stalk and branch. I could even see my breath. We had over-slept, yet it was questionable whether we had slept at all. But at least I had dreamed, because I awoke with the memory of eating pork crackling and giving birth to an insect. Either way, running beckoned, as did the tyranny of the sun, threatening us if we didn't hurry and pack up.

The village of Lumbrera marked our next rural deviation. Here we could leave the dual carriageway, avoid the cities of Salta and Jujuy and head north-east, on a minor road amid the rolling hills. We saw a toco toucan; an extraordinary bird with an enormous bright- orange and yellow beak. It seemed that, should it take off, it must nose-dive to the earth. That beak has been found to have a thermo-regulatory function like that of an elephant's ear; but one of the beak's loveliest uses is during the pre-nuptials, when the amorous pair toss fruits to one another, catching them with a yikkering snap.

A river crossed our road, perfect for our night's camp-site. A long, grassy track meandered away from an open gate. We slunk off the road and followed it until it connected to the river, a few metres from which we strung our hammocks amid thigh-high scrub. David collapsed face-first into the river and I followed. It was blissful feeling the cool water rippling over our limbs. Through slits in my eyes I watched the overhanging branches: a blue-tufted, star-throat hummingbird dashed overhead. The sweat and grime from the last couple of days loosened from our bodies. We filled all our bags and saucepans with water and after cooking slipped into our hammocks. As darkness fell, sweat trickled down our bodies and we listened to a thunderstorm drawing closer. At some point in the night we became conscious of another presence.

I squirmed under the tarp and saw a shard of light flickering over our trailer,

(David wrote). It seemed irritated, emitting a deep guttural gurgling that grew in pitch into a yelling, maddened shriek. It wasn't Spanish, but something else. It flashed the torch around. I yelled, '¡Buenos noches! ¡Hola!' really to explain our presence, but he wouldn't respond. I made to get out of my hammock, my heart racing, ready to flee or fight; neither being an option whilst stuck in my cocoon. Katharine was silent, clutching the pen knife in her hammock. The machete lay just outside of mine. I undid the zip. I heard his feet shuffle and then suddenly he was fleeing, yelling as he went, bare feet pounding the soft earth.

I was petrified. We had been yanked from our dreams into a living nightmare. Was the intruder about to knife or shoot us, rape me or something equally heinous? It was pitch black, and his weird mumblings sounded devilish. My senses were on fire and my heart was at fever-pitch, as if it would explode right out of my body. I knew I had to remain mute; a woman's voice could make us a soft target. I froze when David spoke, my ears sweeping the night for a whisper of response, but there was nothing: just a void. The silence was chilling and clanging in my head. Then the muttering and pounding footsteps; I didn't dare to utter a word in case the intruder came back; just lay in shock. Would he return with more of his kind to attack us? Now that we had been discovered, we were sitting ducks.

After about 20 minutes David whispered, 'Are you OK?'

'I'm scared,' I gasped.

'If we hear anything else, we must get out of our hammocks as quick as possible. Leave your flap open. We can't do anything trapped inside.'

'I'll run. I'm not facing that….' My voice trailed off. I lay rigid, my ears straining the darkness for sounds as the hours slowly dissolved.

I wanted a more logical explanation, but nothing came (David wrote). We heard footsteps drumming the earth at various points during the night. Sleep was impossible. I expect he was hunting, armed with either a machete or gun. Guns are terrifying; you don't need to get close to your victim, it's too easy to fire out in fear or at the unknown: us.

Morning eventually came. Cockerels crowed and we noticed a small mud house, which we hadn't seen the evening before. It lay within half a mile of where we had camped. Perhaps the fiend lived there? But why did he vocalise only weird noises? Why no language? Why just grunting?

Over the next two days we ran 48 miles to Las Lajitas. A range of mountains, pleated and drenched in forest, reared above us. They were beautiful, but on the flat valley floor, things were changing. The forest was being burnt and ploughed up to make way for the green gold of soya that was bringing people salivating and scurrying for a piece of the action. Enormous fields stretched endlessly into the horizon. Billboards advertised noxious pesticides. Aeroplanes jostled on an apron, ready to unleash their chemicals, and huge tractors circled the fields with 20-metre spraying rigs. Troops of gleaming Hiluxes sped past, one with a *picui* ground dove stuck in its radiator. Badly-designed Monopoly houses sprouted up on the road into town, with manicured gardens and high gates marking the rapid acquisition of wealth. The whole area stank, not of pollen, but of the thick, hollow smell of chemicals.

> Hostels in Las Lajitas flip their vacancy signs over to indicate they are full (David wrote). It's harvest time. But this is no ordinary harvest. This is the coal face of the South American 'gold rush' for soya, a small green protein-rich legume which has secured Argentina's place at the top table in a global industry worth $35.7 billion. And it's a shock to find that the UK is a significant consumer of Argentinian soya, requiring an area almost the size of Yorkshire to be planted every year in order to meet demand, largely for manufactured food products and chicken and pig feed.

A police car stopped us on our way into town. The window wound down and a flabby arm waved at us. The owner certainly wasn't going to move from his seated position and instead blurted, 'Where have you come from?' and 'Where are you going?' He and his companion were chewing coca, and after receiving our responses, they nodded and spat out large, masticated lumps of leaves and sped off.

A scattering of earth and corrugated-iron houses marked the settlement of La Estrella. Low, scratchy scrubland stretched as far as the eye could see. The river had long since curdled and dried up. Goats and long-legged sheep ranged through clouds of dust. A convoy of Bolivian lorries shipping gas from Argentina to Bolivia parked by a hut serving hot food on plastic tables. I was so excited to see the Bolivians; excited to be close to their country.

The café-owners said we could camp in the disused petrol station across the road, so we cleared a space outside to tie our hammocks. Just as I was having a strip wash the following morning, a shepherd appeared with his flock of sheep and goats. I think the poor man was more shocked than me, as he scurried away, leaving his flock nonchalantly chewing the scrub. An hour later a woman appeared wearing a collection of long skirts and a bright-red headscarf tied into her waist-length black hair. She mentioned that her husband had found us that morning (she didn't mention my nudity). She watched us pack our bags and strap them to the trailer. They clearly intrigued her: 'What are you selling?'

She thought we were travelling gypsies selling our wares to local communities, as we found many locals were doing on the route northwards. I explained we weren't selling anything, but did have a bag of lemons that we could exchange for some water and bread. She seemed very pleased with the deal and marched me off to her home to seal it.

Running South America

Her house consisted of two dark rooms with hard, baked-mud floors. The first was the kitchen and living-space, which was shared with the pigs, chickens and ducks that trailed in and out. The second room lay beyond a curtain and was the bedroom for her, her husband and their eight children. I prepared our water bags and with the help of one of her burly sons, we shifted an enormous urn that contained their next couple of days' water supply. We slopped some of the contents into jugs and ladled that into my bags, picking out some of the bigger insect cargo as we went.

She returned with me to the trailer to wave farewell. Before we left, David remembered to ask her a question that had been foxing us since first running into Argentina's central provinces. We had watched herds of goats nibbling the roadside verges with bells tinkling around their necks. Often three or four dogs accompanied them. People called them guardian dogs, and sometimes they would herd the goats alone, without a human shepherd. Unlike the goats, which could extract moisture from vegetation, the dogs couldn't survive without water, so how were they managing in such arid lands? David asked the *Señora*, 'People have told us that dogs will suckle from the nanny goats. Is this true?' She grinned, '*Sí, sí,*' she said. 'Why, of course. They are clever. Not only do they guard the goats. They milk them too!'

A few miles on we noticed two children standing barefoot by the side of the road. A silver car with blackened windows drove past. The girls waved something at it. The car continued, but changed its mind and reversed. Three portly men in white trousers and shades emerged to inspect what the girls were holding. One man turned his back to urinate. Then I recognized their prize; the near-threatened, southern three-banded armadillo. The men started laughing and shouting, '*Flaco, muy flaco*'. (Thin, too thin). Smiling and shaking their heads in mirth, they got back into their seats, turned up the music and screeched off. The armadillos weren't big enough to eat. The disappointed children watched their exit through a cloud of dust.

We ran up to the girls. A tiny stream of urine leaked from the little creature. Its natural defence of rolling into a ball offered no protection from their clasp. Its sturdy claws shook and its damp eyes stared petrified. The girls were asking a pathetic 30 *pesos* (three pounds) for their trophy. We desperately wanted to buy it and set it free, but we knew this would only fuel the trade. The longer they held the little animal in their hands, the longer it would be before another armadillo was snatched from the wild.

There wasn't much traffic on the earth road, but a couple of minutes later two men passed us on a motorbike. The passenger held two shotguns over his knees. This was becoming a familiar sight. We often heard hunters running with guns and dogs. Most troubling was the sound of shots resonating through the night. What would happen if they stumbled across us in one of our camps?

The day was overcast and fantastic for running, but my mood was dark, like the clouds above us. With each step forward my mind slipped further into a depressing groove. I couldn't stop thinking about the armadillo, industrial agriculture, the rubbish, pollution and traffic. What are humans contributing to this extraordinary planet? All I could see was destruction. From the *chaco* teeming with wildlife we plant soya; from the rainforest, one of the richest ecosystems on earth, we grow burgers; from the wetlands heaving with incredible diversity we plant rows of rice. What have we achieved since we climbed down from the trees? Simplification, then a reduction and now the deterioration of such exuberance and utterly astounding life. Have we gone mad? Can we really continue consuming and tearing up the last of what is wild and unfoetid? I thought of an extract from Tony Juniper's *'Spix's Macaw'*:

> We spend billions of dollars in the quest for evidence of life on other planets, when we have it here in superabundance and at levels of sophistication that we have barely even begun to comprehend, all of it haemorrhaging out into oblivion as we turn our faces to the dead night sky and our backs on the rainforests and reefs, the deltas and the deep. In our lifetimes the natural world will have shrunk by a greater amount than any human before has ever witnessed. Fairly soon, at this rate, in 100 years' time perhaps, our teeming earth will end up as a sterile, sanitised gridwork of concrete and crop fields.

But the following day we saw something incredible. It afforded us hope that it is still possible to find something truly spectacular and wild in the rural corners of our planet. The day dawned steely-grey and cool, creating another opportunity to run without feeling the sun's red-hot claws. We flew along the long, straight asphalt road bordered by gigantic soya fields. An area of thick bush loomed up ahead. I was pulling the trailer and David was trotting behind. We were both quiet, each contemplating the day and enjoying the easy early miles.

Suddenly, about 200 metres away, something large emerged from the bush on the left hand side. I scrutinised its shape, its sleek, muscular form, its sloping back, the long, up-curved tail, the lilting, easy gait and finally the rounded head. A shiver rushed through my body and I hissed to David, 'A puma, it's a puma! Quick!'

Here at last was the species we had been hoping to see since the very start of the expedition, when we first found paw prints in the snow near Cape Froward. After 233 days of watching, here she finally was: the creature people had warned would kill us. In a heart-beat she was with us, and in seconds she disappeared like a puff of smoke.

We ran on. Adrenalin pumped through our bodies and we were desperate to catch just one more glimpse of this queen of the *chaco*. We tore along the road. 'Shhhh!' I scolded David. 'You're making all the noise!' he hissed back. Jettisoning the trailer and grabbing the binoculars, we tried to sneak through the thick scrub. Branches cracked under our feet and whipped at our faces. There was no way that any self-respecting puma would linger within 500 metres of us. We marvelled at how silently she had slipped through this wall of vegetation. Our ears strained for sounds of fleeing birds – anything that would reveal the presence of the cat. Nothing. A frail image of her parting was all that remained in our heads. We searched the bare, orange mud for signs of her passage – four toe-marks around a central pad circled and criss-crossed. Perhaps she had passed through last night? Perhaps she had passed our camp? Smelt that familiar stench of human?

Two cream-backed woodpeckers drilled by the side of the road. David grabbed some stones and tapped the solid bamboo frame of the trailer. The woodpeckers responded, flying right over our heads, hammering back. A few miles later we passed a wetland bristling with birds. It was a magical morning, topped off by our crossing the Tropic of Capricorn and officially stepping into the tropics. It was 18 March 2013, and we had galloped 3,201 miles of the continent.

A faint smell of burning began to tickle our noses, growing thicker and more pungent until it overwhelmed us with an acrid stench of plastic. The rubbish was even thicker than normal, forming drifts of detritus across the road, piling up against the scrub and draping branches. Makeshift dwellings lined the roadside, loosely strung together with plastic sheeting, old crates and bits of wood. A vast rubbish-dump loomed below. Smoke billowed in black toxic clouds from its depths. Families waded knee-deep, bending to inspect anything that caught their eye, anything they could sell or trade. Green slime leaked from the seething mountain of debris, trickling into a green ditch with a floating cargo of white plastic cutlery. Four dwellings had been constructed out of the waste. They stood on either side of the rubbish mountain, jealously guarding their territories. A group of children ran through the heap fighting imaginary battles, while a lone child carefully examined the latest spoils. A blue-and-white flag flew from one of the shacks. We had never imagined such squalor possible in Argentina.

Things didn't improve on the outskirts of Pichinal. A pack of dogs riffled through rubbish; another tore at the innards of a dead horse, and another pair played tug-of-war with a rotting cat. The stench of decaying flesh filled the air, to be replaced by raw sewage as we drew closer to the town. Groups of dogs fought and humped, buildings crumbled into the street and a scummy liquid flowed through the open gutters. Amid the squalor were some newly-built houses, left standing only because the owners must have been important in the town's criminal circles. Women stood by the roadside selling heaps of Chinese clothes. Others sat by freezer boxes of drinks or tables of *empanadas*, deep-fried chicken and *humitas* (a spicy corn mash boiled in maize leaves), while children squatted snotty-nosed and listlessly by their mothers' chubby ankles.

We were being warned about crime every day now. People were concerned at our vulnerability on the roads. The inequality between the wealthy and the vast droves of poor was undoubtedly fuelling delinquency. But as yet we hadn't been considered worth robbing: this was no surprise, as we didn't look the most lucrative of targets or the most sane! Our shorts and tops were faded and shabby; we had stitched patches over the gaping holes in our shoes; our caps and home-made sun-gloves were tattered and sweat crystals encrusted our skin and clothes. The trailer and its cargo looked tired and battered and was inevitably filthy due to the constant clouds of dust that ballooned over it from passing vehicles. We towered over most of the locals (Dave is six foot four and I'm five foot ten) and we were both tanned/ dirty with sun-bleached hair.

The following day we descended into a low marshy area. Tall reeds and rushes lined the roadside, dragonflies buzzed past, and a group of roseate spoonbills filtered for prey in a ditch with their bizarre, spatula beaks. We were hot and thirsty, so stopped for a quick drink of water and bite of *mantecol* (a sweet peanut block, with a good energy boost, that doesn't melt in the sun). David squeezed the sweat from the scarf around his thigh (which he used to prevent chafing) then slapped his thigh, then his neck and ankle. His thrashing grew more and more frantic. I thought he was under attack from a swarm of bees. Then I saw them: enormous black mosquitoes. Over thirty had descended, and they were after our blood. We flew off, but they wouldn't let us go, chasing us like a pack of wolves. I had never seen anything like it. I grabbed David's cap and belted his legs and arms as he ran. As soon as I had dislodged one group, another joined, while ten more bit me and others hitched a ride on the trailer. It must have looked farcical to anyone who passed by, as we tore down the road wildly flailing at one another.

Just before Tartagal we found a café in a small village. The lady had rigged up iron bars across her kitchen door and windows. After ordering *milanezas* through them, I asked her why she felt them necessary. She shook her head, 'The druggies killed my nephew and daughter,' she said. 'They will rob and kill for ten dollars.' She showed me a photo of her large family, pointing at her deceased daughter. We watched the next-door neighbour arrive home, unlock and lock the gate to his barred garden, then lock himself into his house.

Tartagal marked our final city in Argentina. David's right knee was really sore, but with applications of Diclofenac gel he kept going, and we only had 37 miles left to the border. The hotel owner was very friendly but warned us, 'You had better finish your book quickly if you want to help the forests here. Every tree will soon be cut down.'

Moist forests cascaded down from the layers of hills above us. Long-horned cattle crossed the road in front. Two horsemen, wearing enormous, cattle-hide breeches that stuck out in front of their legs like wings, emerged from the bushes herding them. The nearest man stopped to chat. He grinned a gappy smile beneath his large leather hat, with one cheek distended by a wodge of fermenting coca. He explained that the leather breeches were to guard against thorn trees, and invited me to sit on his pony. I sprang up, sinking my hands into its coat, inhaling that familiar intoxicating smell of horse.

As we took our last steps on Argentinian soil, our feet sank into the boiling tarmac, leaving them printed in the asphalt forever. The border town of Pocitos loomed ahead. The familiar turquoise-and-blue Argentinian flag was painted over walls and buildings. We were bound for Bolivia, but couldn't find it anywhere. It was as if Argentina couldn't believe that any other world existed beyond its own. We pounded down the main road, only to be re-directed back to an obscure, nameless street. This was the magical road that would lead us out, through the wardrobe, to a new, promised and desperately longed-for land.

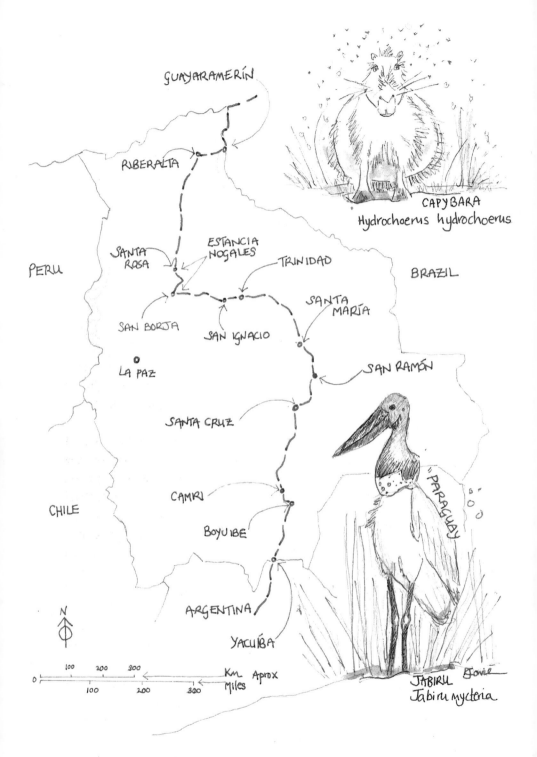

GUAYARAMERÍN

RIBERALTA

CAPYBARA
Hydrochoerus hydrochoerus

SANTA
ROSA

ESTANCIA
NOGALES

TRINIDAD

SANTA
MARÍA

PERU

BRAZIL

SAN BORJA

SAN IGNACIO

SAN RAMÓN

LA PAZ

SANTA CRUZ

CHILE

CAMRI

PARAGUAY

BOYUIBE

ARGENTINA

YACUÍBA

N

100   200   300   Km   Aprox
0   Miles
    100   200   300

JABIRU
Jabiru mycteria

Map 6 – Our Running Route through Bolivia

Gangs of toco toucans clacked
their beaks at one another

Toco Toucan
Ramphastos toco

13 Bolivia: The Promised Land

There wasn't a river, a sea or a mountain to cross. The golden-collared macaws knew nothing of the thick line ruled on our map over which they flew daily; but for us everything changed. We had achieved something we had at times thought impossible; we had crossed into our third South American country on foot, having run 3,322 miles from the very tip of the continent (see Map 6). And although there was no natural border, the anthropogenic transition was enormous.

A kaleidoscope of colours and sounds crashed into us as we hit a wall of humans, cars and their squealing animals. People and vehicles wove between one another in an endless, honking dance, the outcome of which remained uncertain. From behind the tinted window of a shiny black car a man's face appeared. 'Here,' he signalled, 'take this.' It was 50 *bolivianos*, the equivalent of about £5. Before we could explain what we were doing or properly thank him, he had disappeared.

Lorries lined the road waiting to cross into Argentina. Drivers snoozed in their cabs or lay in their hammocks strung underneath the bellies of their vehicles. We stopped to get fruit – and thanks to the mystery motorist, we could buy the sweetest mandarins for one *boliviano* each. The cheaper cost of living was going to be a huge relief, for we had a gaping hole in our finances. This wasn't helped by the fact that, due to our initial miscalculations, we would need to run an additional 1,500 miles, including a significant detour in Bolivia.

The countryside north of Yacuiba was wooded, with a distant, jagged range of blue hills. People would appear at the side of the road from nowhere to catch a *movilidad*, (communal taxi) after walking one of the sandy tracks from the little farmsteads and maize fields which lay hidden behind trees and shrubs.

We gathered papaya that had sprouted in a ditch by the road. They weren't ready, but we knew from living in the Caribbean that green papaya is lovely in stews and would give us our quota of vitamins. We followed a path into a woodland

and set up camp. Two hours later we heard voices. We had no time to hide. A brindled mongrel came bounding around the corner. It stopped dead and barked emphatically. A figure followed, but stood half concealed in the gloom of a tree. We couldn't see what it was doing. We shouted, '¡Hola!' After five long minutes it slowly came forward. It was a 'she', a young girl. She was clearly more frightened than we were and stood rooted to the spot, a look of terror gripping her face.

We invited her to join us for supper and she finally smiled. I watched her nose pucker up as she sampled our meal, 'But it's so bland!' she exclaimed, 'Have you salted it?'

'With at least half a tablespoon!' I giggled. We thought it tasted absolutely fine and as we had run 20 miles that day and sweated rivers, we thought we should have been the ones demanding more salt! It wasn't until we tried the local, homemade cheese that that we appreciated where this salt-immunity came from. This white rubbery cheese is sold by local smallholders throughout Bolivia. The salt used to preserve it gives it an almost eye-watering intensity, which, after a long day running, quickly satisfies any salty cravings. The only problem was that it added to our general state of dehydration.

Silviana (our salt queen) needed to visit her family, so wandered off singing. She reappeared later presenting us with two steaming cups. 'These are from my aunt. It's a special local tea made from a yellow-flowered herb that we collect from the fields here. It's good for your heart and blood.' David loved it and was determined that we recreate it ourselves. In the next couple of days we would find a gaggle of women rushing out of a *movilidad* to collect the plant, which they pointed to us growing on the bank (it looked a little like chamomile) before jumping back into the car.

Silviana started to riffle through her beige canvas shoulder bag. She pulled out two feathers of emerald, purple and gold, exclaiming, *'De pavo real'* (from the peacock). They were exquisite and had been fashioned into earrings as a present for me. And with that she was gone, scurrying home. Silviana's generosity became something of a theme in Bolivia. When asking for onions and garlic from a roadside vendor, David was faced by an enormous grin from a pint-sized woman, insisting she could not take our money. Every single day, from the first day we entered Bolivia to the day we arrived in Santa Cruz, 346 miles later, a motorist would stop and hand us cold drinks and food. Never had we received so much goodwill – and this from the poorest country in South America.

A rural landscape of woods, hills, pocket fields and distant mountains unfolded in a hazy green concertina at our sides. The little towns, villages and straggly settlements were full of clucking hens and snake-necked roosters, the odd grazing cow or a snorting sow and her piglets. The level of personal threat had dropped dramatically since crossing the border, and we no longer had to keep up the daily grind of claiming a false nationality. It was a huge relief. We both felt extremely content in this gentle rural land.

Bolivia also brought an escalation in our daily parrot count. These intelligent birds never failed to fill us with joy as they cart-wheeled and cackled through the air in a flash of startling colours. Our eyes feasted upon yellow-collared macaws, scaly-headed parrots, turquoise-fronted parrots and blue-crowned parakeets. Often they would be feeding in the treetops or commuting between their favourite roosting sites. If they passed over our heads we would see one or two craning their necks, clearly intrigued as to what species we might be with our extra two wheels trailing behind us.

As in Argentina, the grassy strip by the side of the road was seldom left to waste. Flocks of sheep and goats were watched-over by a woman, usually one with a dog, occasionally accompanied by a man. The women wore the same distinctive fabrics we had seen high up in breathless La Paz, generally displayed in two or three bright, bell-shaped skirts, knee-length woolly socks (the use of either being extraordinary to us, considering the heat) and a bowler hat. A strip of colourful striped fabric was often tied around their back, with two chubby legs dangling out. Their long, dark, shining hair would be plaited and commonly looped together with curtain braids. These were the *Colla* people, traditionally of the high Andes, who had over the decades migrated into the lowlands where the *Camba* live.

The origin of the multiple layering of skirts is difficult to pinpoint, but was perhaps a reaction to the extreme cold endured in the snow-covered Andean villages. Geraldine, a Uruguayan friend brought up in Cuzco in the 1950s, recalled the Quechua people wearing such skirts. She suggested that a new layer was added once the last one had become dirty and tattered. She also remembered the skirts' advantage when the wearer wanted to urinate in public spaces, as she could squat without anyone being the wiser.

Geraldine said the women were the work-horses and the men the ornaments. A familiar scene would be of a woman leading a llama down a track, with a baby in a sling on her back, while spinning a skein of llama wool. Her face was the colour of tanned leather, creased and battered by the wind, and her mouth locked in a permanent grimace, which spoke of the extreme physical hardship she endured. Several paces in front would wander the man, sipping on fermented potato liquor. We found that women dominated the workforce along the road, too. They comprised the crews humping wheelbarrows full of rocks and mixing cements. Women were the vendors. Women cooked up steaming broths and manned restaurants. So where were the men?

The next day a little square on our map heralded Machareti. Although we found a town square, it didn't seem to lead anywhere, it was as if the village had long forgotten its responsibilities and decided to slumber in the heat. We collected a few supplies and flopped onto a couple of chairs in a food shack to fuel the rest of the day's run. A middle-aged couple insisted on sitting with us.

Soup was placed in front of us, followed by rice and meat. The couple were tall and overweight, enveloping the little plastic chairs in their copious backsides. The guy wasn't concentrating: his eyes darted around the room searching for something. When an old man shuffled past, he waved him over. They exchanged a couple of quiet words. The man pulled out of his pocket a familiar, emerald plastic bag (thousands of which we saw floating by the roadside like jellyfish) and upturned its contents of leaves into the ham-sized hand in front of him, before bidding him farewell.

Now content, our man relaxed. His lady, with her died ginger hair, unstoppered a small plastic bottle from which she emptied a little heap of white powder. 'This is bicarbonate of soda,' she told us. 'You add this to the coca leaves and it breaks them down, freeing their juices. Try it.' She gathered a selection of leaves, dusted a little of the bicarbonate upon them and wrapped them up into two little bundles. 'Here. Push them into your cheeks and allow them to work their magic. Coca is a wonder plant. I give it to my daughter: it cures everything. When you're down, take it. When you're restless, take it. When you need to concentrate and stay awake, take it.'

She grinned, her cheek bulging, her rouged lips stretched with a small gap at the side through which a green speckle of saliva dribbled out. Well: one thing it wasn't was attractive! I soon surreptitiously spat mine into my hand, slipping it under the table and under my foot as the woman went on: 'It's not just coca that can boost your body's health. Nature has a whole medicine-cabinet of plants and animals. You know the little *hornero* bird? Well, his nest of mud can combat paralysis and cure strokes. What about if your baby is all thin and crumpled? All you need to do is make a hot bath, soak those leaves over there into it – do you see them? Yes. Then add the stomach contents of a cow into the mix. Submerge your baby into it every day, for five days and it will fatten up beautifully.'

Our treacle-tart witch doctor was just getting into her stride, 'But what you two really need is snake fat and serum to cure your aching muscles.' I was starting to feel uncomfortable. 'Come and see us in Santa Cruz,' she said. Here, this is our number.' And with that they strode off.

We decided to gather a few *empanadas* before we left the village. While we waited to be served, we overheard two teenagers conniving, 'If we're going to do it, it'll have to be tonight. Old man Juan has a full clutch of hens. He's not going to notice the absence of a few plump girls!' With that they ran off giggling. The woman behind us shook her head and a wry smile crept across her face. She had also been listening to the youths. 'What were they talking about?' we asked.

'It's Good Friday; Jesus is dead and He's not watching over us as he usually does. So it's time for a little bit of light thieving! No one will notice. It's a tradition around these parts. Help a fat neighbour by freeing him of a few of his weighty possessions. But you only have a few hours, because soon *Señoir* (Jesus) will be rising from the dead, and you had better be behaving yourself when that happens, 'cause he'll be watching you all over again!'

Sixty-four miles north of Villamonte lay the little town of Boyuibe at the crossing of three roads, one of which headed directly east to Paraguay. Many of the people we met there spoke both Spanish and Guaraní, the language of a large indigenous group found in Paraguay, Argentina and Brazil, but with their greatest stronghold in Bolivia. Boyuibe was a small, dusty settlement of earth roads and a mix of traditional earth and concrete dwellings. It was very rural, with animals trailing through the streets and houses, along with the local tribe of children. We noticed a blackboard sign saying, 'Hay almuerzo familiar para 120 bolivianos y soda fría.' (Family lunch for 120 bolivianos and cold fizzy drinks) scratched in chalk.

It was like manna from heaven. We collapsed into the seats for the favourite part of my day; meal time. The food consisted of a strawberry fizzy drink; a chicken broth with a floating piece of boiled yuca and a chicken bone or two wrapped in a few shreds of meat; followed by a piece of hammered beef on a thin bed of rice, with a few more boiled yuca portions and a slice of tomato. This was traditional fare in Bolivia, with the addition of a fried egg and one or two chips a possibility. Portions were always well salted and mean (but then the Bolivians are fairly diminutive people) and would barely touch the sides of our stomachs.

A man and young woman sat to our side. He had a collection of plastic goods piled in the middle of the table, and when it was time to pay he offered the owner a drying rack or a flask in lieu of money. A few minutes later a *movilidad* arrived from Santa Cruz, disgorging a flock of Boyuibens who filtered off to their respective homes. One young man alighted with armfuls of plastic devices. He too came and sat down, and during his lunch began a lengthy discussion with the owner about the merits of his various products. He was particularly keen to sell her a liquidizer, but she flashed a smile, caressing a similar machine which she said she had bought for less money. The banter was still progressing as we retreated to a hostel having paid perhaps her only cash bill that day.

That night our eyes gradually pierced the darkness, finding corners and road-ends where once there was only blackness. Parties of children and elderly couples appeared from the gloom; everyone was out, and stars prickled the night like a million jewels. We came across a stall over-flowing with vegetable produce. The owner stood waist-deep in it. Our eyes roved over the bags of alien roots and obscure fruits and settled on a sack of shrivelled brown-and-cream balls that looked like fungi of sorts. We only needed provisions for a couple of days, so we asked the woman to full our container with them, along with a handful of pink potatoes, garlic, onions and some oranges.

She called the fungi *chuña* and told us that we needed to boil them in water or in a stew. They had an odd, rubbery consistency and didn't seem to add much to our potato, onion and garlic meal. It was only after speaking to a clutch of local people in the following weeks that we started to gain a more detailed picture of the significance and origin of *chuña*, which means 'wrinkled' in the Aymara dialect of the high Andes.

Chuña have nothing to do with mushrooms, but are in fact potatoes, which Andean people have grown for centuries. They are said to have been domesticated in southern Peru and north-western Bolivia over 7,000 years ago. Over 1,500 years these communities have perfected a method of preserving their crop. After the annual harvest, villagers take their potatoes up to the tops of the mountains, spread them out over the ground and leave them to freeze solid for three days in the below-zero night-time temperatures. The women then return to stomp barefoot on the layer of potatoes, removing their skins and the freezing dew. They then allow them to bake in the sun until they turn dark brown. The result will apparently store for many months, ensuring the families have food all year round.

The following day we ran past a small school in the middle of a sea of spiky scrub. We hesitated: if we stopped, we would end up running in the harrowing midday sun, but if we ran on, we would miss meeting our first rural Bolivian pupils and teachers. I knocked at the classroom door. Children jumped from their seats and within 15 minutes the entire school had filed out on to the netball courts, dragging chairs from their classrooms. We wheeled the trailer to centre stage and pulled out various kit items, wildlife photos and feathers to use as props, then began chatting about the expedition and why we love running and wildlife. We quizzed them on the names of local animals and asked which species they liked most and least, and then explained how they are all connected and that you need the nasty ones as well as the lovely ones. It was a magical session. The little school had never had visitors from elsewhere in Bolivia, let alone from another country whose native tongue wasn't Spanish.

The next day we passed another rural school, and buoyed by the previous day's experience, decided to ask whether they might like a talk as well. The Headmaster said he would have to seek consent from the Village Elder. We waited and watched, growing more and more uneasy. After what seemed like an eternity, the Headmaster returned from the old lady's thatched barn and announced that the she had consented to us presenting.

After over half an hour of quizzes and chat, we turned to the Headmaster who thanked us heartily and reinforced our messages. He then began a passionate explanation of the wrongs that Bolivia had suffered, 'We are very fortunate in Bolivia to have such a huge diversity of habitats and animals. But there is something that we are missing that should rightfully be ours: the sea. Before Chile claimed our piece of the Pacific coast, our children knew what it is like to feel the waves wash over their feet, to watch an infinite horizon of blue, to know the animals of this watery world. Now they are blind.'

It was a moving declaration, and a discontentment we would learn was widely felt throughout the landlocked country of Bolivia. What we hadn't envisaged, however, was that Britain had been involved in the dispute, siding with Chile against Bolivia in the War of the Pacific in the 1880s. Was the Argentinian confrontation about to repeat itself? We were contending with the fallout, hundreds of years later, from our ancient seafaring nation's exploits. At least the school didn't seem to hold it against us, as the teachers invited us to share some of the children's break-time fare of heavily-sugared black cinnamon tea and bread. Indeed, we would never feel judged for our nationality in Bolivia. The only coldness we ever felt was from the *Colla* people, but this wasn't a result of our nationality, more a consequence of our being some of those insufferable *gringos*. The harsh, forbidding and austere land they hail from seems to leave them with little space for public shows of affection?

The growth-rate in the tropics is phenomenal. A rainbow of flowers sprout from the verges and trees spiral to the sky. Sun and rain conspire to provide perfect growing conditions. No opportunity is wasted: even the cow pats which spotted the road (and felt so soft under our bare feet) would be covered within days with tender pea-green sprouts. Among this green lust for life were any number of species that darted through the branches as we ran, feeding on the output of this mass of vegetation. Gangs of *toco* toucans clacked their beaks at one another, and purplish jays eyed us. A tethered donkey provided the perfect platform for two sulphur-yellow cattle tyrants. Every few minutes they would launch from their hairy table, catching the flies disturbed by their grazing host.

With such abundance came wasps. I find wasps fascinating. The elaborate paper nesting galleries created by our British version, from fine threads of wood masticated with saliva, are feats of engineering. But in Bolivia we got little chance to marvel at their behaviour. Instead, we would be scudding along, our minds in a fog of random thoughts, when one or other of us would shriek and start batting our legs or arms in response to one of the brutes having stung us. It became a regular event every couple of days, but I couldn't understand why.

Most animals will not attack a human unless provoked, whether backed into a corner or defending their young. It is just not worth their precious energy. Perhaps the wasps scented our sweat and were homing in on our salty secretions, and when our swinging arms and striding legs trapped or knocked them, the collision caused and involuntary response? Whatever the reason, we became accustomed to the sharp, needling sting, as a minor irritant, which sometimes lasted an hour or more.

School children also accompanied us. Spewing out of school gates at going home-time, they would race after us, laughing and giggling at our foolishness. One wee lad was so determined to keep up with us that we thought he might keel over, as his breathing rasped from his thin little body. We stopped and even though he was bent over catching his breath, his eyes sparkled and he gave us the most enormous grin.

We wound our way up into the hills towards the town of Camiri. With an altitude of 819 metres, it felt noticeably cooler than the sweaty lands we had left behind. We found a hostel bedaubed with plants. Vines hung from trellises, flowers snaked up pillars and pots overflowed with colour. The cheapest room was 90 *bolivianos* (about nine pounds). We unpacked the trailer and flopped onto our bed, gazing at a line of ants forming traffic-jams on invisible roads up the wall. Every time they met oncoming traffic they would hold little mothers meetings.

One of the highlights of our time in Bolivia was always finding the market, where we would pull up a plastic stool and sample a new food or drink. Among our favourites was *api,* a hot, purple, glutinous liquid, with something of the mulled-wine about it. It is made from blackberry and maize-flour, ground cloves and cinnamon, lemon and sugar and is truly delicious, especially with *pastels* or *empanadas.* To make the *pastels,* the women roll out incredibly fine pastry, slip a thin slice of cheese in the centre, fold the dough over and pucker the sides. This is all done in a split second, after which the little packages are deep-fat-fried. In the market in Camiri, one glass of *api* cost fifteen pence and a *pastel* ten pence; finally we could feast like kings.

We scanned the stores for the most interesting-looking lunch. The market-place was divided up into small cubicles, and inside each was a woman, often with her teenaged daughter. A couple of gas rings were mounted on the worktop. Upon these sat huge black cauldrons, simmering with chicken broth, spitting with rice and bubbling with meat stew. A plate of chopped onions and tomatoes sat nearby and probably some savoury *empanadas* or *tucumáns,* as they were called in northern Argentina and southern Bolivia, the equivalent of a pasty, which usually contained potato and meat.

Menus were chalked on the blackboards propped up on each of the booths. Strangers and friends would pull up a bench and eat at the work surface. We selected a fiery-haired lady who had some unfamiliar dishes emblazoned on her board. I chose *majadito,* which turned out to be a bed of fried rice, with pieces of battered jerky, speckled with vegetables and crowned with a fried egg and a sliver of fried plantain. *Ranga* tickled David's fancy, but we couldn't make out what it comprised, apart from the fact that it was beef-based and that it was, according to the cook, 'Muy muy rico' (very very delicious). But as he tucked in, I watched his face visibly contort, 'This isn't great,' he said between mouthfuls, stoically soldiering on. After a few more he commented, 'I think it's off. There's something desperately wrong here.' At which point he offered me a forkful. Both of us will eat absolutely anything – but that was the most disgusting mouthful of food I have ever tasted. It could only be likened to faeces. How David ate 90 per cent of his platter of *ranga* without throwing up I will never know.

It was not until a couple of days later, when talking to some people on the road, that we fully understood what *ranga* was. It refers to the intestines of an animal, and it was more than likely that the lady had not properly cleaned them out. David had indeed been eating faeces, cow-dung to be more accurate, which had been on its way to the outside world just before it was slaughtered. *Las partes menos nobles* (literally, 'the less noble parts' of the animal) was a collective term for animal innards, and something along with *ranga* from which we would be keeping well away during the rest of our journey through South America!

On leaving the market, we decided to buy a glass of *mocochinchi* (syrupy peach drink) from a stall-holder outside. A small, plump woman was perched on a step by her stall, with a friend stooped over her plucking grey hairs from her head. We laughed and I explained how I had to pull out the stiff hairs that grew at right-angles from David's eyebrows and ears. They giggled and asked us, '¿Tienen hijos?' (Do you have children?) We shook our heads. 'Perhaps in the future.' They retorted, '!Están flojos!' (You're so lazy). The fact that we had run a marathon that day didn't seem to count!

A little girl yanked on my sleeve and started talking. She wanted to show us her mother. I held her hand and she pulled me through the market beaming, '¡Ella es mi mamá!' (She's my mum). I looked over to view this shining belle, and found a great Bolivian walrus. But to her daughter she was the most radiant queen, and on seeing her little girl, the mother cracked a great smile and enveloped her in a colossal hug.

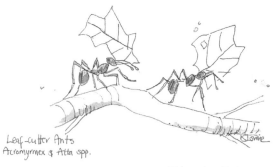

Leaf-cutter Ants
Acromyrmex & Atta spp.

We're under attack, come
and help,' he yelled.

14 A Series of Afflictions

David started to turn green. He felt faint at midday and collapsed onto the
road a few hours later. Energy and colour drained from his body. The cause
could have been many contenders (*ranga* being a prime culprit), as we followed
a strict policy of eating everything and anything edible that we found by the side
of the road. This had served us well up-to-now, but clearly something had slipped
through David's robust internal ecosystem and his body wasn't combating the
onslaught. Water was another suspect, because we didn't always filter it. A virus
might have struck him; or perhaps it was the Doxycycline antimalarial pills
we had started taking? Either way, he couldn't stomach food or the pills, and
collapsed in the mosquito net tent.

Next morning we awoke to the heart-warming sound of *habladores* (blue-
fronted Amazon parrots) flying over the hills. Each one appeared to have
something to say as they screeched and gurgled to one another, tumbling through
the air and streaming over the tree- tops. We saw these garrulous characters
throughout the continent, stuffed into tiny cages or clinging onto a bar of steel.
Their fantastic mimicry skill and intelligence make them a number one favourite
in the pet trade, but it was devastating to see the flea-bitten, distressed captives,
imprisoned in metal tombs, chewing on a piece of hard white bread.

David was determined to head on, even though he still felt nauseous, with
barely the strength to run. Early in the morning we stopped at a wayside kiosk
to buy some of the salty white cheese. As we chatted to the stall owner, we were
joined by a couple of workmen who bought a bottle of Coca-Cola, pulled up
some chairs and asked us to join them.

It transpired that the younger guy, Javier, was a keen naturalist and we ended
up spending the next couple of hours with him. Together we walked up the road
to a family who served lunch from a couple of tables at the front of their house,
but when we went to pay the bill after Javier had left, we found he had beaten

us to it. Before he departed, he pulled a package from his coat containing two enormous scarab beetles. They were a husband and wife team. The male was the size of a three-year-old child's hand, and black and shiny with a rhinoceros's horn protruding from his head. The female was a dull brownish colour. We found out later they were a *Megasoma* species, but in the meantime he said we could keep them.

We felt most honoured with our fascinating cargo, although it seemed unlikely we would get them through customs to grace our natural history collection in the UK. In the end we carried our more and more stinking friends all the way to Santa Cruz, where we deposited them in the Noel Kempff Natural History Museum, much to the delight of the curator.

The restaurant owners were another lovely, warm family. The father sat with us, the corners of his mouth gently curved upwards at rest. He was long and thin, with hazel hair, a *Camba* with clear Hispanic blood. He described the difference between *Colla* and *Camba*.

'The Colla people have been coming down to the lowlands in search of an easier way of life, in our warm, productive climate – and I don't blame them! I love it here; we have a simple, but beautiful life. You plant a seed in the soil and it grows. The sun shines and the rain falls. We have the most delicious fruits and plenty of water. Rice sprouts and cattle grow fat. People are content down here, we're blessed. But the Colla cannot relax. They bring their ruthless business traits and lust for money. Yes, they work hard, but for what? Gold coins to pile into their coffins?'

The great thing about the run was its clear daily goal and end goal. We just had to put one foot in front of the other, find a clearing to hide in at night, gather enough water, make a fire and carry enough food. Pretty basic stone-age necessities; activities we humans have perfected over millennia. But David's condition had become our most urgent preoccupation. He couldn't kick away his nausea. It stifled his appetite, producing a general lethargy and weakness. We were carrying Ciprofloxacin, amongst our extensive chest of medicines, which a friend had given us in Uruguay, but David was determined not to take it. It would not be until weeks later, in a desperate attempt to shake the condition, that he would finally start a course. Even to this day, however, we will never know if he had contracted Chagas. I conversely, had escaped sickness (so far), but I was still suffering from the needling sensation of prickly heat.

In addition to the general feeling of sickness, red rubs were flaring on the top of David's legs and nipples from the near-100 percent humidity. One friend had suggested hair conditioner, another fine tights, someone else talcum powder, the aim being to reduce friction. David tried everything, but nothing worked. The culprit was his sweat; torrents of it, that outran and out-produced any potential cure. Within minutes of starting the day's run, he would be dripping from every pore. When he was on trailer duty the problem was ten times worse. He began a regime of wringing out his top every five miles during the trailer and shoe change-overs. An easily accessible pond or stream would allow him to rinse his top en route, but at the end of the day we often didn't have enough water to drink, let alone any spare to wash ourselves or our clothes. And so the inevitable happened; David developed crotch rot.

The hot, sweaty conditions were ideal for fungal growth, which explained this raw, sore, itchy development. He tried puffing anti-fungal powder over it, but it didn't work. The problem was that we couldn't remove the causal effect of running through a humid, incubating environment, and the chances were that conditions would deteriorate even further in Brazil. Washing ourselves and our clothes needed to feature higher in our daily priorities (if only we could find water). Luckily, a series of days off in Santa Cruz would spell the end of David's affliction, with the administration of an antibiotic powder.

Contributing to the nausea was the smell of our clothes, which stank overwhelmingly of urine. Neither of us thought too much about it, but after researching the topic, I've discovered our diet was too protein-heavy, lacking the carbohydrates that are the body's best energy-creating friends during periods of intensive exercise. In lieu of carbohydrates, the proteins we had been consuming (beans, beans and more beans, and the odd bit of cheese and meat) were being converted into glucose, of which one of the waste products is ammonia. Usually ammonia is converted into urea and expelled through urine, but when the kidneys can't deal with high levels, it is expelled through sweat. Due to lack of water to dilute the ammonia, our sweat was almost 100 per cent NH_3.

We were climbing up and up through layer upon layer of misty forest, spiralling into the clouds. Massive trees, draped in lianas, cloaked the roadside. We were nearing the golden figures of 18' 54 south and 63' 24 west, which represented the start of something mighty in our expedition: the Amazon River basin. From here on in (until Venezuela) all the rivers and streams that we ran past would be draining into the greatest of all rivers in the world. Yet it was amazing to think that we were still a good 1,500 miles south of the river itself. On summiting the pass, David found the exact line where the watershed of the river began. We watched water from our bottle trickling south from one side of the line and north from the other. The northern trail pointed to the path our journey would carry us, through Bolivia and onwards into the jaws of Brazil and Venezuela.

As if to signal what waited ahead in the most species-diverse ecosystem on earth, we counted 32 bird species that day, from the mighty King Vulture to a crimson-crested woodpecker. We descended to the town of Abapó, crossing the silt-laden Río Grande and running into an ugly ramshackle settlement beyond its banks. Every eye swivelled towards us. Faces high and low pierced our progress, less in wonder, more in shock and disbelief. The faces were blank, uncomprehending, grappling to work out exactly what and who we were. It was formidable, I wanted to hide.

The first hazy lights from a scattering of street lamps and vendors' stalls stuttered into action. We jogged through long shadows, searching the murky darkness for a possible camp. This veil of shadows was defeating us. We had broken our rule not to run in the dark, especially in urban areas. It was almost impossible to work out what lay where; where the pot-holes were, the heaps of rubbish, the sudden appearance of cyclists or walkers, morphing from the darkness.

A track snaked off to our left. We had to get off the main road, so we followed it. A couple of motorbikes passed; a watery light heralded a dwelling down a path that forked off to the right. Another path curved into the darkness; we chose it. Fireflies pulsed their glowing bums into the night. A bird fluttered from almost under my foot – a little nightjar. Eventually we found a spot to the side of a gateway and unpacked our tent.

The following day, 1,996 miles after we had last seen them in the Aluminé valley of Argentina, we met David's sister Fiona and her friend Octavio. It was Octavio's birthday and also mine, so they whisked us away into the mountains for two blissful days of rest. We talked and talked until there was nothing left to say. We practised self-defence moves with Octavio: sprinting backwards from a pursuer, before turning and belting away; weaving to avoid gunshots; never allowing an attacker within arm's length, but if one did get that close, to grab him by the wrist, forcing a knife or gun to drop. We also talked through a possible rape scenario, and how David and I could counter it. Seriously crime-ridden zones awaited us in Brazil and Venezuela, I felt vulnerable; the possibilities of being attacked were real and serious. I hate confrontation, and I knew that fleeing would be my fall-back, but I also knew that that wouldn't always be possible.

The road to Santa Cruz marked the start of Bolivia's own green-gold harvest, with soya fields creeping into the deep distance. White Brahman cattle speckled the fields, with white cattle egrets perched on their humps or snatching insects by their feet. We ran 28 miles and then 24 miles to reach the city. When we followed a disused railway a couple of miles south of Santa Cruz's great bulk, overhanging scrub and trees threatened to ensnare us as nature reclaimed her land.

A long-legged road-runner burst into our field of vision: the most extraordinary- looking bird, like a pheasant on stilts, with a red beak above which sprouted a tuft of unruly feathers. It was a red-legged *seriema* that stalked through the grassland, its sharp eye searching for reptiles and amphibians. We had seen a black-legged *seriema*, the only other species in the family, in savanna north of La Rioja. The birds intrigued me. They can reach speeds of fifteen-miles per hour, preferring to run than fly. They have a fierce reputation as one of the only birds that can kill a coral snake. Farmers tame them as guard birds to keep foxes at bay. Needless to say, our *seriema* bolted into the thigh-high pampa as soon as it caught sight of us.

Finding the primate in David is not difficult. He can scuttle up the masts on our boat and skip across her five-metre bowsprit as if he were walking on solid ground.

He has scaled cranes dangling above the skyline of London and hot-footed up craggy peaks needling through the clouds. I, on the other-hand, have the climbing abilities of a gnat. I cling onto the mast with all my limbs as the colour drains from my body, and force myself to scale vertiginous peaks with suffocating progress. So when we rounded a corner in our railway line and found a chasm in the dry river bed, and a rusted bridge with slats missing from its already airy arc, I froze.

David was already a quarter of the way across, pulling and half-carrying the trailer when he asked for my help to manoeuvre it over a two-metre gap. Great! I was still fixed to the ground on the wrong side of the bridge. I sucked in air and willed my feet to move. Soon I was on all fours, staring through formidable holes at the river bed far below. David was shaking his head in despair. My eyes gradually moved from the bridge to him; he had nearly reached the other side. I knew I should go on and conquer this illogical phobia, but I had seen an alternative. I reversed and pushed through thick prickly vegetation, sliding down the bank on my bum into the riverbed. Quickly I ran through the sand and scrambled up the bank on the other side back.

I was now plagued by the possibility of another bridge, but luckily the track continued on solid sandy ground until we reached the outskirts of the city. By then the sun was beating down. A woman was selling homemade lemonade under an umbrella. We necked the sweet liquid she ladled from her fridge-box in long draughts. The roads had probably once been asphalt, but were now a mix of mud and stones, with lagoon-sized puddles and craters, with pigs, children, chickens, street sellers and *movilidades* milling amongst it all.

We had arranged to meet Sebastian, who worked for our second conservation charity, *Asociación Armonía*. He had given us a geo-locator, so we knew we only had three miles left. We passed a market fronting the towering stone walls of a prison. Our watch began flashing, announcing that we were fifty metres from our destination. We followed it, splashing through puddles, counting down the numbers, while trying to keep it partially hidden from watching eyes. 'Zero!' We looked up. 'But this can't be right,' muttered David. We were standing beneath the prison's northern wall. Something had gone gravely wrong. We tried again, approaching from another angle, but no matter what we did, the watch was determined to send us to prison. We grew more and more short-tempered, each accusing the other of causing the problem. I asked a woman where Sebastian's street was, but she just shook her head. I tried the lady selling fruit; she cackled and slapped her hand on her great thigh, 'Ah, very far, north of the city!'

In desperation, we found a shop with phone booths. After several incorrectly dialled numbers, Sebastian's voice echoed in my ear. 'You're so close! I'll come and show you the way!'

Cars and trucks strangle the roundabout. People screech from their windows as they hoot their horns. A donkey weaves through the chaos, branches flying from the wooden cart it's pulling. What are the branches used for? There's no time to think. I take off through the amber light, straining forward with the trailer to beat the traffic behind me. Faster, faster, all my senses are pulsing; I'm on overdrive, my heart thundering in my ear, black fumes expunging my vision, exhilaration flooding through my veins. Perhaps I can fly? This must be how it would feel inside a video game, battling adversaries on all sides.

We were extracting ourselves from Santa Cruz after a brief break from running. Sebastian and his wife, Carolina, had taken us under their wing and we had willingly moved into their nest. We had scrutinised her extraordinary scarab beetle collection, met the *Armonía* staff and learnt of their conservation work, finally got hold of a delivery of new shoes and given a presentation to the university. We had also been interviewed by heavily made-up Bolivian celebrities for a couple of national TV shows. In one I inadvertently switched one little 'a' for an 'o'; *pasas* (raisins) for *pasos* steps, saying, 'With small raisins we can all make a massive difference to the natural world we live in and its wildlife!'

Now we were bee-lining for one of the busiest roads in Bolivia, with no siding for two-footed traffic, crazy death-wish drivers and a soya harvest underway, with three-strong trailers towed by lorries hurtling down the road. On several occasions we escaped being swept under oncoming trucks by a hair's breadth, but the rest of the animal kingdom wasn't faring so well: we made daily counts of over thirty-five bodies rolled flat across the road.

One species we now found dead most days was the lesser anteater (or *tamandua*). This caramel little fellow, with his elongated snout, containing his 40-centimetre sticky tongue, is another of South America's unique animals. Unlike his colossal cousin, the giant anteater, he is equally at home excavating ant, termite and bee colonies on the ground or in the treetops, secured by his prehensile tail. My eyes would dart through the roadside vegetation for the rest of our journey searching for one, but it was not to be. Instead, we encountered the most tragic of sights; a female *tamandua* squished on the road, with her baby straddling her back. I couldn't hold back tears as we picked up the little team. It's such human behaviour to carry young on your back, and it's difficult not to empathise with it in the wild. Without arms or teeth for carrying their pups, all four species of South American anteaters can carry their young like this. Seeing life expunged from such an amazing animal made me hate cars, for the destruction and death left in their wake.

Snakes were another regular sight pancaked on the road. They were a preoccupation of school children, who often asked us about our reptilian encounters. Four days after leaving Santa Cruz, we had one of our most bizarre snake meetings. We were re-joining the road after breakfast with a family who owned a little *chacra* (farm), when we saw something darting towards the traffic –

a tiny emerald snake. David flew after it to usher it back to the verge. Instead it shot straight towards me, aiming for the only dark place it could find, under my shoe!

Why my foot wasn't firmly planted on the floor, I don't know, but the crevice provided the perfect bolt hole for the little guy. We had no idea what species it was, or whether it was venomous, but I couldn't guard my snake all day, so I very gradually picked up my foot. Would it launch into the air, fangs bristling with a fatal goodbye blow? No. It remained curled in its beautiful, sinuous coils, hoping the alien species staring at it would clear off.

A few nights later another Hollywood monster plagued our sleep: vampire bats. A mile down a wooded track we had found an abandoned farmhouse, and hung our net tent from a veranda. The watchman was pleased to have company, insisting on collecting us water from a river in exchange for conversation. The farmhouse had been built as a wood-yard by an Italian, but had soon fallen into disrepair. Now termites and fungi were claiming it.

There were no loos, electricity or piped water, and so the subjects with which the man was preoccupied felt most out of place: September 11, Osama Bin Laden, the nuclear disaster in Japan and nuclear threats from North Korea. Of more immediate interest to us was the news that our friend had been bitten on several occasions by vampire bats.

I would have loved to see one at work on a cow or chicken, but actually dealing with one sucking my own blood might have stretched my bat fervour a bit too far. As it was, we needn't have worried, for our zombie night-watchman decided to work all through the night under the shadows of a sickle moon, hacking away at the buildings, singing, talking to himself and dancing to his radio. There was no way a vampire bat would come anywhere near us, except in our dreams.

Another creature did seek us out: the ant. This little insect is represented by many hundreds of species; 11,700, to be exact, but it's thought that at least the same number again are still at large undiscovered. The first incursion happened one evening when we set up the net at the edge of a patch of secondary forest. David got up to grab something from one of the bags and found the harness vibrating with gigantic leaf-cutter ants. Attached to the thick rubber with their powerful mandibles, they were carefully cutting rounds out of it. 'Shit!' he yelled. 'We're under attack! Come and help!'

I leapt up and joined him as he pulled handfuls of ants from the harness. 'They're not budging. They won't let go.' David was screaming with anger, mixed with frustration and exhaustion. 'Oh my god, we're decapitating them,' I cried. 'Look – they're locked on and leaving their jaws behind!'

We finally removed the hordes from the harness, but as I ducked back into the tent, I couldn't believe my eyes. 'Now they're devouring our tent!' I hollered. They were everywhere, swarming all over the netting and floor, cutting neat little circles out of everything. But as David was sprinting over to me, he noticed our shoes were black with ants too, as were our running tops and shorts. 'They're everywhere,' he growled. 'It's war.'

Ants are amazing insects, and they are super-important as one of the mega production houses of ecosystems around the world, from the poles to the tropics. They reduce plant and animal debris to their constituent parts, creating and aerating soil for free. They harvest seeds, herd and milk other invertebrates, farm intricate fungal gardens, slave-make and construct elaborate thermo-regulated fortresses. If you were asked what munches the most vegetation in the neotropics (Americas), perhaps you would plump for monkeys, tapirs or even sloths? You would be wrong! Although they may be a pin-prick in size, it's the tiny, industrious leaf-cutter ants that are the kings, munching nearly a quarter of all leaves produced, with (it appears) running tops and shoes thrown into the mix. We were afraid that they were capable of compromising our entire expedition.

Any holes the ants created in our tent laid us open to mosquitos and other biting insects. Holes meant hours of repair work, which was the last job either of us wanted at the end of a long run. One night, a small, shiny, black species trucked in through one side of our tent, exiting through the other side. We squished a good part of the platoon and thought we were safe, but in the morning we awoke to find a matrix of holes snipped out of our pants, shorts and tops. David was seriously worried about the ramifications of the latest invaders:

> I've just realized how tough the Amazon section is going to be. We were attacked again by ants tonight. We're both covered in itchy bites and welts, my inner thigh is raw, my nipples sore and I have sunburn. Never mind the human issues and diseases which now include leishmaniosis, leprosy, malaria, dengue and *chagas*. We're also easily downing 20 litres of water per day, all of which has to be hand-pumped.

In a secondary rainforest the voracious, unruly vegetation spirals upwards, as if on speed, when light pours onto the forest floor after an old stalwart of the primary forest has toppled or the canopy has been hacked down. What we didn't realize until we ran out of the last, tangled remnants of the forest was that the battalions of leaf-cutters were a product of this disturbed habitat. During the weeks of running through mainly high old forest on our way to Manaus, we would be magically left in peace, with hardly a leaf-cutter in sight. And the reason? Leaf-cutter ants love the fast-growing, juicy, weedy species of the secondary forests because their leaves are palatable and super-nutritious, and lack the chemical defences of the shade-tolerant trees of the old forests. Later we learnt that one of the two genera of leaf-cutters found in the Brazilian Amazon (*Atta*) have thirty times higher densities in secondary rainforest.

We had run into a region of marshes and ponds; mosquito-heaven, and the clouds of insects we were having to fend off were scaling up. Five o'clock became the new bogey hour. If we hadn't found a camp by then, we would need to rapidly slash a hole in the nearest undergrowth to make one, because by half past five, as the sun began slipping under the horizon, the hordes would descend. We wore full waterproof gear, but still the critters would find a way down our sleeves or between our socks and trousers to our ankles, wrists and necks. The torture of cooking outside necessitated a new invention. David was onto it.

We called it the 'nuclear reactor tunnel'. It involved cutting a large round hole to the right of the entrance of our tent. He then created a tunnel using a length of the spare mosquito netting. One end of the tunnel was sewn to the side of the door and included a flap of netting, while the other end was the exit to the outside world and also culminated in a flap. The idea was that we could push our hands through the tunnel and cook food, but the mosquitoes couldn't get in and tuck into us.

The other fallout from the mosquito explosion was a new way of emptying our bladders in the night. Although bad practice, we would invariably do the greater part of hydrating once the day's running was over. This necessitated at least one or two toilet trips per night. But exiting the net would allow mosquitoes in and also provide the opportunity for severe attacks while squatting outside. To avoid the need for this nocturnal excursion David had started using a bottle, and he was determined to construct me a female equivalent from one of the discarded plastic bottles that littered the roadside. It was basic in principle, but beautiful in practice. He cut through a two-litre plastic bottle to create a funnel, then made a series of half-centimetre slashes in the rim and melted these back onto themselves, using a fire-lighter. The mouth of the funnel was directed into a large plastic yogurt bottle. The result was a perfectly soft and comfy surface upon which to settle my buttocks.

The road had become much quieter since forking north-westerly through San Ramón, and the population of wetland birds was rocketing. Long-legged *cocoi* herons, wood storks, *maguari* storks and *jabirus* probed through the swamps on their long, narrow legs, while sharp-eyed snail-kites looked-on from lake-side perches. The shells of gigantic snails littered the fields, their soft bodies ripped out to feed this formidable avian army. It was an extraordinary bonanza, like an enormous chocolate cake for birds.

The GPS watch beeped 31 miles. It was our longest run to date, fuelled by a meal from a roadside restaurant and the determination to reach the tiny spot that marked Guarayos on our map. But after chatting to the owner of the stall and her many attendant children, we were faced with the sun diving for bed. So there was no chance to celebrate, as we needed to pitch our tent before the mosquitoes descended.

A lonely farm stood about half a mile back from the road. We plumped for hiding behind the roadside scrub in a soya field opposite and prayed we would be left alone. Only ten minutes into unpacking our gear, two figures appeared. Their hair was so blonde it was almost white and they wore blue dungarees with long-sleeved white shirts. They were Mennonites; Anabaptist Christians. We had been seeing an increasing number of these distinctive people since entering Bolivia. The women were conspicuously absent from public dealings, remaining seated in cars in their bonnets and long skirts. Their unusual, dated dress, quiet ways and obvious desire to remain removed from conventional society stirred our interest. These two were aged nine and nineteen: the elder was clearly busting to talk to us, and we leapt at the opportunity to find out about their secretive lives.

'We go to our own special community schools until the age of 13,' he explained. 'We learn religion and languages, but after that we're expected to work on the farm. Our parents grow rice and soya. I have ten brothers and sisters. All my friends have similar sized families. We aren't allowed to watch television, or drink alcohol. We were born in Bolivia, but my parents come from Germany.'

He then fired a ricochet of questions back at us, 'So you can travel wherever you like? What are Argentina and Chile like? Do you have televisions in the UK? Do you grow soya and rice there? Do you drink a lot of alcohol? What do you think about North Korea? What religion are you?' and so he went on enthusiastically.

His brother was too shy to talk, but listened intently. Soon the darkness and mosquitoes became too oppressive, so they jumped onto their bikes and cycled home. The following day we saw a sister and brother in a little shop. Like all the other Mennonites we had observed, they were both tall and thin, and as white as lilies under their large, floppy hats. The girl, who was probably about 13, plucked up a huge amount of courage to say, 'How far have you run?' before collapsing into herself from the social effort. They each bought a handful of sweets, and the little boy offered us both one of his collection, before scurrying away on their bikes.

We saw many more Mennonites along the way: large groups of children sitting on wagons in floral dresses and dungarees as they returned from the fields; men buying provisions in market-places, and women sitting meekly in the backs of cars. We asked local people what they thought of them. The response was overwhelmingly positive. They said that unlike the *gringos* who travelled to Bolivia, they didn't booze and swear or behave aggressively. They kept themselves to themselves. Their large farms provided jobs, and they were known to be decent, fair employers. They were happy with the progress and prosperity they brought to their country.

We trotted onwards, with every step taking us closer to Trinidad. We were officially in the Amazon basin, but the view from the road was unlike what we had imagined. Since leaving Santa Cruz we had passed through the low, dry crop areas (soya and maize) and the diminutive hilly areas around San Ramón and Guarayos, where forest still dominated but was being overtaken by cattle. Now we were back in the low wetlands. The field boundaries revealed that the land could support forest and savanna, but it had been converted to cattle grazing and paddy fields.

We ran on a bank about one-and-a-half metres high. Almost the whole way to Guarayos there were little homesteads and farms, some visibly scalped from the forest, others hidden down little paths. Orange and grapefruit trees bloomed in the gardens, and palms provided shade in the cattle fields. The odd *palo borracho* tree added a streak of bright pink. The buildings were a mix of mud or wood walls and palm-leaf thatch, with occasional corrugated iron or pantile roofs. Many of the homes made us yearn for their inhabitants' simple lives; others astounded us with their level of basic sanitation. Children paddled in pig manure, which mixed with burning rubbish and geese-poo to form a black slime that slipped into the dusty houses and wells.

Water was never far away. The wetlands were full of wattled *jacanas* and egrets. Cows waded up to their waists, with scattered palm and *cecropia* trees standing on high ground. We watched people lighting fires to create more grazing around the swamps and road margins. Hard-baked termite mounds pockmarked the land like enormous zits. These vast flat lands allowed room for the sky, which was a deep blue in the mornings, before pillows of white clouds puffed-up, to dissipate slowly by the evening.

Although I had suffered from colds, fleas, sore knees and ankles and prickly heat, which I managed with a good dollop of moaning, I had so far escaped the sickness that had knocked David in Argentina and Bolivia. Now it was my turn. We had a great day of running, clocking the usual 20 miles, before finding a camp-site outside an abandoned farmstead. I made a salad for supper and we hitched up the net. At which point I began to feel a slight headache and unusually, couldn't eat all my food. Feeling odd, but with exhaustion overcoming the sensation, I fell into a deep sleep. Sometime during the middle of the night I woke bolt upright, my stomach wrenching. Within ten minutes I had vomited; two minutes later I vomited again, and this continued in an enormous vomiting blur, the like of which I had never experienced.

Fiery bile erupted from my mouth, searing my throat. Spasms clawed at my stomach. David could do nothing but watch, patiently passing me containers which rapidly filled up. Then my backend joined in, leaving me desperately sprinting from the tent. The resultant evacuations were dramatic and swift, my biggest worry being my ability to flee the tent in time. To add insult to injury, enormous black clouds of mosquitos followed me, enveloping my poor, tender exposed parts. Not until the sun waved a sliver of gold over the eastern horizon, did my body finally cease retching, and I slept.

We awoke to find a red squirrel bashing about in a nearby tree. The scene around our net was disastrous: a minefield of slurry and stinking slime. David was desperate to get away from the overpowering odour. When we did finally leave, I felt terribly weak and couldn't eat. The run was a disaster. I only made six miles before I collapsed in front of a gateway, to which we tied the net. The next day wasn't much better

> We're both heavy-legged and drained of energy (David wrote). Katharine
> is feeling dreadful. In reality it's because we don't have enough food inside
> of us, despite our best efforts. Fizzy drinks just don't suffice.

We were determined to reach Casarabe, which lay just over 30 miles from Trinidad. We were running into a wall of darkness. Frogs played their castanets in the roadside woodland, and the odd fire glowed in a house. Fireflies pirouetted and winked at our side, eddying into the sky in a mesmerising display. It reminded us of the magical phosphorescence that illuminates the sea at night and shoots through the loo on our boat in a galaxy of stars when you flush.

But it wasn't just fireflies that were active that night: almighty plumes of flying insects clogged our eyes and filled our mouths. Others plumbed our ears or stuck in a peppered soup to our sweat-laden skin. The humidity wouldn't drop. David's elbows dripped a constant flow of sweat like two taps. Cars occasionally whizzed past blinding our night vision, necessitating a plunge into the roadside vegetation. Then there was the other problem with running in the dark; snakes. Some snakes like the deadly fer-de-lance do not move when you approach. If you are unlucky enough to step on one, you trigger an attack. Being a woman who regularly squatted in roadside vegetation, my risk of provoking a viper was 100 percent greater than David's. We did carry a snake-venom extractor in case we got bitten; but miraculously, during nearly 15 months on the road, I didn't shower a snake, or at least no snake that was concerned.

Orinoco geese flocked around the reserve building

Orinoco Goose
Neochen jubata

15 Taking to the Air

To avoid the main roads, which had been blockaded, we bumped down muddy side-tracks to Trinidad. The whole of Bolivia were protesting about something – we weren't sure what. A stack of branches barred our way. A little lady hovered nearby. David got out of the car and pulled the barrier aside to allow us through. He didn't realize, until we had passed, that the lady was part of the protest. Miraculously we found a way into the airport, where 20 or so armed and bored-witless military stood teasing one another.

We were taking a break from running, on a mission to get under the skin of our charity *Asociación Armonía,* which, along with Birdlife International (our third charity), is working to save the critically-endangered blue-throated macaw *(Paraba barba azul).* Bolivia, specifically the Beni province, is the blue-throated macaw's last and only stronghold in the world, with only 200-300 individuals remaining. Our run would help to fund an extension to the macaw's reserve, and we were on our way to see how this could be achieved.

Cross-country routes were sketchy due to the rains, so we opted for taking to the sky. It was half-past six in the morning. We slumped in the terminal with a few other passengers. The guy in a *Top Gun* leather bomber-jacket, pressed jeans, aviator-glasses and slicked-back hair was our pilot. We were told we were waiting for more passengers to arrive, but nothing was very clear.

Two hours later, it transpired that we had the passengers: it was just that the plane had broken. Three hours more and we were ready, but now a storm was brewing. Little planes were trolleyed around so that their noses would face the escalating wind. Streaks of rain battered the tiny terminal building and wind hurled itself against anything in its path. People ran through a blur of storm, but the planes, although jumpy, somehow sat still. At one o'clock we were hustled into action as there appeared to be a narrow gap between the weather fronts, and the plan was to fly low underneath the cloud. It was time to depart for Santa Anna, the nearest town and stepping stone to the Barba Azul reserve.

There were five passenger seats in the decrepit little plane, including one up-front by the pilot. We were lugging an 80-kilogram outboard motor to the reserve, and had pre-paid for a seat to house it. That left room for two other passengers, but three Bolivians stood by our side. The pilot eyed us, assessing our respective weights and heights. He signalled for six-foot four David to sit up front, me to sit at the back as ballast with the motor, the sacks of maize and sundry other bags of cargo, and the three short, stocky Bolivians to sit in the middle wedged into two seats. To earn himself another wedge of *bolivianos*, the pilot had re-sold the seat paid by us for the motor.

David curled his legs into a grasshopper fold and concentrated on avoiding touching the steering wheel and controls that lay millimetres from his elbows and knees. Two guys wheeled across a rusty barrel of fuel and proceeded to fill the tanks through a funnel. The knackered old plane creaked, with its frail, peeling parts barely sticking together. The luggage-handler pointed at the side of the plane against which I was pressing myself: *'Cuidado, la puerta se sale'*. (Careful, the door doesn't close properly).

The pilot twitched in his seat, his apprehension augmenting everyone's unease. We sat rigid. All three Bolivians crossed themselves, as did the pilot. The plane spluttered and jumped towards the runway. The two Bolivian women let out an involuntary squeak. The engine buzzed like an asthmatic bumble bee. We turned the corner; the engine roared, we skipped and hopped, faster and faster, until the end of the runway was upon us, but we were still land-based, barely bumping into the air. 'We're not going to make it!' I hissed. 'We're too heavy, we won't take off.' Then suddenly we were airborne. Just.

Like an over-fattened goose, we flapped our wings, barely scraping over Trinidad, watching the pan-tiled roofs metres from our flabby undercarriage. How were we ever going to survive this? I was frozen to my seat, desperately trying not to move for fear of upsetting this delicate, overloaded, out-of-date, flying machine. But the view was incredible. A diaphanous layer of cloud lay above us. Vultures spiralled past the windows, then up and over us. The languorous Mamore River meandered her voluptuous thighs through a saturation of green. I could pick out lily-pads the size of rooms. Palms formed a sliver of gallery forest, and rushes wavered in marshy islands. A *jabiru* stork sailed beneath us, skeins of roseate spoonbills spilled through the sky above, flocks of egrets and herons speckled the green below. It was utterly beautiful; a geography lesson unfolding below us. I realized that rivers are best viewed from the air.

The Mamore is the lifeblood of these grassy savannas, the focal point of wildlife in the dry season and then in the wet season, when it pours from its banks to inundate the grasslands, it provides rich foraging for the hundreds of wild animals that depend upon it. It's also crucial to the herds of white cattle that smother its banks, wading through its shallows to its rich vegetation, clipping away the new growth of palms. Their tracks radiated like wood-worm trails from the river, out into the vast plains, wrinkling and stressing the face of the earth.

Throughout the flight the pilot had fiddled with his instruments in a most disconcerting fashion. He was now newly twitching as the rooftops of Santa Anna pricked the sky just beneath us. We were banking furiously. I was sure we would drop straight out of the air, but suddenly the landing strip was beneath us and we were jumping and scuttling along it. Miraculously, we had survived. The Bolivians were kissing one another. The woman in front of me had scrunched her eyes closed the entire length of the journey and now very gingerly opened one.

We had two full days to explore the *Barba Azul* reserve and search for its treasure. Our bags were bulging with food, so that we could feast like kings and replenish lost calories, now I had recovered from my recent illness. The simple accommodation hut was used by research students and sat metres from an enormous swamp. We drifted through its choked waterways in a little boat, searching the banks for white-headed water tyrants and the yellow eyes of sunning caiman.

The reasons for the macaws' fateful demise are similar to those that have endangered many other parrots; one is a toxic pet trade, the other dramatic habitat-loss. Without a home, which for the blue-throated macaw includes motacú palm islands for nesting, roosting and foraging in, the birds cannot survive. Over the years their habitat has been relentlessly removed through overgrazing of the palm islands that they rely on, and the burning and seeding of non-native, aggressive African grasses, to increase the pasture available for the enormous herds that provide cheap beef to countries around the world.

With the help of ex-poachers and pet-trade collectors, *Asociación Armonía* established where the main flocks of the macaw were. They then worked with the estancia owners to ensure their land-management considered the macaw's needs, erected nest boxes and initiated 24-hour surveillance during the nesting season. The next step was to buy a reserve which they could manage specifically for the macaws.

We arranged to head out for a long day's ride with Jernan, the warden and local gaucho of the reserve. David's pony was far too small and his legs dangled in mid-air somewhere near its ankles. We couldn't get the stirrup leathers straight and so he rode skewed the entire day, on a knife-blade of a saddle. Needless to say, his unaccustomed behind was in a parlous state by the end of it all.

Tall grasses and reeds swept the horses' bellies as we edged around the swamp. We were making for the distant palm islands, which lay far beyond the research centre, where blue-throated macaws commute for feeding. A volley of barks exploded from the vegetation in front of us. Enormous guinea pigs galloped for the water, detonating a wave of spray from under their hairy legs. They were *capybaras*, the largest rodents in the world, and they reminded me of a gaggle of overweight Edwardian bathing ladies. They came in all sizes, with the smaller ones being mirrors of their robust, tubby parents and grandparents. Shocked by our appearance, they disappeared under the water. But after a few minutes, faces began to pop up beside the lily pads and rushes, like little hairy hippos, curious about us; as curious as we were about them.

An enormous party of American wood-storks were patrolling the shallows a little further on, like expectant undertakers with their 'arms' held behind their backs and long, downward-pointing, thinking 'noses'. They were joined by Brazilian ducks, sporting scarlet beaks and black mullets. Wetlands are always wildlife magnets, through the richness of plants and invertebrates, which attract a cornucopia of birds and animals. Even as we left the swamp, the sky was full with skeins of storks gliding towards it from the surrounding grasslands. We fixed our heads back against our necks, watching these aviators. Then something crashed into the corner of our view. A cloud of macaws was streaking overhead.

We counted 16 in total. They called to one another, piercing the air with their repetitive, hoarse shrieks. Could this be them; a party of one of the rarest birds on earth? We could see only their silhouettes at first, and neither of us could tell the difference between what is meant to be the more *brutas* call of the blue-and yellow macaws and the slightly lighter call of the blue-throats. But Jernan knew; he had listened to these birds all his life, unaware that the flocks flying over his ranch represented one of the last hopes for saving the species from extinction. Our three sets of eyes met and he nodded, grinning. It was them. As if answering our wishes, the birds broke off to the south, flying directly over us. As they drew closer we watched their dark forms transform into a dazzling display of gold and indigo. I wished I could burn their images onto my retinas for eternity.

As we moved out into the wider grassland of the reserve, the contrast with the surrounding farmland was startling. Without the constant gnawing of cattle, grasses were once again able to grow tall, and a thick layer of thatch was forming at their base, providing a home for tunnelling small mammals and nesting birds and the reptiles that seek them. In the palm islands new life was returning, as gangly-legged *motacú* palms started their spiral to the heavens.

We turned for home, splashing our way back through the water-logged grasses. In the distance almighty black clouds billowed into the sky. These weren't rain clouds, but forebears of the start of the dry season and the burning of the grasslands by the cattle handlers. The annual aim was to clear the build-up of dead grass to provide fertile ash with which a new flush of verdant grass would sprout when the rains came. In the following months the reserve would sit like an emerald in the black haze, while Jernan and the *Asociación Armonía* staff would pray their fire-breaks and precautionary measures would repel the flames. But for the time being, our main preoccupation was the thought of the return journey to Trinidad and what craft awaited us this time.

Hoatzin
Opisthocomus hoazin

The once heard, never-forgotten grating call of the hoatzin emanated from a pond

16 Meeting Mary

Someone shouted from below. Suddenly people were yelling and cars and trucks revving, as a small, flickering white light glided towards us. At that point the Río Ibare was about 100 metres wide, with thick, muddy banks. We pulled the trailer down to a floating pontoon and over the thick, tropical-hardwood boards that formed a gappy lattice between its exposed frames. The car at the front was instructed to leave its headlights on. A bilge pump was being operated by a thumping generator, sending jets of water splashing from the pontoon to the river. Flotation was a fine line.

A thin fishing boat with a large outboard engine pulled alongside us and somehow pushed the pontoon off the bank with the help of the ferryman prizing us away with long poles. We rapidly began floating downstream, with the boat alongside us just creating enough power to push us across and diagonally. The ferryman sat with us. He said he had seen us on TV. He was lovely. He talked for a while about how he lived for seven years in Madrid and had visited London; the contrast with his river life must have been enormous. He warned us that vipers would be up near the road, as they couldn't use the inundated land at the moment, so we had have to be extra vigilant, especially in the dark.

Back on land, cars and trucks from the pontoon streamed past, leaving us in an oily darkness. We ran on, tripping and shuffling over the potted track. The going was virtually impossible, but we were determined to cross the second river, the Río Mamoré, that night to avoid further delays in the morning. Something crashed through the swamp at our side. We couldn't decipher what it was, but it was unlike the sporadic heavy splashes of caiman.

It was only about four miles to the Mamoré, which was heralded by the fragrance of wood smoke wafting through the air. The same sepia, tungsten and paraffin-shadowed landscape of the last river greeted us. A young girl kicked a football with her little brother. A large crowd of people perched on plastic chairs, mesmerised by a small, flashing television, slapping ankles amid clouds of mosquitoes.

A dark village perched on the opposite bank. We ran through, coughing in the plumes of dust sent billowing into the air by the departing ferry traffic. Orange sediment cloaked the huts. A wavering lamp lit a flock of Maran chickens roosting on a row of wooden bars behind a hammock. Then even that faint glow petered out as the thwack of the generator grumbled to a halt. Now the night was still, with only a distant conversation floating on the air as we ran into an almighty swamp-land. Towering sedges and enormous lily pads lined our path. A chorus of burping, ping-ponging frogs crooned to one another, and our pathetic head torches reflected the eyes of a caiman. We weren't alone.

Morning revealed that, despite the track being a dog to run along, with mounds of desiccated mud and crater-sized pot holes, the bog beyond was amazing. Every fold and crease, hummock and hillock, seemed to contain even more wildlife spilling from its fecund arteries than the last. On one corner, we counted over 2,000 snowy egrets nosing through a marsh. The five splayed toe-prints of *capybaras* marked family night-time wanderings. We watched a huge ringed kingfisher hovering, as if held by a silken thread from the sky, as it scanned the water for fish. This super-adaptable species accompanied us the entire length of the continent; from the freezing rivers of the south to the steaming lakes of the north. Great splashes near the bank stole our attention: Amazon River dolphins. The pod was whacking their flippers and tails on the surface of the river, herding their catch of fish into the centre of their ambush. But amid the wealth of beauty, David had since leaving Trinidad, been steadily turning green:

> My stomach's sloshing as I run. I can't keep anything down; not that I want to eat or drink anyway. I've started taking a course of three 500-milligram Ciprofloxacin tablets a day. Fortunately, it's a cool today, as I am becoming severely dehydrated.

A passing jeep-driver said that the track to San Borja was *'muy feo'* (very bad) and likely impassable, due to flooding. This was really bad news. We had less than 30 days left on our visa; running an extra 100-mile diversion via Yucumo and Reyes would mean we wouldn't get out of the country in time. The route we were already on was frustrating enough. Since leaving Trinidad, we had been running due west, often south. We were making absolutely no progress northwards, and wouldn't until San Borja, 150 miles away. We had spoken to so many people about a possible alternative, but the options in the vast *Llanos del Norte y del Noreste* (floodplains of the north and northeast) were non-existent.

That evening we found a wire gate leading to a cattle-handling area. Some old boots and a holey jumper had been cast onto the hard-baked floor of a wooden shed, by the side of which we set up camp. A few sooty cauldrons hung from the thatched ceiling, along with a ladle. Salt and flour bags were stacked on a wooden shelf and a machete lay by an upturned log.

No one arrived that night, but as the sun began to wheeze over the horizon, a man clipped past, corralling a group of cattle. There was no way he could have missed our home, newly sprouted from his land. But he ignored us, and it was not until a good hour later, when we had dressed, eaten and packed up, that he appeared. His black Wellington boots had long slits down the back to the ankle. He was thin and dark-haired, and wore an old tattered T-shirt and threadbare trousers. He had the warmest face, with glittering eyes and a wide smile. He chatted for a bit and then plodded off, as if there was nothing out of the ordinary about two strangers squatting on his land. Before he went, we asked how far it was to San Ignacio de Moxos, 'Ah,' he pondered, 'Let me think, yes, that'll be about five hours on foot.' During the entire run, only three people estimated our distance enquiries by foot. And each of them, including this man, gave us the most accurate estimation of anyone on the continent. Even people with GPS gadgets in their cars mystifyingly managed to get it wrong. It seemed that only those who walked were aware of true distances.

Arriving in San Ignacio was like stepping into a sci-fi movie. Squadrons of camouflaged militiamen, dressed in masks and wielding fire hoses, filled the main road. An outbreak of fatal malaria had besieged the town, so all the houses were being fumigated with a fine mist of insecticide. It did seem a somewhat futile behaviour, considering that the town was sited on a mighty swamp. I just hoped the townsfolk (and we) weren't going to suffer a double blow from the pesticides and the disease.

We found a scrappy room in a tiled hotel with green water that everyone drank, and went off in search of food. David was delighted to feel hungry, but as soon as we had eaten he felt tired and sick again. In the morning we ate fried rice, *yuca* and beef from the market with a hot, bitter chocolate. The woman serving us was *Colla* from La Paz and held her long bell-pull plaits together with fabric braids. She was really interested in the run, 'What terrible hardships you must have been through! I can't imagine how you survive, sleeping at the side of the road. But think of the story you will tell!'

We asked her about the malarial risk in town, commenting on the spraying we had observed. 'There's is a huge problem here,' she said. 'I came down to the lowlands nineteen years ago to escape the cold, but instead my family must face these terrible diseases. When my son was a baby, he had blood dripping from his eyes, nose and gums. But he was a chubby baby, and that protected him from the ravages of malaria.'

We had heard a medley of different droning mosquito species during the night. Neither of us felt that we would be particularly robust in combating a disease; we had both shed masses of weight in Bolivia, and David couldn't shake off his sickness, so I was happy to be leaving the town and the increased malarial risks that populated areas harbour.

We chose to gamble on leaving the main track and taking the 60-mile, winding 'muy feo' path north through Estancia Nogales and risk having to wade through floods. Our bags were still basically waterproof, and if we had to modify the trailer into a raft, so be it. This turned out to be one of our best decisions, and one of the most charming routes we ran.

When we reached the little community of Pueblo Nuevo, a large group of villagers and construction workers greeted us. They were unloading bricks from a truck that had passed us a few hours previously. Everyone was grinning; the truck must have warned the village we were on our way. We were presented with glasses of Coca-Cola by the headmaster (Julio) and his teacher girlfriend (Sylvia). They ushered us to a bench in the shade and told us about the place and their life in Oruro, in the high Andes, which they had left behind. Sylvia adored her pupils, but said how much she missed home, which they had forsaken seven years ago. 'I cried every day at the start, I was so homesick,' she said. 'But now I will find it extremely difficult to leave.'

They selected a classroom for us to camp in, and we were shown a communal shower and loo. A mother and her five children watched us unpack, with one chubby boy on her hip and the other children of various heights winding their hair around their fingers or picking their noses. Being British and private, I found this hard to bear. I felt like a caged animal, as their eyes darted over us and our things. I was desperately tired and needed to sleep and eat, but how could I do this, with all these eyes drilling down upon us? Finally I muttered, 'We're going to sleep.' But they didn't react, it appeared they would be watching over us all night.

At eight o'clock, Sylvia and Julio roused us and invited us to the procession of the Virgin Mary. Torches flashed around the thatched houses as we padded down the grass streets to a palm-roofed outdoor meeting area. In the flickering candle-light villagers sat in rows on wooden benches in their Sunday best. Gap-toothed smiles looked up at us as we all sat waiting, with stifled laughter and whispers tickling the air. A figurine of the Virgin Mary stood on a little bamboo raft in a sea of plastic flowers. The gaudy statue was apparently 150 years old, but had been made-up and improved over the years.

Bats threaded intricate pathways around our heads. An enormous fat beetle collided with the floor in a pool of torch light. He whizzed on his head for a while in a break-dancing move, before a small boy squished him. An invisible signal triggered a man to stand up, open a book and start chanting. Twenty minutes later we were still thanking Señoir (Jesus) and still repeating the same benedictions, that now even we were singing like prize parrots. At which point a squealing pig hurtled through the barn, nearly but not quite taking the Virgin Mary with it, followed by a group of boys with sticks. Someone kicked it as it passed; it squealed again and fled into the darkness.

Three-quarters of an hour later, the eulogising finally petered out. People began to shuffle in their seats; two young women picked up the statue, and we all followed into the star-speckled night. The walk was beautiful, the best bit. An entire galaxy of stars blinked and fuzzed. A soft, warm breeze titillated the darkness, wafting the fragrances of cut grass, marshes, wood smoke, chicken stews, fried rice and coconuts. Another barn had been decorated and was awaiting the arrival of the statue.

Sylvia explained that during the month of May the statue was moved from house to house so that everyone could share in the Virgin Mary's blessings and that she could bring fortune and good luck to their homes. This meant an entire extra service in the new venue, and so we began all over again. As we had run 21 miles that day, I was finding it incredibly difficult to keep my head upright and my eyelids from banging shut. We were close to one hour of praise, and yet there was no sign of abating. David was scrutinising the roof of the barn, which had been beautifully joined and crafted, while delivering a poke in my ribs every-now-and-then when my chin began to loll too noticeably.

The audience was gradually augmenting during the service. Why were they coming now? I clutched my seat in disbelief; there was no way we could survive another service; even the stalwart appeared to be waning. Then suddenly it ended, and we realized why the crowd had grown. A feast had been prepared and villagers were arriving with cauldrons of steaming food. Sylvia explained that the Virgin Mary's new owners would provide the meal. Pork, chicken and rice were ladled onto our plates and grapefruit juice passed around. It was delicious, and we revelled in our second meal of the night.

> It was an odd experience (wrote David). Mostly I was struck by how curious it was to have forty indigenous people praying to a god that was nothing to do with their own heritage or culture. That they had subscribed to a religion that was relatively recently pressed upon them by their ruthless Spanish occupiers.

We watched a huge lightning flash illuminate cumulous clouds on the horizon, and walked back with Sylvia and Julio to our classroom tent. Next morning we exchanged emails and hugged them, certain we would never hear from them again. We were wrong. Eighteen months later I received an email from a name I couldn't recognize. I opened it, to find that they were getting married and had invited us to their celebrations in Oruro!

The woman who had watched us for so long the night before now invited us to lunch with her five children and silver-toothed husband. We ate the chewiest, free-galloping chicken imaginable, on a bed of fried rice and noodles. It tasted great, as did the *toronja* juice (a relative of the grapefruit) which she had squeezed with lashings of sugar. We asked her about her children; 'I don't want any more. I'm 28.' I wasn't sure how she was going to prevent more coming, however, as the emancipation of women didn't appeared to have arrived in Bolivia's rural heartlands.

A couple of miles further up the track there was another community; another Pueblo Nuevo, just smaller. Cheers were ringing around a little thatched rondavel on wooden stilts. The crowd swayed, and roosters leapt through the air. Drunken voices called us over. We waved back but kept running. A motorcyclist passed us a few hours later; two cloth bags hung from each of his handlebars and another strapped across his back. Scaly legs poked through the bottom of each, and three feathered rooster heads peeked out of the top.

A small coppice looked ideal for camping, and so we slunk under its leafy canopy and pitched our tent. There were two houses below, and so we went over to them before they found us. The man we met was very keen that we should give a talk the following morning and instructed us to turn up at eight o'clock. The air was heavy with humidity, rain looked to be imminent and so we started to put up the tarps. Suddenly David jumped into the air yelping. Something had stung him. Great black ants were swarming over the tree and now over his hands. He beat them away, but not before at least four of the critters had managed to bite him.

The man from the village appeared at 7.30 next morning, calling us to class. David mentioned that he had been stung by some vicious ants. The man pointed at the sapling, 'Was that the tree you tied your tarp to?' David nodded. The man curled over and let forth a great deep-bellied rumbling laugh, '¡Jajaja!' 'That's the Palo de Diablo (stick of the devil) tree,' he spluttered. 'The fire ants guard it. No one in their right mind would touch it!' News of the incident must have rapidly circulated through the community, because one man stood up after the presentation and said, 'The fire ant's sting cures arthritis. Nine ants must sting the affected joint. This must be repeated every nine days until you're cured.'

The track had descended into a narrow path, with footprints and motorbike trails marking the way. White cattle thronged the savanna, grazing a tapestry of swamps, trees and bush. The once-heard, never-forgotten grating call of the *hoatzin* emanated from a pond. This dinosaur of a bird has a bare blue shield around its beady red eye, a crown of long, orange mohican spikes and a long flecked neck. It is one of the most unusual birds alive today, hanging around in large gangs with its mates and crashing about in waterside foliage.

The curious thing about the *hoatzin* is that it eats leaves. The reason so few birds have adopted this abundant food-source is that in order to fly they need huge amounts of energy, which leaves do not provide. To process this unusual diet, the *hoatzin* is equipped with a fore-gut fermentation system like a cow. Anaerobic bacteria within its oesophagus and enlarged crop secrete enzymes, which break down the tough cellulose, allowing it to make a meal out of plants. The weight of that enormous processing unit, and the need to eat such a large amount to keep it going, mean that the *hoatzin* is not a nippy flier. In combination with its distinctive call and bungling behaviour, it seems rather amazing that it has not been hunted remorselessly. But river people we met when sailing in Venezuela confirmed, 'The meat's nasty.... anyway they smell!' Considering all the gases that must be produced during the fermentation process, it's no wonder!

The land was becoming more and more waterlogged; the cowpats sprouted fine parasol mushrooms, but the little windy path continued, now raised on an embankment with a series of rickety wooden bridges. As the light started to ebb, we found a slightly wider span to camp upon. A group of four motorbikers blazed past, barely missing us. As I started to fall asleep, I felt a sharp needling sensation under my eye, followed by others on my wrist and chin. 'Something's attacking me!' I gasped. The holes in the mosquito net tent we had made weren't small enough to prevent these swarming, miniscule biting flies from coming in, and there seemed no way of curbing the onslaught short of asphyxiating ourselves in our sleeping bags.

Capybaras had created the lawn on which we had pitched our net. Their droppings, which are like those of an over-grown sheep, with each 'raisin' measuring about three centimetres, were clustered on the bank. During the night we heard families snuffling, grunting and barking as they came out of the water to graze. As we listened, while desperately attempting to beat off the flies, we wondered whether the *capybaras* and the insects were linked. Were the *capybaras* providing the walking meal the flies delight in? Or perhaps it was just the commonality of habitat, with both animals thriving in bogs? Either way, we gave up on sleeping.

We emerged sometime during the early morning, well before the sun had traded places with the moon. Thousands of itchy bites pock-mocked our bodies. After a few minutes' run we startled a trio of *capybara*s munching long grass. They snorted, but seemed reticent to leave their café, and after a few further token barks started grazing again. Great clouds of flies surrounded them. We envied their thick pelt of coarse hair, and ran on. On arrival in Santa Rosa we were met by wry knowing smiles when we described the painful little critters that had accosted us during the night. Their local name was *puri puri,* and their insatiable appetite and parting itch were famed throughout the swamps of Beni.

Santa Rosa signified our last brush with civilisation for over 250 miles. So began an enormous provisioning operation as we scoured the streets for power- foods. Our cargo was crippling and included: bananas, garlic, beans, limes, peanuts, crackers, rice, oats, tomatoes, onions, jerky, biscuits and packet soups. Unfortunately, we would remember Santa Rosa not for its little thatched cottages, the cattle weaving across its sandy roads, nor the charming Canadian who photographed us departing, but for something altogether less savoury for poor David:

> A hugely disturbing bout of fungus/rot has covered 90 per cent of my groin for two whole terrifying nights' sleep. Katharine spoke to her Mum about it and they seemed to enjoy discussing my affliction at length!

Lorries passed us like ships in the night. We could see their navigation lights for an eternity as they crawled over bumps and holes, lumbering slowly, ever northwards. Our tent was tied between the barbed wire and branches outside the entrance to an estancia, 20 miles from Santa Rosa. We awoke to rustling. I pulled my head torch on. Something was moving under the groundsheet. It was long and thin. 'A snake!' I screamed. David sat bolt upright, 'Where is it?' We made a barrier out of the bird book, some shoes and a cooking pot, but it pushed under them. We were now squished into a small corner, with a fine layer of material between it and us. David banged his foot. It thrashed and lunged away, breaking for cover into the bushes, with a crackling of leaves marking its retreat.

At five in the morning we stumbled through the darkness to a stand of trees in front of a large swamp. The *estancia* owner, Victor, had appeared the night before and asked us to breakfast. We could just make out the form of buildings beyond, but there was no evidence of anyone stirring. We took our shoes off and began wading across, the thick mud and warm water reaching above our calves. A torch flashed. A voice barked. A shape was growing closer, clearer; it was Victor.

We splashed behind him. He led us through a wooden fence where animal buildings and a small hut had been built. A large barn was dimly lit by a few candles. It had open sides, a thatched roof and thick wooden pillars between which wove eddies of bats. Hammocks were tied to hooks on the beams. 'Here, there's water, please wash if you like,' he motioned. A young, chubby girl, Cati, emerged from the hut. She had long, raven-coloured hair and was cleaning four glasses for us. Two young children clutched her shorts.

I asked her if she went to school and how old she was. She said she was 16. 'So you must be Victor's daughter?' I continued, unaware of the enormous hole I was diving into. She giggled and said he was her husband. Victor was over 50 years old. At least one of their children was two years old and the other perhaps four. Working out family dynamics in rural areas was never straightforward, and often troubling.

Victor emerged from the darkness with a speckled cow. She ambled behind him snipping the odd blade of long grass. He tied her to the fence and asked us to bring our glasses over. I held mine under her taught nipple and he squeezed out frothy jets of warm, yellow milk. Cati passed me a jar of dried crumbly *yuca* pieces and I mixed them in. We hadn't drunk from a living vending machine before: the milk was utterly delicious, with the addition of the *yuca* creating something of the Horlicks about it.

We hurried back to the trailer as the first rays of sunlight speckled the distant hills. We were no longer debilitated by sickness and were consistently clocking over 20-mile days. The red, parched, flat lands allowed us to run fast and rhythmically, and for David to meditate upon how the future of the expedition would map out:

I'm dreaming of reaching 5,000 miles; imagining the feeling, the exhilaration and conquest. But then I spring back from too much hope by a tinge in my knee or ankle, reminding me that it could all still go disastrously wrong. It started when I totted up our total mileage last night – 4,264 – which means we're on track for 5,000 miles in 12 months. We're so close now to that original target. Brazil may be possible. But then I remember to think in small steps. We must be happy to achieve just one more mile, then the next, to conquer today, to reach Riberalta, not the rest.

Anyway, I believe we have three major physical challenges awaiting us: the remote rainforest path to Manaus, the Guiana Shield and ultimately, the Venezuelan coastal hills. I am also coming to realize that for me at least, skin may prove to be my most fragile organ. Bites, rashes, prickly heat and psoriasis are conspiring to create a really difficult time. Sometimes at night my whole body is on fire as I desperately scratch it. I really hope we haven't contracted *chagas* or *leishmaniosis*.

We were seeing many more blue and yellow macaws, with their screeches signalling their approach from far off in the savannah. One afternoon over 200 peach-fronted parakeets exploded from a thicket of trees near our camp. Somehow the countryside absorbed these colourful beauties into its soft pallet of hues, so that only movement or sound revealed their presence.

We finally caught sight of an animal we had started to think we would only see squished on the road. As I bent over to change my shoes, I noticed a slight shaking of the grass by my foot. I watched the quivering stems draw closer. A liquid body flowed through the vegetation, a flickering tongue sensed the air, its soft red, black and cream scales gliding effortlessly towards me: a coral snake.

There are over 65 different species of coral snakes in the Americas, and I had no idea which of these venomous snakes it was or if it was one of the mimics who has all the flashy colouration, but lacks the poison. They're known for being unaggressive and although highly poisonous, kill very few people, preferring to flee than to attack. This guy was certainly not in the least bit bothered by us, streaming past and then doubling back and disappearing into the bush, his livery merging into the scarlet earth and vegetation.

That night we realized that the packet soup we had bought contained 36 calories per portion. To meet our energy requirements, we would have to eat 100 portions (20 packets) a day! Luckily we still had a good larder of more nutritious food to compensate for this shortfall, but even with this addition, it was clear that our bodily balance-sheet was severely skewed, and that we weren't consuming enough. In three days' time we would observe the results of this oversight. Two skeletal bodies would stare back at us from the hotel mirror in Riberalta. My shoulder blades jagged, my hip bones sharp, all the little vertebrae pricking through my skin as they tracked down my spine. The scales would reveal that I had lost two stone since the start of the expedition, and David one-and-a-half. We would need to make a concerted effort to up our intake.

Before arriving in Riberalta we were invaded by termites as we slept. Thousands streamed in, perhaps simply because we were in their way, making them try to incorporate the two great slumbering beasts into their elaborate earthen walkways. They built an immaculate covered highway down one side of the net, neatly snipping entrances and exits on either side. Arterial routes forked off across my sunglasses, the GPS watch and the binocular case and along our sweaty tops. Perhaps they particularly enjoyed our odour, because they also cemented our shorts to a branch outside, and engulfed the harness and trailer wheels, hundreds strong, creating a flickering roundabout within the spokes. But these minions have no defences against humans, especially as, during a pre-run expedition into the Amazon, we had found they tasted rather deliciously of carrot! It's just that we would have had to devour a heck of a lot of them to fill our gurgling tummies. It took time to clear away the earthy havoc they had created, but they were too easy to dispatch to be a great nuisance.

Another invertebrate was also making its presence felt; butterflies. Clouds fluttered like confetti on the air, lining the road in multi-coloured drifts. We had never seen anything like it, and ran ecstatically through them as they pirouetted around our heads. The village we passed that day was aptly called *Mariposa* (butterfly) and the school children and teachers to whom we presented said it was always like that at this time of the year (early June).

Then there were the 'butterflies of the night', the moths, who were strangely attracted to our hammocks. Hundreds would cluster upon them before we snuck inside each night, like the scales of a palm tree, their golden eyes glinting in the beam of our head torches. But by the morning they were gone, disappearing into their hidden homes. We also discovered that we had been running oblivious to a couple of hitchhikers, who had taken up residence in the trailer. David noticed two sets of long hairy legs, poised at the top of each of the bike forks. He had sawn off the ends of the forks to cut back on weight, and the hollow tubes provided the perfect lair for two large spiders.

The day before Riberalta one of the trailer-tyres had a flat. We noticed a little path leading into the forest and hoped that whoever lived down it might give us a bucket of water to find the puncture. A thatched wooden hut perched on stilts rose from a swept clearing. A man was sitting on a bench, with clods of coal-coloured hair flying to the ground, as a dainty woman snapped shears in an arc around his head. Children lay slumped on hammocks in the shadows of the building. Their faces were a mix of smiles, nervousness and intrigue as we approached. I quickly described our predicament and the mother summoned one of her daughters to pull a bucket of water from the well. We were ushered towards a bench and glasses of *chicha de maíz* (maize cider*)* were handed to us.

While David fixed the tyre, I talked to the dimpled-cheeked, smiling mother. She proudly showed me her garden, full of *yuca*, tomatoes, rice, maize, papayas and mangos. She was only 34 years old; a year younger than me, yet had five children from ages six to eighteen, and now two grandchildren. Her 18-year-old son had a child of 14 months, and her 17-year-old daughter one a year old. This she suckled as we chatted, while the other grandchild was rocked in the hammock by the children and their friends.

We reached Riberalta after a 27-mile day and 12 days of continuous running. In town we heard the wonderful news that the Transglobe Expedition Trust had approved our application for a top-up grant, as had Sculpt the Future Foundation. The John Muir Trust also agreed to help out again. It was an enormous relief, and meant that we would be able to scrape through, financially at least.

Riberalta also brought a letter from Buckingham Palace. While camping on a forested river bank, I had written to Prince Charles – a hero of mine for speaking out about the environment and conservation. I explained what we were doing, and said that if we could meet him after the expedition, it would give us a tremendous boost during the hot, sweaty miles that lay ahead. David said I was crazy, that he would never reply. But he did:

> Bearing in mind the length of time your letter has taken to reach the UK from Bolivia (it must have been walked in a cleft stick around the country several times) I thought I should reply swiftly! I am hugely impressed that you are undertaking such a gruelling and challenging 5,000 mile run for such a vitally important cause and I pray you will not have too many blisters, mosquito bites and other travel scars by the time you return from such an extraordinary marathon . . . I send you both my kindness, good wishes and admiration.

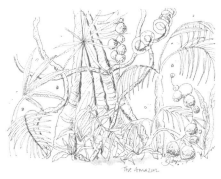

The Amazon

If we had been there only 40 years previously,
we would have been running through rainforest

17 Brazil: a New World

The journey across the border took barely 20 minutes. The riverside town changed its name from the Spanish Guayaramerín to the Portuguese Guajará-Mirim, and with that we stepped into another world (see Map 7).

The hawkers and street-side sellers had been swept away. Everything was sanitised and sterilised. Grey concrete buildings grew from orderly streets. Ranks of cars glinted in the sunshine. Highly-polished women tottered on sky-high platforms into designer boutiques. Motorbike taxi-drivers were *women*, wearing helmets, with sheaves of paperwork strapped to their backs and extra helmets for their passengers. An enormous supermarket sat in an enormous car park. Inside, everything was air-conditioned and extortionately expensive. We felt dizzy and slightly nauseated by the mountains and variety of food. The petrol stations even had chilled-water machines. Where was the chaos and colour of Bolivia that we craved?

Then there was the language. A friend from home put it like this, 'It's a cross between Spanish and French, so you need to pepper a healthy mix of the two into sentences. But if that fails, then just shout!' We had known it was going to be a hurdle, but this was a disaster. Portuguese is decipherable when written with the help of Spanish, but put it into a Brazilian's mouth, and it becomes mind-boggling. People stared at us as if we were idiots, which we were when it came to conversation. We soon realised that the enjoyment we had felt chatting to locals in Bolivia would now be impossible. But it wasn't just the language: the immediate problem was the heat. It was scorching, with no cloud-cover or shade from trees. There wasn't a verge, the asphalt was full of gaping holes, and juggernauts were hammering past.

We were galloping alongside millions of hectares of grasslands stretching into the distance, dotted with white cattle and clumps of palm trees. If we had been there only 40 years previously, we would have been running through rainforest.

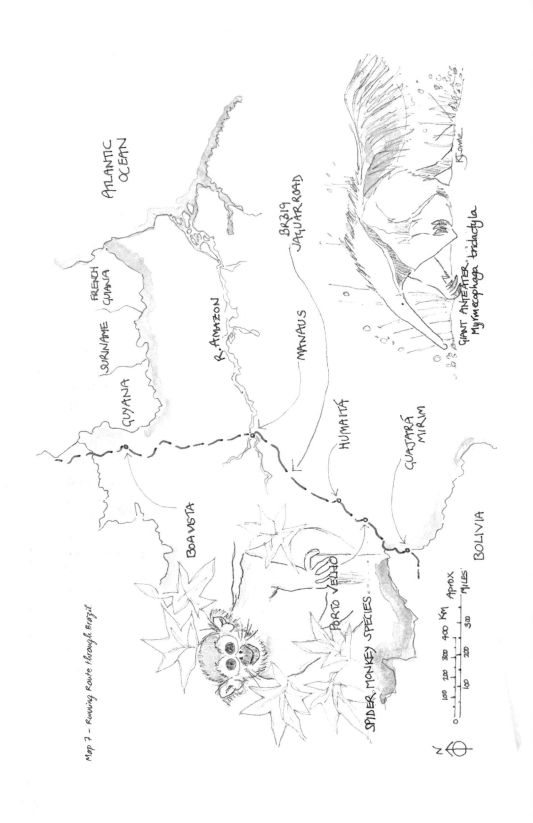

Map 7 - Running Route through Brazil

ATLANTIC OCEAN

FRENCH GUIANA

SURINAME

GUYANA

R. AMAZON

BR319 JAGUAR ROAD

MANAUS

HUMAITÁ

GUAJARÁ MIRIM

BOLIVIA

BOA VISTA

PORTO VELHO

SPIDER MONKEY SPECIES

GIANT ANTEATER
Myrmecophaga tridactyla

RJoune

100 200 300 400 KM Aprox
0 100 200 300 MILES

N

I felt physically sick casting my eyes over the simplification of a once-incredible natural land. We were also scared. We were running through the start of a series of lawless states where environmentalists had been killed. Sister Dorothy Stang was just one of the victims. She worked with peasants, helping them make a living within the forest without deforesting it. She was outspoken on the environment and the rural poor. She was often photographed wearing a T-shirt with the slogan, 'A morte da floresta é o fim da nossa vida' (The death of the forest is the end of our life). She had received several death threats from loggers and landowners, and was finally murdered on 12 February 2005.

With evening approaching fast, we were doing exactly what we vowed we would never do in Brazil – still pounding the roads. David was imagining how and where we could be robbed, and that our only reprieve would be to reach the Caribbean as quickly as possible. A small, black Fiat stopped. Beto, the driver, miraculously talked Castellano and we chatted briefly about what we were up to. 'Look, he said. 'I'm on my way back to Nova Mamorá, but you can stay in my house tonight, which is only about a mile up the hill. I'll probably be back this evening, but either way, just make yourselves at home. Here's my key,' he went on. 'I'll leave a sign at the fork in the road showing which track you need to follow.'

With that the ever-grinning Beto screeched off. Our hearts soared. We were overwhelmed. Where else in the world would somebody entrust their house key to two complete strangers? Brazil? The country whose folk we had been convinced would be ready to hang, draw and quarter us.

But it wasn't going to be quite that easy. After running a mile we found no sign of a track. We asked a group of children whether they knew Beto, but they shook their heads laughing at our weird 'Portuñol'. I knocked at a house, but the woman couldn't understand a word I said. And so it continued, with perplexed faces staring back at us. We snapped at one another; feeling tense and scared. We had already run an extra two miles, but we agreed to carry on to the bottom of the hill, where there looked to be a stream, by which we might be able to camp. As we neared the water-course, we noticed a track meandering off to the right – and then suddenly I saw it. A couple of branches had been configured into the shape of an arrow, and they were pointing down the track. Euphoria swept over us.

We walked down the sandy path: it was nearly a mile long and ended in a cluster of hardwood huts on stilts. We could barely make them out in the gloom that had descended. The area around them had been razed, and there was a small lake in the middle. David tried the key in the closest hut, but it didn't fit. He tried another: same story. Perhaps we were in the wrong place after all? Then the rumble of an engine grew louder and louder, and Beto emerged from the darkness with his daughter, Hilda. We were saved! Hilda insisted on cooking for us, and we chatted late into the evening. It was a dream. We showered and slunk off to a hut. I cut David's hair under a full radiant moon, and then we lay on our mats and sunk into a deep sleep.

Beto was incredibly hospitable and invited us to stay another day, so we decided to take our rest day with him in the countryside. During the morning a battalion of army ants charged through the house. It was a spectacular raid. They were black and of all sizes, but ruthless in their attack, seeking out anything living, half-dead or vaguely edible in their path. They swarmed up the walls, over the floor and beds and into the cupboards. Nothing was left unturned. 'They can kill and carry off a new-born baby,' Beto warned. 'But they're very useful cleaners.'

Discussions ranged widely during the day, but one thread that remained constant was Beto's extreme nationalism. He became very animated that 'we' (internationals) should not have a say on the Amazon, that it was a matter of Brazilian domestic policy. He said that we had cut down all our trees (more or less true) in the U.K., and now it was Brazil's turn. It was difficult to confront such bigotry; especially given that his forefathers had been as responsible as ours for deforesting Europe. David asked, 'What if we pay to preserve the Amazon?' That, said Beto, would be great, but it's not for sale. He warned us that ninety percent of people in Amazona and Rondônia felt the same as him, and that interfering foreigners (and indigenous people who were hindering development) were despised.

We ran early the following morning to Nova Mamoré and stopped for frozen coconuts. These were one of the most amazing foods we ate during the expedition. We would often find the nuts growing along the way and would slurp their juices, then hack out their rich, creamy pulp. But sipping their silky water, ice cold, was of a different magnitude of sublimity.

Two school children skipped down the road, hand in hand, one black and the other white. People of every skin-colour and ethnicity walked the streets together. A striking multiculturalism was revealing itself. Brazil seemed to be a truly 'rainbow nation.'

We hoped to camp in someone's garden, but cringed at the thought of having to speak to any owners. It was ironic that we were now desperately seeking Spanish speakers with whom to communicate. A patch of wood at the bottom of a hill contained a house. I walked down its pathway. A wiry black guy with a thin, grey moustache answered the door. He seemed troubled. He explained that he had been robbed a month ago, that the men were armed and had punched down his door. I thought there was no way he would let us stay, I wouldn't blame him. But he nodded and motioned us towards a patch of trees.

Chickens' dust-bowls riddled the ground. We were having difficulty finding a flat patch upon which we could pitch the tent, when I looked up and saw the man watching us. He seemed irritated and was calling me over to the house, wildly flapping his arm. I padded over, bracing myself for the eviction notice. But when I stood before him, I could see that he wasn't annoyed with us, only perhaps with himself. 'You can't sleep out there. Come into the house. Look, I can clear the floor and make a place for you to sleep in here.'

I couldn't believe Pedro's generosity, in fact, I didn't trust that I had understood him correctly. But he seemed happy for us to unpack our gear in his room; moving chairs and plants and sweeping the floor for us. He then disappeared and returned with some string and a pole, tying it to various fittings as an attachment for our net. He reminded me of my Great Aunt, like a character on a World War II footing, with his neat, simple house, utilising everything to the full. When David started using the MSR, he quickly ushered us into the kitchen, showing us around, inviting us to use the cooker and to share his chicken and rice stew. The room was spotless and old-fashioned, with two sets of plates and cutlery, one to be used only for special occasions. In many ways we could have been standing in any grandfather's house in the U.K., except there were live wires running in the open eaves and everything electrical ran off their scraggly ends.

Pedro coughed nervously around us. David cooked. Pedro picked things up and put them down again. I wondered what his wife would be like if she was still alive. It turned out she was very much alive, she was just visiting friends in Porto Velho. He showed us photos of her and his grandparents, all of mixed race. When he learnt that we were ecologists, he brought out a nature encyclopaedia, lovingly leafing through it while pointing at the amazing wildlife. He was very proud of it. It was very touching and provided props for communication.

A friend of his appeared: a lorry-driver who often stopped by for a shower and chat. He was short and pot-bellied, with sun-baked skin. He giggled and called us *locos* (crazies) and warned us to beware of *tigres* (jaguars). Apparently, two men had been killed recently by them. We finally ate together, sharing our meals and a papaya we had picked up which we smothered in lime juice. Pedro whistled nervously, but seemed to enjoy the food. It must have felt very odd to be sitting and eating in his own house with two strangers with whom he could hardly communicate. But we looked at more of his books, and then I gave him our Spanish card. He examined it wistfully, proudly revealing that he had recently learnt to read. I asked if I could take a photo of him for our memories. He agreed, and disappeared into his bedroom, returning in a newly- pressed white shirt and neatly combed hair.

We still hadn't quite lost Bolivia. It lay across the Río Madeira, alongside which we were running. Most of the time there was at least a couple of miles' separation of grazed pasture between it and us, so that if it hadn't been for the map, we would have been unaware of its presence, but then at one point our road swung close. We could hear its rapids and just make out the forest beyond. I left David with the trailer and ran over, scrambling down the steep river bank to take a last look.

The vision was spell-bounding. The river was at least a quarter of a mile wide; white water crashed over the boulders and forested islands anchored in its rushing torrent. A silver mist fingered over its surface, but beyond rose the forest; thick, mighty and awe-inspiring. I imagined canoeing down that river 50 years ago, through a wall of trees on either bank, echoing with the calls of monkeys and birds. Now my side of the bank had been cleared, but on the Bolivian side the forest was still intact.

Although we ran through a sea of tall grass, occasional forest remnants were still present alongside rivers and high on hillsides. These were the pockets of trees that the Brazilian Forest Code sought to protect. This progressive piece of legislation, introduced in 1965, is on paper an environmental jewel. In addition to watershed forest conservation, each Amazonian landowner must preserve eighty percent of existing forest-cover on their *fazenda* (farm). But the reality on the ground was strikingly different, with landowners rotating patches around their farms, logging or burning primary forest, and thus ensuring only poor-quality secondary growth made up the required percentage. Any surviving patches of primary old-growth forest were probably too small to provide any biodiversity value. No fines or penalties were taken against such indiscretions: in fact amnesties on all past deforestation were applied.

Another stark fall-out of the code were lone Brazil-nut trees, protected from logging, growing in a vacuum of grassland. Although well-meant, these trees soon die in such a harsh, hot environment, so alien from their steaming, fecund rainforest home, while their flowers are not pollinated so that their nuts never fruit. It was heart-breaking, running alongside countless numbers of these old stalwarts and witnessing their gradual demise. But the more I learnt about this extraordinary tree, the more I realized it could offer a key to saving the Amazon.

> As cumulus clouds tower above the intact rainforest on the Bolivian side of our river, ready to discharge vapour with the coming wet season, the humidity is tangible. And the sound is deafening. Far, far above the forest floor, some 50 metres up, an army of bees are supping on the sweet nectar of hundreds of custard-coloured Brazil-nut tree flowers. But these are no ordinary bee, they're orchid-bees: strong enough to lift the coiled hood of the Brazil nut flower, with an extraordinarily long tongue, adapted to extract the sticky-sweet delights hidden deep within the complex flower. In a silky-scented twist to the tale, the bees are believed to be attracted to the Brazil-nut trees by perfumed orchids, while the orchids' nectar is thought to provide special chemicals that enhance the colour of the bees' wings, making them even more dashing to the females. Over a year must pass for the Brazil-nut's 'toes' to fatten. Twenty jostle for space within a single canon-ball pod, waiting for the trigger – the rains. As more and more rain falls, for longer periods and more regularly, so the canon-balls start showering down. This is no time to linger; a single knock from one of those balls can kill a man.
>
> And so the next jigsaw piece in the Brazil nut tale reveals itself: a silvery moon-shadow casts light on a Brazil nut pod, lying unsuspecting at the base of a nearby mahogany tree. Your ears detect a rustle. A Jaguar? No, too light. Suddenly an over-grown, guinea-pig-ratty type of creature snuffles

Running South America

154

over. An *agouti*. He stands on his back legs. Sniffs the air. Nothing there? Quickly he gets to work. Sharp, 'tin-opening' incisors grinding away at the seemingly unconquerable pod. And he's in. Ruthlessly, efficiently, he chews a few choice nuts. Acutely aware that the bounty is short-lived, he begins digging larders, ensuring caches for the future months.

So another generation of Brazil nut trees are secured thanks to '*Super-Agouti*'. Because, as we all know, we can count on the agouti, just as we can upon our red-squirrel, to forget exactly where he put all of his stores. The forgotten treasures will soon be sprouting and belting for a place in the Amazon's canopy.

Voices echo deep in the forest. Most of the Brazil nut pods have dropped to the ground and local men, the '*casteneros*' are arriving to harvest their 'plots'. They have already cut-back the vegetation that strangled last year's paths and cleared the floor under their trees in preparation. With an ever-present machete and a basket on their back, secured with a strap over their forehead, they begin collecting. Baskets bulging, they head out of the forest. A Brazil nut tumbles to the floor. In the following months a new seedling sprouts in the light of the path.

So what is this nut you hold in your hand? It's full of protein, calcium, iron, selenium and a whole host of other riches. It's a perfect segment of intact rainforest. Because unlike just about any other food you might pop into your mouth, this hasn't been industrially produced or spat out from the tired ranks of a plantation. People have tried, but it just hasn't been economically viable. Because without the orchid bees, the orchids or agoutis and the intricate fabric of a functioning tropical rainforest that it depends upon, the nuts won't form. It's a nut with a story, a history, a local person's life, a rainforest that can remain standing.

It was blindingly hot. We felt we were being incinerated alive. We wore our spare T-shirts over our heads, and David rinsed his clothes whenever he found a trickle of water. From eight o'clock in the morning his body gushed like a shower. When he stopped, he sweated. A few seconds after drinking, he leaked like a bucket and soon his top smelt of the acrid uric odour of unkempt horse stables.

We arrived at the point labelled Mutumparaná on our map. But there was no sign of a village, not even a single dwelling. David had seen it on Google Earth, so why was nothing visible on the ground? We ran an extra two-and-a-half miles. A bus-stop appeared with a man sitting in it. 'When's the next bus to town?' We implored. 'There's no bus and there's no town for 30 kilometres.' He shrugged, then looked away. 'So why is there a bus-stop here?' I hissed at David, 'And what's he doing sitting in it?' We felt we were living in an *Alice in Wonderland* dream world.

Three men appeared walking down the road. They had to be going or coming from or to somewhere. We asked them the same question. 'No, there's nothing here,' they replied. 'No bus, no town, no shop'.

'But it says on our map that there's a settlement!' we insisted.

'Well, if you walk 500 metres up the road in front, there is something.'

We decided to follow them up the track. At the top a wall of odour punched us in the face. It was musky, pungent, acrid and slightly rotten. It seeped everywhere, as if we were wading in soup. I had never smelt anything like it, and yet it included something familiar: wood. The striking difference was that the smell was coming from Amazonian hardwood timber, and was a world apart from the fragrance of the wood I knew from the UK. We were standing in a huge timber-yard. We cast our eyes down to the slogans on our T-shirts, *Corriendo por la naturaleza* (Running for the natural world). Our ears burned. It felt like we were minnows in a pond of very large sharks. And so we did what any noble eco-activists would do: we turned our shirts inside out!

We were marched towards a large building. Perhaps this was where the public blood-letting happened? A man beckoned to us, wiggling his fat fingers in front of his mouth, in a gruesome octopus gesture. Minutes later he was piling *feijon* (fried beans), beef stew and pasta onto our plates and handing us glasses of ice-cold juice. Beyond the hardwood walls of the canteen, gigantic tree trunks were being loaded and unloaded in the yard. Some sections were so big they needed two forklift trucks to lift them. Mountains of wood reached towards the clouds, and yet lorries kept arriving with more. Enormous off-cuts were forming the base of a bonfire. We mused about how the cutting edge of climate-change and habitat-destruction often has a friendly smile on it.

Over the following five days we ran 100 miles to reach Porto Velho. The road was flat and fast. The forest had been nuked on either side of us. A web of pylons criss-crossed the open plains as the new rainforest *emergents*. But, amazingly, life hung on in the scrub and scrambling secondary forest patches that were grappling for a foothold in the wake of the ancient forest's destruction. Among the survivors was a tribe of little red monkeys which stared quizzically at us.

Cockroaches were the new currency in this disturbed land. We awoke one morning to find a small brown variety scurrying all over us. It was difficult not to be repelled; it seems the reaction is hard-wired in human sub-conscience. At least they didn't sting or bite, unlike the wasps that had recently puffed up our hands and legs with swollen mounds.

The next day flamed once again. Distant cars and lorries shimmered as if in a dream, fanned by the blistering heat that rose from the tarmac. By eight-thirty in the morning our footprints were scoring the asphalt. We stormed down the undulating dual-carriageway towards Porto Velho, high on the thought of stopping for a day or two. I clutched a damp scrap of paper in my hand. Scrawled on it was the telephone number of Leo, a friend of Renan, whom we had met when he was cycling in southern Chile. It was our key to space on a floor while in the city. We came to a giant roundabout. The city sprawled loud and ugly down a hill to the left. A few shacks lined the road. I sauntered over asking whether I could borrow someone's mobile phone for a few *reais*. A ginger-bearded man handed me his, watching me as I dialled the number. I introduced myself in Spanish, but a clear English response explained how we should get to the flat.

We charged back down the road and up into a sprawling housing-area which soon dissolved into shanty squalor. Electric wires hung limply from roofs and were shoved into make-shift satellite dishes and radio masts. Holes in the road looked capable of swallowing us. Plastic sheets and corrugated iron were the universal building materials. We had found the backdoor into Porto Velho.

Perhaps all the reprobates were busy looting the rich estates. Perhaps their targets were never brazen or stupid enough to venture into their backyards. Perhaps two filthy runners, with holey shoes and stinking, perforated clothes, pulling a rag-and-bone cart, were not considered the most prestigious or lucrative targets. Either way, we snuck through one of the dodgiest residencies of this shady city, famed for its crime, without so much as a word.

Leo lived four flights of stairs up in a concrete flat with two housemates. He sprouted lots of brown curly hair and a beard. He was super-welcoming, wonderfully laid-back and fascinating, after the depressing red-neck attitudes we had encountered along the road. He told us about his work helping local people to be custodians of the forest, by finding markets for non-extractive products, allowing the forest to remain intact, while providing a livelihood for its people.

The following morning he introduced us to the blood-purple berries of the açaí palm, pouring them over a gravelly bed of *farina de mandioca* (ground manioc). This form of manioc seemed to be a staple for every Brazilian dish, whether breakfast, lunch or dinner. The result, combined with *açaí* and a few heaped teaspoons of sugar, was absolutely delicious. The berries are native to the Amazon rainforest and have recently been recognized as a super-food. Apparently bodybuilders in the USA were going nuts about it, but we were oblivious to this in our running cocoon.

Leo also made us tapioca (*goma de mandioca*), another derivative of manioc, but ground down into a fine, moist powder. He sprinkled it over a hot griddle, and the starchy grains fused together, forming a thin crepe. Apparently it's a favourite game to pour gallons of the powder on to the surface of a swimming pool and to charge across. If the competitors run fast enough, the powder behaves like steel, but if their nerves falter and they're not speedy, it collapses, as do they into its slurrisome depths. Leo cooked both sides of the crepe, smeared it in butter and filled it with cheese. It was delicious.

As we ran out of Porto Velho, a small green car stopped us and a family erupted. The large, beaming father introduced himself and handed us drinks, before rummaging in the boot for some T-shirts. 'These are for you!' he proclaimed joyously. We were loath to carry any extra weight, not even three T-shirts, but we couldn't turn down his gift. The caption was decipherable even in Portuguese, 'Projecto Clube Escolar ParaOlímpico' (Paralympic School Club Project). Well – at least he thought we had some potential for the Para-Olympic team!

Two nights later we were on a rural road north of Porto Velho, writing under torch- light in our hammocks.

> I'm thinking about home (David penned). It seems so distant, so irrelevant. Perhaps we should do a Moitessier* and keep on running?

It took us six days to cover 127 miles to Humaitá, the next settlement on the map. This marked the start of one of the greatest challenges of the expedition; running the *Rua do Onces* (Jaguar Road), *BR319 TransAmazonica,* through the heart of the Amazon rainforest. Whenever we told locals of our destination, they would gasp and shake their heads.

The *Rua do Onces* was the most remote and wild stretch of the expedition. We would run deep into the Amazon, far from human habitation, carrying all the food we would need for three weeks, plus emergency rations. The road had been built in the 1970s by the Brazilian government in an effort to link Manaus to the rest of the country by land. The project failed. The annual floods inundated it, sweeping whole sections away, allowing the forest gradually to reclaim it. We were told that hundreds of rickety bridges crossed the countless streams and rivers, but that in some places they had disappeared altogether.

We might have to swim rivers with all our food, equipment and trailer. If anything went wrong – say a snake-bite, or one of us chopped off a finger with the machete, there would be no rescue; we were the rescue services. All we had to depend on was our first-aid kit, our own strength and guile, and the trailer which could act as a stretcher – not that there was anywhere to take a body. If we got held up for some reason, we could only carry enough survival rations for an extra week.

*Moitessier was a French national sailing hero who competed in the first solo non-stop round the world race in 1968. He was on course to achieve the fastest time, but elected to carry on sailing rather than return to the UK to claim his prize. The race and its commercialism had become pointless to him, 'Because I am happy at sea and perhaps to save my soul.'

South American Tapir
Tapirus terrestris

Never far from our thoughts
when finding signs of tapir
was its predators...

18 The Jaguar Road

We needed to carry a vast amount of food. Then there was water, camping kit and all our other belongings. Our trailer had to transport all this and survive the rigours of the crumbling track that lay ahead. It wasn't possible. This was the point at which we made a second trailer and split everything between the two. Except we didn't get that far.

After running only three miles, the new trailer collapsed. The bamboo that David had found in Humaitá wasn't as tough as the solid Chilean *collihue* and had caved in under the weight. We were stuck, with the potential of losing another day to renovations. But there was an army base a couple of hundred metres up the road. Lorries, dumper-trucks and bulldozers were streaming in and out of the compound, repairing a stretch of the orange road that lay ahead. It was our only option.

We were ready for high surveillance, fences, guard dogs and hostility. Instead we were greeted by smiling faces and ushered into a welding shed. Up to that point we had tried to keep the trailer as light as possible. But now we had no option: we needed to get moving. Someone found a metal rod, and within minutes white sparks were flying as our trailer metamorphosed.

A few hours later our shadows were lengthening across the road and we were on the hunt for somewhere to camp. A sign straddled the road. It had rusted over so that the numbers were barely visible, but we could just make it out, 'Manaus, 640 km'. A slight opening in the forest on our side was just big enough for us to hide the trailer and set up camp. But we weren't the only occupiers of our new premises. Within minutes of dumping our belongings, my legs and thighs were on fire. In fact, any exposed skin was under attack from hundreds of tiny, biting black ants. I peered down at my feet through the pale light of my head-torch; ants were swarming all over them and over our bags and hammocks.

We found we had plunged back into a world of strange and inexplicable noises, which pierced and moved through the darkness. Troops of monkeys crashed through the branches and muffled footsteps crunched through the leaf litter. We peered through the fine mosquito gauze of our hammocks, probing the forest with our pathetic torches, but nothing revealed itself.

David groaned with terrible leg cramps. The hammocks were locking our joints into agonising positions. As a result, we often hitched our hammocks only centimetres off the ground, so that we could effectively lie on the ground and stretch out our limbs in our pods, but this often wasn't possible in marshy or thickly vegetated areas. David also had a fiery rash all over his legs, which, considering we had failed to wash again last night, wasn't surprising. By morning the black ants had regrouped, streaming over our hammocks and all our kit. We flew out from our silk liners, grabbing belongings and shaking them wildly, before hurling everything onto the road.

A steady trickle of motorbikes, bicycles and cars passed us. On the fourth day we stumbled into Novo Realidade. The cluster of houses we had expected had bloomed into a proper settlement, its arms stretching in all directions in its grab for the forest. Migrants were pouring in from the southern states of Paraná and Mato Grosso, desperate to cash in on the forest bonanza. Houses were flying up in front of our eyes.

It felt like storming into the frame of a modern-day wild-west film, but the men sauntering down the dusty road carried chainsaws instead of guns. Clapped out 1950s American trucks rattled cheek-by-jowl with horses and traps. Hardware shacks and convenience stores had sprouted. We felt exposed, and dived in the direction of a swamp-green motel. Luckily it was open, and so we unbuckled all our stuff, hauled it and the trailers into a small concrete cell and collapsed onto the musty bed.

The hotel owner was cooking for a white-haired sparrow of a man who was sporting a panama hat and carrying a toy-pooch. She agreed to extend the meal for us. She was pertly plump and wore a bright green-and-yellow swirly floral top, with a knee-length denim skirt hemmed in pink and white stripes. Her slightly silver Afro curls were eked back into a bun, and she grinned broadly. She was determined to talk to us, remaining stoical in her resolution even in the face of our blank faces. I offered a smattering of eager, 'Sís' and nods, some of which clearly hit the mark, receiving vigorous nods and smiling approval, while others were regarded quizzically, as she cocked her head like an hen, examining her subject with a look of concern, before doggedly progressing with the interrogation.

With a startled twitch she stopped talking, frowned and bustled off behind a faded ply-board screen. 'Oh God, may this be our dinner!' we whispered as our stomachs groaned with the interminable wait. After a few minutes she rounded the corner, proudly placing a series of bowls on the trestle table containing: *feijon*, rice, meat stew and *farina de mandioca*. Never had we been more happy to eye-ball the old favourites, and we began to devour everything in sight, alarming the old sparrow with our powerful competition. The arrival of the food spurred him to twitter, though luckily his chatter was of an accent slightly more discernible.

'This place is a goldmine of opportunity,' he said, his eyes glazing over. 'There's wood everywhere. It can be yours for almost nothing and no one's watching! This is it; the last of the good times. I'm telling you, it's the Promised Land. People are lining their mattresses with sacks of *reais*!' His whole body had begun pulsing with pleasure. In front of our eyes the town was being assembled like a Monopoly board from deep-mahogany- coloured hardwood, from a forest now barely visible from the road. But this was a fragment of what was being milled and sent rumbling off to market. Prospectors, whether in suits or cow-boy hats, all wanted a piece of the action, as the new vanguard of illegal squatters. We were witnessing how a road could kill a forest. The road allowed access for felling, the cattle would follow and when the land failed, the settlers would move on to the next gold mine. The 'Arc of Deforestation' was on the march.

We had to do something about our clothes. The landlady ushered me along a concrete drain at the side of the motel. I hopped from side to side of a green, oozing liquid. She banged open the lid of her stirring machine, shovelled some powder into its cavernous innards and departed humming. Red grit and scum poured from our kit, out of the open silver pipe, mixing with the green to form a deep-brown frothy smear. No matter how many times I emptied the machine and added more cold water, the red stain kept coming. Eventually I gave up, rung the sodden clothes out and hung them on a metal wire.

That night it was due to rain. The air settled thick in our lungs and bunged up the town. My attempts at washing our clothes were farcical; there was no way we could win against this onslaught. In the morning we would pull on cold clammy tops and shorts, it would be grim, but largely irrelevant as we would soon be soaked in sweat.

A small cupboard opposite our room served as a shower, shared by all the guests. A pair of red silk pants dangled from one of the taps. The thin trickle of water soon petered out, but we were used to washing in a few cup-fuls and anyway that soon became irrelevant when I noticed another occupant, of the non-paying variety. He was tiny, white-and-porcelain with black, beady eyes, and at first I thought he was an ornament. He sat on a thin ledge by my right shoulder and blinked thoughtfully at my nose while I scrutinised him back. A large cinnamon moth flew in. The statue burst into life, and a long, pink, sticky tongue darted from the frog's gaping mouth, snapping the moth up between gummy lips.

As we ran out of Novo Realidade, the rainforest chorus was headed by one of the loveliest and most distinctive duets: that of a pair of white-throated toucans. Sitting on alternate branches, the amorous couple yelped and yipped, their enormous black bills pointing to the sky, as they rotated their heads from side to side.

We stopped by a river for lunch. It was David's birthday, so I cooked a special birthday concoction on one of the dug-out canoes that had been upended on the bank. The river was the same ochre colour as the road. An entire fleet of half-submerged dug-outs were tied under the thick wooden columns of the bridge. Frogs croaked in a metal pipe, their voices amplified in the sound-tunnel. We slipped into the water fully clothed. I felt fish nibbling my feet. They liked any loose skin and scars, and were particularly partial to a small white wart that had recently appeared on my ankle bone.

We found a cleared red-gravelly area beside of the track, where the rain had washed away any topsoil. These patches would provide the basis of many of our camp-sites during the following weeks. After Realidade only the occasional cyclist or motorbiker passed, often carrying a gun or a chainsaw. We heard hunters shooting in the night. We didn't want to be caught in their cross-fire or startle them. While I set up camp, David began unstrapping and re-configuring the new trailer with some poles he had found. The rutted road surface would really test both the trailers, and then there was the problem of the two green food-bags that David could barely lift. We were carrying far too much and we couldn't afford either trailer to fail over the comings weeks; they were our lifelines.

A little nightjar flitted round our net in the gloom, searching for insects. She would sit close to us for a few minutes and then take to the air like a feathered butterfly, before alighting in the leaf-litter again, her huge eyes alert and whiskers bristling. We had come to expect visits from nightjars in the rural areas of the run; from mid-Argentina northwards numerous species had accompanied our dusk-and-dawn runs and fluttered around our camp-sites.

That night disaster struck; the MSR stove failed to light. Without it, we couldn't eat. So David set to for the next hour, attempting to pull the constituent pieces apart, but they wouldn't come, and he didn't dare break them. He needed WD40, but we had none, so he liberally lubricated the stove with cooking oil and waited. He had mended it before, but this time it didn't look hopeful. He began building a fire, but everything was drenched. Without a stove, we would have to build fires twice a day, whatever the conditions, as well as running, cooking and sleeping. Fires were a worry, as they would give our position away to anyone unsavoury.

The rainforest wasn't going to give us a break, either. At ten-thirty that night the wind started howling through the trees. Leaves the size of dustbin lids showered onto our net. A branch cracked nearby as it split off and dropped to the ground. We knew what this heralded. Crawling out of our silk liners and grabbing waterproofs, we clutched the two tarps and scrambled out of the net tent. We hadn't bothered to tie them up, and now we were going to pay for it.

It was as if the forest was writhing with an army of ghosts intent on finding us, as the wailing, deathly force grew closer and closer. I was scared. My nerves were frayed after Argentina's mighty electrical storms. Everything moved, every tree and branch groaned and wheezed. Billions of leaves shook, the frogs' yelps reached fever pitch, the wall of noise was almost upon us and then suddenly,

'Bang!' Water cascaded from the sky, drumming and ricocheting off every surface, hammering down upon us, drenching us in seconds. We were freezing cold, desperately tying the tarp lines to branches which had morphed into river beds down which raged rivers. How were we ever going to sleep or keep our bedding dry? We grabbed the cooking pots and any containers into which the tarps could drain. At least we would have fresh rain water to drink tomorrow.

The rain seemed never to tire, never to squeeze the sky dry. We lay listening for hours, curled into one another in an effort to keep warm, drowning in the deafening sound that was saturating our senses. It was impossible to think or talk. Then, as quickly as it came, it went, as if someone had turned off the taps. It took a few minutes for everyone to work out what had happened, but then we heard a click, next a bark, a squeal, a trill, and soon the forest was singing with frogs, toads, cicadas and ranks of unidentified insects crooning into the night. What better than the new puddles and pockets of rainwater, the steaming moisture, the damp leaf litter; the delightful wonder of water?

Day seven was punctuated by a big *fazenda* (farm) of long cattle-grass and the end of a veneer of civilisation. Then it started: closed, thick, glorious forest. It wasn't virgin forest – at least not immediately adjacent to the track – but in the distance we could see pristine forest and enormous giants spiralling into the sky. Our white-throated toucans were bombing across the road with a flick of their bright-red tail vents. Such a lot of beak-to-bird seemed sure to make them bomb head-first to the ground. In fact their beaks have a honeycomb structure, allowing them to cruise easily around the tree-tops and crunch fruits, invertebrates and birds' eggs.

Day nine was our rest day. We found a small, brown stream and sited the net in its scrubby banks. Thick forest lay downstream and a wooden bridge upstream. It was a lovely, simple day spent ambling around camp and into the forest, watching for wildlife as we darned the mosquito net and the great, gaping holes in our trainers, washing and laying out our clothes to dry, spending hours pumping water ready for the following day's run and filling in missed diary entries. We kept a fire stoked most of the day, collecting wood and cooking vats of lentils and beans to provide for that day and the next.

Tending the fire was hot work, a job I hated, but at least we had the magical stream to cool us down. We would dunk our heads in it or hang on to a branch, allowing its soothing water to ripple over our bodies. As I lay back, I could feel the water trickling around my ears and I watched a flock of red-bellied madeira parakeets preening and screeching in their favourite tree on its bank. And if I stayed really still, an Amazon kingfisher would occasionally dart over the surface of the river and I would will it to perch on my head, but it never did. Instead, the nibbling fish paid me attention, far too much, nipping at my elbows and toes, until I had to retreat out of the river into the shade.

I discovered the four-toed prints of a tapir etched in leafy clay. We were sure we had heard them nosing through the forest during the night, and had found fresh spore close to our tent. Never far from our thoughts when we found signs of tapir was its predators, jaguars and pumas. We would have loved to see them, and knew an attack was unlikely; but still, we kept the bottle of pepper spray and the machete close at hand at night, just in case. From the disturbances we heard in the night, and the reports of people who had travelled the road, it was clear that even if we didn't see jaguars, they sure as hell saw us!

As ever, we were far more pre-occupied with the smaller beasties of the rainforest. A jet-black spider with blood-red abdomen spots carefully created her silken orb in the shrub propping up our tarp. Marmalade bees swarmed onto our clothes, while the microscopic black bees preferred the sweat that settled in the folds of our skin. There were also gigantic black bumble bees, like mini-helicopters, with furry boots, who ignored us completely, homing instead on nearby nectar. There were ants and termites streaming from chandelier nests and elaborate earthen gargoyles hanging in the trees. But the star of the show was what we christened, the 'lichen bug'. I would be staring at a branch and all of a sudden the small piece of crusty lichen would up-sticks and move, like the old hag who carried all her chattels upon her back in the the film 'Labyrinth'. This little fellow, more like a piece of fluff, constantly amazed us, turning our world upside down and inside out, as we were reminded that nothing is ever as it seems.

A few days later I was searching for a place to camp and was hacking a path through the forest, when I felt a prick on my nose and another on my arm. Wasps poured over me with a deafening drone as they crawled under my shirt and up my trousers intent on attack. I dropped the machete and charged out of the forest like a wounded animal, hammering down the track, madly thrashing at my face and body, desperately trying to rid myself of my assailants.

Gradually, I felt fewer and fewer stings; it appeared they had gone. I was burning and in shock, but knew I had to get back in and retrieve our machete. I pulled on all my waterproof gear until there was only a small slot for my eyes and gingerly re-traced my footsteps. The machete lay on its side. I grabbed it and hastily retreated. Perhaps with experience we would start to recognize particular tree species that specific wasp-species prefer? Or perhaps it was more to do with the structure of the forest? The only clear lesson from this debacle was 'Never, never, let go of the machete!'

In the tropics machetes are like an extension of your arm. Young, old, fit and frail use them, whether for slashing open coconuts, weeding a watermelon patch or excavating a lobster, there seems nothing beyond their reach. For us too they were essential for life: for hacking paths into prospective camp-sites, for clearing the ground for our tent, for stripping lianas to hang our clothes upon, for making kindling, cutting vegetables – and so the list went on.

On 22 July something remarkable happened – something we had begun to doubt we would ever achieve: we clocked 5,000 miles. It was just a number, but for us a massive accomplishment. We couldn't afford to lose sight of all the extra miles that lay ahead of us, nor the lurking threat of Venezuela. But now we could always say we did it; we ran 5,000 miles in a year, with five days to spare. That evening we camped at the side of a denuded gravelly area, strapping our tent into the vegetation that grew at its edge and prayed we would be left alone. It wasn't to be.

A huge, yellow moon climbed into the sky and flooded the forest with an eerie silver wash. The net tent was made for exactly this; those rare moonlit nights which might allow us views of some of those secretive forest inhabitants that we so craved to see. The tarps were off and we gazed through a narrow window at milky stars directly above us, framed by interlaced branches and leaves. It was magical. Suddenly we heard a loud crashing through the forest. A deer, a tapir, or perhaps a jaguar? The moonlight couldn't penetrate the black interior of the forest surrounding us; our only hope of seeing the animal would be if it came into the open by our camp, but as usual we were left guessing. After that, I couldn't sleep. My ears and eyes searched for meanings from the crispy leaves falling, the water dripping, the paws or hoofs moving through leaf-litter, the unexplained sounds. Daytime rationale slipped away, as I entered a reeling, waking dream-state haunted by jaguars.

We ran a split shift the next day, stopping to bathe in a river. It was roughly the size of the Thames in London, but in this continent of giants it was miniscule. Someone clearly spent time there, as a fireplace had been roughly created in a shelter, and so we set a pan of lentils to cook for lunch. That was when we heard a squeaking sound in the palm roof above us. We dismissed it at first, imagining it to be a bird or perhaps a rat. But soon the squeaks turned into high-pitched shrieks accompanied by a vigorous thrashing. We jumped up to inspect the source of the commotion.

Two glassy, unblinking eyes stared at us. We froze. They belonged to a large yellow- and black snake which lay barely a metre away from our noses. Its jaw was agape with a wriggling grey mouse. Quick as a flash it whipped its tail and retreated deeper into the palm roof. But we could still see it working on the unfortunate mouse, dislocating its jaw to ease its passage downwards, until all that was left was a small, brown tail lolling limply from the snake's mouth.

The snake was all too aware of our presence, tasting our scent with its black tongue and aggressively lunging towards us. Then suddenly it leapt forward onto the centre supporting pole of the hut, and rapidly coiled over two metres of body down it, before it hurled itself into the undergrowth, smashing through the foliage, practically flying through the air to be rid of us. It was a riveting but terrifying experience, which left us shaking, with our hearts drumming in our ears. The snake was so very close to us, and so long. Watching the mouse undulate through its body, intact, was amazing.

We would learn that it was a tiger rat-snake (*caninana* in Portuguese and *mica* in Spanish) and that specimens as long as four metres have been recorded. Apparently its vision is exceptional, and the weaving motion we saw was probably it triangulating its distance from us, as it does with its prey. Its aggressive behaviour was probably explained by its need to appear dangerous, so that we would back away, as it is non-venomous.

We washed in the river with rafts of butterflies who were sipping the damp earth and smothering our drying clothes, until it seemed that our T-shirts and shorts would take off into the air carried by a hundred fluttering wings.

> They're astonishingly beautiful and seem to like my rotting odour! (David wrote) Their colours, shapes and sizes: the wings marked with *ochenta-ocho* (88), the big blue that drifts nonchalantly through the dense forest, the clouds of yellows and purples that are stirred as we run. They balance on my ear, nose, or forehead, licking beads of sweat with their long, recoiled tongues. I'm always happy to have them about, their flash of colour and their confidence, the feeling of flapping wings as they pass close by or land upon me. It's different at home; they're so much more flighty, unlike here where I can lightly coax them onto my finger.

We ran beside a long line of yellow butterflies flitting north; the next day they would probably be travelling south. David wanted to pee '5,000' on the road and let them settle, but he was too dehydrated! A reminder of man came from the sky when we heard three jets. We had been wondering whether there was a no-fly zone over the Amazon, to respect indigenous zones. Perhaps there was over some of the most remote areas of the forest, where some of the last untouched human beings on earth still reside? We hoped so.

Ranks of spiralling vegetation were on the march, within places, barely a path marking the gash of the former road. The forest was gradually, imperceptibly, healing its scar. This filled me with bubbling rushes of joy. I love plant-succession; that with a tiny toe-hold nature can once again burst into life. And as if to salute this magical fecundity, the following day we awoke to a riot of blue-and-yellow macaws twisting and circling in the sky above us. They accompanied us for over half-an-hour, craning their necks, screeching to one another, then flapping away, only to loop around again and dive over our heads. Occasionally they would settle in the tops of trees in front of us, but as soon as we were near, they would free-fall out, squealing with delight, to chase us down the road.

That evening we followed a rough path deep into the forest, hacking back the vegetation that would have soon disguised it forever. We passed a little tea-coloured lagoon, which led us to a gap in the canopy where three mature trees had been felled and light was streaming down to the forest floor. Young saplings and climbers were already bursting up, eager to win the battle to be the next kings of the canopy. Large chunks of timber had been left on the ground. Why? Perhaps it was only worth transporting the best heart-wood to the market hundreds of miles away? Or perhaps the illegal fellers had been disturbed and left in a hurry with only part of their booty?

One of the lianas we had cut to allow us through was leaking a milky latex liquid. When we returned with another haul of equipment, we found a horned black ant stuck in the glue. We were amazed that this little Trojan had succumbed to the plant-sap. It reminded me that plants were the real killers of the rainforest: that in their war to survive against an army of creatures intent on milling and digesting them, they had developed an arsenal of some of the most deadly chemicals on earth. Which is why scientists are rushing to understand the Amazon's mind-bogglingly diverse chemical laboratory, and to record the remedies used by rainforest people, in a bid to discover the countless unknown medical cures waiting in the shadows of this mighty forest.

After days of seclusion we ran back into the world of humans. For about 500 metres an incongruous stretch of dual carriageway had been built high above the floodplain, like an aeroplane strip dropped from the sky. We ran down the middle of the warped tarmac like two fleas on an elephant. But at its end lay the village Igapo Açu, where civilisation was said to start. We had no idea how the people would view us emerging from the forest, so we tucked the pepper spray into the trailer handles just in case. Eyes peered from windows and people stared from the roadside, but all was peaceful and the pepper spray remained unsheathed.

We found a corrugated-iron shelter to sleep under. It was exciting to consider that Manaus was within our grasp, but sad to think that we were reaching the end of the wilderness. Odd shacks littered the roadside; the latest arrivals of squatters were hacking open the forest and setting it ablaze in their march to claim the land. We were amazed that land-grabs were still accepted, or at least that a blind eye was still turned to them. Once the squatters had colonised, they demanded a road and electricity, which suited the federal politicians and the government, who overwhelmingly sought to 'civilise' the Amazon and excavate its resources.

Each of the settlers had a gun. They padded down the road at dawn and dusk, so that for the first time in weeks we didn't see a monkey. But it wasn't just guns that were killing the monkeys; each new incursion into the forest meant that more habitat was lost. It began with the hacking down of a 100- metre strip, then two kilometres, then ten kilometres, in 'death by road'. It was like leaving the mice in charge of the cheese store.

We met the road-builders the following morning. Thick, red clay was being shipped, dumped and smeared all over a new mega-causeway by colossal machines and a massive workforce, thus answering any doubt about the government's determination to progress, despite having read that all works on the road should have been suspended until a proper environmental assessment had been carried out.

When the mighty thunder clouds that had been gathering above our heads exploded, tropical rain saturated us within minutes. The hard, red clay turned into a skating rink of thick, oozing mud, so that we slid one step sideways for every two steps forward. The final four days saw the landscape becoming ever more waterlogged as we ran towards the *várzea*, the seasonally-inundated areas of the white-water Amazon tributaries. But this isn't flooding as we know it; this is whole-scale transformation of the forest, as the rivers rise to meet the tree canopy. For up to five months of the year entire animal communities migrate to the upper-storeys of the forest: frugivorous fish pluck fruits from the tops of trees, pink-river dolphins and Amazonian manatees thread through branches, and trees shed their cargo of seeds to float on the eddying waters, to colonise new areas.

It's an astonishing phenomenon to which man, also, has adapted. Houses are constructed on stilts or cast floating upon the river. Little moats surrounded a mosaic of ponds being excavated for the new Amazon export, *tambaqui*, a meaty river fish. An old man, sitting high up on a balcony on stilts, explained that *tambaqui* was his hope for the future, as his foxy little dog yapped at my feet. He said he fed his fish a combination of soya and fish bone-meal, and they were thriving. And therein lay the dilemma; fantastic to be farming local fish, but intensive aquaculture demands protein, which means soya (equals deforestation) and fish meal (equals overfishing).

Río Geigo was the final river we had to cross before we met the monster of all rivers, the one I had so long dreamed of seeing, the Amazon. But as we gazed out across an enormous expanse of water, we found ourselves transfixed even by this unknown tributary. An entire town had grown upon it. Three-storey wooden houses, topped by corrugated-iron sheets, were connected by a latticework of planked walkways raised on hardwood pillars. Other streets of the neighbourhood were tethered on wooden rafts, imperceptibly rising and falling with the river. Animal arks floated near the houses, filled with pigs and chickens. A girl sat on the steps to her house with coffee-tinted water lapping around her knees as she -brushed her teeth, spitting into the giant sink beneath her. A yellow former school bus floated past a medley of other boats, some large, roofed and chugging, others dug-out tree trunks, their owners gently paddling.

Southern screamers, flocks of parrots and *hoatzins* called as we ran our last few miles to the Amazon River. We were on a high: we had barely slept, but adrenalin was charging our bodies. A green iguana leapt from a roadside tree, and two teenagers darted into their house. Once we had passed, I looked behind; both the girls had reappeared and were staring at us with their parents. We often got this reaction; I suppose we must have looked very odd, even scary? Come to think of it, we hadn't met a *gringo* since leaving northern Argentina, so we really were obscure, let alone being latched onto an orange rickshaw.

We sprinted past a long line of vehicles queuing to board one of the Manaus ferries. The ferry, more of a floating pontoon with two engines, had capacity for 30 vehicles plus foot passengers. Once on board I found a concrete block to perch on, and gazed out at the grey river that stretched into the distance with no end. After several false starts, the ferry slipped away from the bank, with its clamouring shacks and shops, and we were unleashed onto this mighty inland sea, the River Amazon.

An inviolable line marked the confluence of the white River Amazon and the black Rio Negro. For miles they refuse to mix, their different temperatures and velocities barring any marriage. As we neared Manaus, we jostled for space with colossal tankers, cargo-ships, houseboats and ferries, all impatient to reach the city or continue beyond to the Atlantic Ocean. For us it was a moment of mixed emotions: of delight to be nearing another milestone that we hadn't dared to dream possible, but also of deep depression at leaving behind our three-week foray along the *Rua do Onces*, one of the wildest and most wonderful legs of the run.

A crested oropendola
collapsed at its knees
in its elaborate popping
salute to the world

19 Running into a Road-Block

Crested Oropendola
Psarocolius decumanus

'Where are the trees?' I remember thinking as we scooted along the inner motorways of Manaus, the jungle city, with traffic barrelling past our sides. Trees hadn't always been prominent in the cities we had run through, but their absence did seem particularly ironic here, in what was once the heart of the biggest rainforest on earth. Indeed, when chatting to two professors, Mario and Rita, after presenting at the University of Manaus, we discovered that many of the city's children had no idea what rainforest was. Rita had been working on an initiative to increase awareness in the natural world among school children, and had taken 300 pupils to the botanical gardens. When she asked whether any of them had seen rainforest before, they all shook their heads, apart from two who explained they'd seen it on Animal Planet!

For us, Manaus was filled with the usual city anguish, but this time there was something else – something that was really unsettling us, something that had the potential to cut short our entire expedition. It lay ahead of us in the form of the Waimiri-Atroari Reserve, a block of indigenous people's land which severed our only route out of Brazil. Vehicles were allowed to pass through the reserve in daylight hours, but no one was allowed through on foot, or by bicycle. And the reason? During the 1970s the government had steam-rollered the *Ruta* 174 through the Indians' homelands without their consent. Next it had built the Balbina hydro-electric dam, which flooded and putrefied a vast area of the Indians' territory. It then sanctioned mining companies to prospect in their forest, cancelling reserve status where necessary.

The State army had been sent in. Guns and heavy vehicles rolled into battle to squash the protests. The tribes were reputed to be among the most belligerent of indigenous people, but their superior knowledge of the forest and poison-dipped arrows had no chance in this modern Armageddon. Over 2,000 indigenous people are thought to have been slaughtered, but no one is exactly sure, as the government successfully eradicated any evidence of its onslaught. Even after the heavy vehicles and gun-shots had faded, blood continued to flow in the forest. Gold miners claimed their prize, killing anyone who got in their way and poisoning rivers and land. The road also provided access for diseases like the common flu and cold. The Indians had never been exposed to them, and entire communities succumbed. By the early 1980s the population had declined from its original 3,000 to a couple of hundred. A few survivors still live in the forest. Some have fled, deeper into its realm, eschewing any further contact with the outside world. Others wear Western clothes and embrace modern culture.

When you look at a satellite image of the reserve, it's clear why the Indians needed to fight the road; either side of their gates, the forest has gone and a herring-bone of roads dissects a matrix of fields dotted with charred tree stumps and grazing cattle. Only through their determination and hostility have they managed to keep squatters away from their forest.

We were on the Indians' side, but it wasn't going to be easy convincing them of that. In their eyes we were just like any other outsider. I suppose they were right. Although our motives were sincere, and our determination to help protect their forests indisputable, we carried the illnesses that had killed their families. We had already consumed more in our lives than they could ever imagine. Our ecological footprint on this planet would have metaphorically squashed their entire population. Perhaps most pressing of all was the fact that we couldn't begin to tell them what we were doing, because we couldn't speak their language. On top of this, the mention of our predicament to Brazilians was inevitably followed by an audible sucking inwards of the lips. 'On foot? No one passes the Waimiri-Atroari Reserve on foot!' they squeaked. 'These people are not like you or I. They're savages! They fire bows and arrows at passing motorists. If you dare dally, they'll have you.'

The official process was to apply for special dispensation from FUNAI, the government agency heading indigenous affairs, to pass through the reserve. We thought it unlikely that they would let us camp in the reserve, but hoped we might obtain a permit that would allow us to run during the day, and catch a bus to and from the reserve in the morning and evening. David tracked down relevant bus companies, but no one would give us a concrete agreement. Then there was the problem of the notorious protracted waits that accompanied an application, without any guarantee that permission would be granted. We were running out of time; also, going down the legitimate route would place us firmly on the FUNAI radar, which would prevent other more creative solutions such as ignoring all the protocol, running through the indigenous village and road-block and hiding in the forest each night (which we did most nights anyway).

Our only other hope was Mario and Rita: they knew a man who lived in Presidente Figueiredo and had brought up his children in the Indian reserve. Could he offer us the Holy Grail in the form of a personal introduction to the

Indians? We clutched onto this glimmer of hope, and Rita scribbled a map showing the route to his house, hoping we could run to the edge of the reserve and persuade the Indians to let us through.

David found a basic alcohol stove which would serve as our back-up cooker and an alternative to lighting a fire when we didn't want to expose ourselves. We charged out of Manaus on an adrenalin buzz, as buses and lorries roared past our trailer wheels. We summited and plunged down the surprisingly-steep and undulating terrain of this section of the Amazon, narrowly missing becoming one of our road-kill statistics, as two juggernauts' tyres screeched within centimetres of our ears.

As the sunset fired the sky we stumbled into an abandoned shed. Ten minutes later we realised that it belonged to a shocked night-watchman, Roberto, who discovered two Brits, one of whom (me) had luckily just finished her strip-wash, but the other (David) was completely starkers. David's nudity didn't faze him and the following morning he plied us with coffee and offered us to stay.

We had organised to stop off in Campo 41, an enormous biodiversity experiment, just north of Manaus. Its aim is to identify a minimum size of tropical forest habitat that can maintain the animal and plant diversity of an intact forest. The Camp's manager, a charming, badgery-looking Brazilian, explained how the project started. 'Cattle ranchers were opening up thousands of hectares of primary lowland rainforest for grazing.' He told us. 'Brazilian forest law stipulated that 50 per cent (now 80 per cent) of primary forest should be maintained within the ranches. We worked with the ranchers to ensure that the patches of forest they were obliged to keep could provide the focus of our studies. A series of one, ten, 100 and 1,000-hectare rainforest plots were demarcated and preserved within the pasture, allowing comparison of plants and animals between the plots, as well as comparisons with the standing pristine rainforest within our study areas.'

Over the decades, an army of scientists have been listening, measuring and recording the extraordinary lives of the inhabitants of the plots and their lucky neighbours in the continuous pristine forest. From leaf-cutter and army ants to tree-frogs, social spiders, capuchin monkeys and towering trees related to peas, very little has remained uncovered. Our plan was to spend two days camping in the untouched forest, borrow some ecology books about what the experiments were proving, and explore the glorious intact forest.

One of the Campo workers, Aleixo, grabbed us from the side of the road, and we took a quick GPS position so that we could resume running from the exact spot. Then we sat in his pick-up and watched the world stream past. It felt altogether wrong! We swung off the main road into a wall of forest. Nothing marked it out as different from the hundreds of miles of former forest, but between wads of indecipherable Portuguese we gathered from Aleixo that eminent characters had trodden the paths we were about to follow, including: Bill Clinton, Al Gore and Tom Cruise. We swerved around giant pot-holes and fallen trees and our driver nonchalantly remarked that the last time he was here he had seen a jaguar saunter across the track.

He deposited us at the end of the mud track and we chucked our bags onto two wheelbarrows, hid the trailer (from what I'm not sure) and picked our way down a narrow path. We ducked under branches, negotiating leaf-cutter ant motorways and picked off thick strands of sticky spider web, praying their super-sized builders were not perched on our heads. Aleixo made a cursory check of the camp, showed us the composting loo and the gas stove and hurried off. We were completely alone.

I couldn't sleep. A stream of sweat ran down my chest. My diary absorbed the moisture and soon my pen gave up. Distant rumbles of thunder triggered an Amazonian orchestra, with crickets, cicadas and grasshoppers whining in anticipation. The forest was at fever pitch. A pair of white-throated toucans yelped from their lofty perches and three screaming *piha* birds joined the crescendo with their lilting calls from hidden perches in the green latticework. For me the calls of these two species would forever be synonymous with the Amazon, conjuring it up in my head, so that even the most sordid concrete environment would melt away. In its place my mind's eye would watch aerial roots spiral down from lofty canopies; seedlings burst into leaf as they belted skywards for a chink in the forest's leafy armour; a lattice-work of fungi spreading its fingers into the fine leaf-litter; jaguars passing under the fading sun; macaw parties screeching on high and inky-green algae sprouting from the hanging sloth's coat.

I willed the rain to arrive and relieve the tropical fug that filled my head with soggy cotton wool. It wasn't only the humidity that was preventing me from sleeping: the camp manager's words kept repeating in my head. He had told us about a team of researchers who had camped where we were now. Each night they would go out to survey bats. One night, at about two in the morning, they were shuffling back to camp in a long crocodile formation when they heard a blood-curdling scream. They looked back to see two yellow eyes glinting in their torch beams and an enormous cat sprawled over the last man.

Everyone shouted and flapped their arms as they charged towards the jaguar. The cat snarled and leapt into the forest, disappearing within seconds. Miraculously the researcher suffered only superficial wounds. I had always been adamant we would never be attacked, but had been thrown off guard by this story. In all probability the cat had been old or injured, as these are the animals most likely to attack people, because they can't hunt their normal prey. Whatever the reason for the rare attack, the question remained: was the jaguar still at large? If so, we were right in the middle of its hunting territory.

Behind the camp we found a little stream. A section had been widened into a pool, with wooden panels forming its sides. Crystal water chattered into and over it. We lay back into a thick mud of plant detritus that formed a silky, black blanket and billowed up into the water like a volcano plume. Frying-pan-sized leaves drifted down into our pool. Enormous dragonflies darted over our heads. A butterfly wafted past: it was huge, another incredible azure-blue morpho species.

We gazed into the forest canopy, pricked by sunlight, some 35 metres above. I imagined two glinting eyes inspecting us; those of one of the largest birds-of-prey on earth, the mighty harpy eagle, which can weigh up to nine kilogrammes, and snacks on monkeys for breakfast. This amazing bird included our camp in its enormous home range. Feeling immensely privileged, I allowed the cool water to trickle into my ears, as I visualised a harpy eagle snatching a sloth out of the trees above our heads.

During that brief but sumptuous break we learnt a little more about rainforests. Considering that they provide a home to half of the world's species, on less than seven per cent of the planet's surface, it's not surprising that the answers that Campo 41 were extracting from their experiments were often as complex and surprising as the ecosystem itself. Among other discoveries they found that the ever-peripatetic army ants disappear from fragmented forests, as the trees do not provide them with sufficient food; that when the ants fail, so do all their right-hand men, such as the insectivorous birds, which are deprived of their fallen prey; that when peccaries abandon a forest fragment for lack of territory, their wallows dry up, and with them go the unique species of frogs who crooned to their mates and spawned the next generation in the pigs' muddy holes.

These extraordinary and unforeseen links reminded me how easy it is for us humans to over-simplify and underestimate the natural world and the immense repercussions of our own actions. The secondary-school concept of food-chains and food-webs should rekindle the idea that all living things (including ourselves), in whatever ecosystems we live, are connected, often in the most unlikely relationships.

Back on the road, the rains had arrived. It felt invigorating to pound through lashing storms soaked to the bones. But as soon as we stopped we would freeze in our saturated clothes, despite the tropical heat, as we had few fat reserves. The storms were not soft and gentle, but sudden and brutal, usually starting with a rumble of thunder, a blast of cold air scented with burning electricity and then forks of lightning speared into the sky, and thrashing rain drummed down.

Our first job on reaching Presidente Figueiredo was to track down Ben, Rita's potential key to the reserve. Our meeting didn't go well, with neither of us understanding much of what the other said. He eventually seemed to recognize the nature conservation commitment of our run, but doubted the Indians would be sympathetic due to the atrocities that non-native people had committed upon them. The only glimmer of hope was if the Indians thought we were researchers and would allow us to pass by day. In which case, there was a disused energy-compound at 31 miles and a petrol station at 50 miles, which we could camp in when the road was closed.

We felt hugely apprehensive about our chances. If nobody attempted to stop us running through the road block, we would have to decide whether to go or not and if so how much gear to carry. Was it worth the trouble? Would our smiles carry us through? Would the Indians talk or fire first? How many people would see us anyway? Our lack of Portuguese was denying us the level of detail which could ultimately endanger our lives. After six in the evening, Federal Law did not apply to the reserve: the Indians could attack without committing a crime. It would be alarming to hide at night knowing we were targets.

In addition to these worries was the problem of our replacement shoes. David logged onto postal tracking and followed the shoes' movements. A prompt flashed up the galling news that our parcel had been returned to the UK *again*. We had darned patches in both of our pairs of shoes, but David's soles had enormous holes that were letting in water and grit. We were becoming desperate. Our only chance now was to have the shoes shipped to Venezuela, 550 miles away.

A small, lop-sided sign speared the verge: Waimiri-Atroari Indian Reserve. We had reached our nemesis-point. On our left lay a lagoon fringed by a thick belt of rushes. A car sat up to its waist in water, its hazard-lights flashing. Was it the Indians' latest victim? We were still disagreeing about what to do. We had endlessly discussed possible options, but none of them were very appealing. A metal chain blocked the road. The large, indigenous village we had pictured comprised two small thatched houses. There were no families, no crops, no dogs – just three short chaps in bright-yellow T-shirts sitting on the kerb. They didn't appear concerned about our presence, in fact I don't think they'd actually noticed us. We eye-balled one another, assessing whether we had the audacity to sprint past. But I couldn't do it: there was no way they wouldn't spot us, and it wasn't worth being hunted down by them and their families in the forest. We resolved to try reasoning with them.

We told them about our expedition. We showed them a map of the continent with our route. They giggled. We said we cared deeply for the natural world and that we wanted to run through the forest so we could share their story. They looked more serious. We weren't sure if it was due to our stumbling Portuguese, or the prospect of us in their reserve. Either way, they resoundingly chorused, 'No' – 'Não' in Portuguese.

We sat and waited. We told them about Ben, how he had lived in their community with his children. A flicker of recognition flittered across their faces. They nodded. We brought out the map with the two buildings he had highlighted for us to sleep in, explaining that we would stay on the road and that they would know exactly where we were. We committed ourselves to running through the forest in just three days. A long, extended finger of disapproval waggled in our face. 'What about if we run during the day and catch a bus out of the reserve before dark?' David asked. They waggled their fingers. 'How about one of you guys run with us?' I asked. They shook their heads, but at least wry smiles spread across their faces. 'Has anyone been allowed into the reserve on foot before?' asked David. 'Não, Não, Não! Everyone must apply to FUNAI for a licence to cross our reserve.' The older man was becoming irritated. I flinched.

We had hit a brick wall. One of the guys started a pick-up: they wanted us out of the reserve before dark. They chucked the trailer into in the back, drove us through the reserve and deposited us at the other end of it. We ran on in fading light with a group of boys on bicycles who pointed in the distance to where a hostel lurked. The landlady said we could stay and that she would find something for us to eat, after which her dog bit David's ankle.

We spent that night bent over the map, devising a new plan. We couldn't allow the reserve to scupper our whole bid. The only option was to run the mileage somewhere else. We looked at side-routes that led off the road ahead. Then our eyes fell on Rorainópolis, a small town just north of the reserve. This looked the best option. We could find somewhere to stay, and run every day from the town until we had made up the lost 67 miles.

We would be on terrain similar to the reserve road, and the weather and road surface would all be the same, so the alternative route wouldn't be advantageous in any way. We wouldn't need to pull the trailer, as we would be back at the hostel each day. We would run the same stretch of road every day, becoming acquainted with its nuances – where to up the pace, where the hills were, when to beat back the time. It would be like running the home patch. It was exciting, it offered a change of life as we knew it.

Before we embarked on this new phase of the expedition, we had to cross something monumental, something that had taken us 5,447 miles to reach. On day 390 we crossed the Equator. The monument that marked the imaginary line was not great, but our elation was. This was a line, a transition, a border, like no other. It couldn't be moved or merged or engulfed by changing geopolitical conditions: it was set in stone, an invisible concept that meant we were exactly half-way across the world and had run most of that chunk of the planet, and had crossed into our own hemisphere.

Instead of waking up and packing everything onto the trailer to run into the unknown, we left everything in our room in Rorainópolis and set off with the sun rising on our left shoulder over a road we had already run. It was David's turn to start with the GPS watch. We weren't going to stop the protocol just because we didn't have the trailer. It was ingrained in our psychology now. We would just swap the watch and rucksack every five miles instead.

We were both on top of the world. It was amazing to feel the freedom of running without the trailer's long bamboo arms at our hips, and its weight dragging us back. We were also relieved to be covering the missing miles. I felt light and springy. The first five miles disappeared without either of us noticing them; but by the 18th mile I was starting to feel heavy and tired. We needed to run only five more miles, but it seemed impossible. Sweat was pouring off me, my feet felt jarred, my knees hot and sore. I had chosen to wear my barefoot shoes. I figured that I had run nearly half the expedition in them, so a 23-mile run would be child's play. I was wrong. Each time my foot landed on the tarmac it was painful. My chin was heading for the floor. I ran curled up, my feet like claws. No wonder it hurt so much; I had discarded everything I had learnt and practised about running barefoot in all the expedition months.

When we finally hit the 23-mile mark on the edge of town, I collapsed into tears, annoyed and frustrated with myself. After over 5,400 miles, how could this have happened? The truth is, it had never been easy. Usually discomfort had arrived between miles 15 and 20, with the next miles demanding every ounce of determination I could muster. What's more, it was clear that, trailer or no trailer, the kind of mileages we we'd been demanding from our bodies would never be a walk in the park.

On the last day of the reserve catch-up miles, for some reason I felt fantastic. Some days it was like that, whether down to a good night's sleep, to the fact that my muscles had recovered well from the run the day before, or that we had cracked our food requirements so that our engines were purring. We weren't scientific in our diet: we couldn't have been, without an army of people sourcing food and carrying it for us in a support vehicle. But we did follow certain ideas, such as eating protein within 30 minutes of a run, which is thought to aid muscle-growth and repair. We also nailed vitamins and minerals, to counter periods on scarcity in the run, and Glucosamine, which is thought to support the structure and function of joints. We also used Ibuprofen and Diclofenac intensively when we had any specific pains.

Orange-winged parrots were gurgling in the tree-tops around us. Their chortles had accompanied us every day. We decided to run down one of the gravel tracks that forked from the main road. We had taken one on the left yesterday and enjoyed the change of landscape, especially as there was woodland and an *agouti*. This time we struck off up a hill to the right through grassland with scattered trees and wooden bungalows.

Something swooped at David´s head: a parrot. A gorgeous, vivid-green mealy parrot. It looked down at us from a branch, craning its neck, chortling contentedly. We chatted back to it, watching it as we ran. Then something remarkable happened; it followed us! As we ran it would fly forward over our heads and then suddenly dive-bomb David before flapping off to a perch. And so it continued, until I stopped to tie my shoe-lace. While I was leaning over, I suddenly felt a light weight on my back: it had landed on me!

I was in heaven. Gradually I stood up, and as I did so it walked up my back to my shoulder. For someone who loves wildlife, for someone who loves birds –

well, this was just too much: one of the best moments of my life! We walked on, an unusual trio, me with an apparently-contented parrot gently nibbling my ear – which, considering it uses its formidable beak for cracking palm-nuts, was very trustworthy (or plain idiotic) on my part. I tried preening its back, but it squealed. That was clearly too forward a move at this delicate stage in our relationship. Then I slipped in a puddle, and it was gone, flapping high into a tree. We called for it as we ran on, but it didn't follow. David was sure it would still be there when we returned, but no,

Running with wild parrots, parakeets and macaws, was one of the most breath-taking features of our expedition. The birds pulled us out of lows and evaporated disputes. We grew to know the different species and their behaviour; watched their raucous flocks tumbling on high, couples preening one another, feeding their young, excavating nest holes. For far too brief a time while running through their world we had a privileged window into their lives.

It took us eight days to reach Boa Vista. The temperature ranged from 28 to 34 degrees Celsius. The highest temperature fell on the day we ran 31 miles. But despite the tormenting rays of the sun, we felt charged, galloping through the miles in a haze of euphoria. The only dent on the proceedings was when I tripped on a cat's eye. I flung out my hands and grated along the tarmac. Blood gushed down my knees and curdled on my wrists. I bit back the tears. Luckily my wounds weren't too grave, and we were only a couple of hundred metres from a hostel, so that we could clean out the grit and bandage me up, ready for the next day's run.

A fuzzy lump pierced the horizon on the road into town. The country was open savanna plateau. As we ran closer we recognized the mangle of hair and flesh as a female giant anteater. We knew she was a female because we could see her teats tipped with milk. Her claws were enormous, bear-like. Her long, pink, sticky tongue lolled from her beak-shaped snout, and her sooty tail, once a great animated brush, was now flat and smeared with black blood and grit. It was painfully sad; we gave up hope of seeing an anteater alive.

Traffic clotted the road. We aimed for the centre of the city, without any more of a plan than that we needed a room to sleep in and internet close by. A guy in our hostel wouldn't stop berating the Indians. Like so many people we had encountered on the road, he was annoyed that they should be treated differently and that their forest couldn't be 'put to use'. 'Brazilians detest them because they stop progress,' he said. 'They might create laws in their reserves, but when they're attracted to the bright lights of the city, there's no law that will protect them. They're vermin to the police; they'll knock them down and then they'll train on them, punching any ideas of grandeur out of them. They're treated like second class citizens, because that's what they are.'

Just before we left the city, a most peculiar sight presented itself; a man crossed the road pulling a dead dog behind him on a lead.

We ran north, under a dark, wet cloud which appeared to be moving at our pace. Our shorts stuck to our thighs and rain-water streamed down our faces, collecting in our sodden T-shirts. We were moving through a big grassy plain. We were still within the Amazon basin and would not leave it until Venezuela, but the area we were charging through is believed to be natural savanna rather than rainforest. The only accents in the landscape were an occasional dark boulder and swamps punctured with palm trees. My eyes swept from side to side. I wasn't paying attention to the landscape, nor thinking, just allowing my mind to wander, when something distracted me. It looked like a boulder, but I was convinced it had moved. I wiped my eyes and refocused; there was no doubt, it had changed position. I grabbed the binoculars, honed in on the rock, which morphed instantaneously into, Oh my God, a giant anteater! I was ecstatic. I yelped and jumped in the air. I couldn't help myself. He looked up. He must have heard my scream. I felt so foolish, I had ruined our chance of observing him. He bounded awkwardly over the tussocky mounds on his long, curled front claws and then stopped. Something had caught his interest. A termite mound. That was our chance.

We abandoned the trailer and slipped down into the marsh. We landed with a splash, as our legs sunk up to our knees. We waded onwards, aiming for the tussocks, oh so quietly, stopping when he looked up and then dashing forward as soon as he continued his excavations. We were down wind of him. He hadn't detected our scent. He was within 15 metres of us. We couldn't push our luck any further and so we selected the largest tussock within a three-metre radius and hopped onto it. At which point a snake shot out from under David's foot. 'What the hell are we doing here?' he hissed. Wading through a swamp in Brazil wasn't the wisest of moves – but then the odd risk had never stopped us before. Anyway, we were far too deep into it now. We stood, barely breathing, David with the camera balanced on my head and his cap above that to shield it from the rain, me with the binoculars fixed to my nose, both of us soggy but buzzing. He was extraordinary, amazing – beyond superlatives.

He appeared totally oblivious to us and the road; no wonder so many are killed. He pushed his nose into a termite mound, then moved on to another. He had tiny, beady eyes, and he was coming our way. A strong, musty fragrance wafted around him. Of course! We recognized his pungent odour now, as the smell that had imbued a recent barn we had slept in. We had smelt it on the road, too. We wouldn't forget it. He was a couple of metres from us now, but thanks to his poor sight and him being up-wind, he still hadn't noticed us.

Stories of people being attacked by anteaters rushed through my mind, but the chance of this happening is probably 0.00003%, and only if the poor animal is backed into a corner and has no way out. His enormous nose pointed in our direction and quivered for a second. He must have finally scented us. But there was no dash: he just ambled off and addressed himself to another anthill a little further away.

The encounter put us on a high. Barn-swallows darted over the long grasses and scattered boulders, looping effortlessly above our heads, before swooping within inches of the ground as they gathered flies in an intricate ballet. A small wooden house was set back from the roadside. We needed water, so I unharnessed and went to enquire. At least seven or eight people were laughing, preparing food and suckling babies. Troubled chocolate eyes looked back at me as I spoke. The matriarch didn't understand me. I dread to think what she thought I had said. I plumped for simplicity, choosing one word, 'Agua?' (water) A light flashed in her head and her sullen black face cracked into a beaming smile. 'Of course!' She cried with a wobble of her many chins. 'Bring the ice and water!' She instructed one of her daughters. 'Come and eat with us too!'

I hesitated. We needed to mission the mileage before it became outrageously hot. It had been in the mid-30s for days now. She took my silence as a sign that I couldn't understand her, and so began an elaborate mouthing manoeuvre, smacking her fat lips. I dashed back to David and persuaded him to eat with them. A great cauldron of rice, *feijon* and pieces of white fish steamed on a gas stove. 'Now let's see, how many of us are there?' She started counting. She reached up to ten on her fingers. Then cast about, looked down at her bare feet and began counting her toes. At which point she burst into peals of laughter. It was infectious. Soon everyone was cackling and so she started counting again amid uproarious squeals and guffaws. The children were very excited by it all. One little girl wouldn't leave my side, gazing up into my eyes. 'I have six children,' the mother said, slapping her thigh. 'I had them all by the time I was 35!'

'I'm 35 and I haven't even had one!' I said. At which point everyone dissolved into laughter again.

We ran off with ice and water strapped to the trailer and celebrated how warm people had been to us. Further down the road, someone would give us 20 *reais,* and someone else would pay for our drinks and food in a café without even telling us. People were constantly looking after us, inviting us to their homes and feeding us. Would we receive the same treatment in our own country?

We lay in our hammocks on the ground amid the musty, lemony smell of anteater – for we had seen another one snuffling through head-high grass. I penned thoughts, unable to believe our luck. Thunder and lightning clattered around us. Half a moon hung in the sky. Sweat rolled off my chin and down my neck. I was craving crisps and chips. I suppose it was the salt. We must have been losing pounds with all the sweating, which was also attacking my skin, as was the constant humidity. I couldn't stop itching the rashes and welts. Bites behind my knees were swollen and infected, and I had developed athlete's foot – at which point in my recollections I swallowed a small cockroach. They were crawling over everything in the thick leaf-litter, and a family had clearly moved into my hammock. Apart from the cockroaches, the camp was magical. We stripped and washed in the river on the other side of the road. It was so cold, I sank into a deep pool, letting the water trickle over my shoulders. Fireflies flickered above my unzipped hammock, their amber lights flashing on and off, mingling with the stars.

We were still running through savanna, but it was becoming more undulating, with more palm-filled valleys, streams, marshes and dark rocky outcrops. David constantly milled numbers in his head, assessing our progress based on latitude and longitude, online maps, wayside signs, local people's advice and physical cues. One phenomena really preoccupied him: that of the sun and our relation to it. So when 11 September dawned and something unusual occurred – something that could never physically happen in the UK – he was over the moon:

> I have waited a long time for this day – the day the sun passed directly overhead! Every day the sun passes in an arc from east to west no matter where we are in the world, excluding the very poles. Well, we spin really, but let´s take an earth-centric view of things. So, if you live in the Northern Hemisphere, north of 22.5 degrees, the Tropic of Cancer, then that arc will always be slightly to the South of you and vice-versa for the South. If you live, or RUN, in between the Tropics, the sun will pass over your head twice a year. Today was that day, and the only time it will happen on our 6,500-mile /10.400-km run!
>
> Today, with the sun's declination (or angle from the equator) *at four degrees,* 16 minutes north, we ran right under it. I had to prove it by stopping running for a minute at midday and making myself as tall as possible, but casting no shadow. Even more fascinating it that we are both migrating at about the same speed, us running at 23 miles per day northwards and the sun tracking at 23 miles per day southwards! From now on the sun is on our back and our noses will burn less!

A day from the Venezuelan border, the terrain was getting serious as we climbed the mighty Guiana Shield. My quads and knees were screaming from the vertiginous hills we were summiting and plunging down. Scruffy houses made of mud and wood dotted the landscape. Dirty faces appeared behind doorways and popped up behind grassy banks. It reminded me of Lesotho. We stopped among a thick clot of houses and people which we took for the centre of the village. David, scenting a shop, went in search of meat. Children sped about on little bicycles around my knees, and a group of teenagers slunk over to me, guardedly asking questions.

As usual, there was nothing in the shop. And so we ran off with two chubby boys pedalling frenetically by our side. As we dropped down the escarpment, we plunged into forest. Enormous twisted trunks and knotted climbers rose up on either side. A little black-throated hermit hummingbird surveyed the canopy from an exposed branch and a crested *oropendola* collapsed at its knees in its elaborate popping salute to the world. I loved these birds, I loved the forest; its sight, its smell, everything.

The sun had long since sunk and we had to find a camp, quickly. We chose a cluster of trees in the centre of a forest garden. We could carry the trailer up off the road, through the manioc field and hang our hammocks from the boughs of trees. We picked our way round crops and began setting up camp. We hooked our tarps high over our hammocks to protect us only from a mild rain storm, as we wanted to see out. The sky was clear, but terrific explosions of light in the east were sending shock waves across it, accompanied by crashes and bangs. With the sky-show came a blast of cicadas, frogs and every insect capable of speaking within a ten-mile radius of us. The noise was deafening.

A couple of hours later we felt a gust of wind, then stronger gusts. Then we could hear it coming; a wall of rain rushing towards us. We had nowhere to escape. 'Quick,' we shouted, jumping out of our hammocks and frantically attacking the tarps, desperately undoing the knots, watching our fingers work too slowly, feeling the first drops landing with a splash on our shoulders and then the wall of water was upon us and we were engulfed. Water hammered down upon us, raged and roared in our ears, sloshed around our ankles. It was everywhere, soaking us within seconds, filling our ears, soaking our hair, rushing down our bodies like a flash flood. At last we secured the tarps millimetres above our hammocks and we swung our legs back up into our pods and lay back, soaked through, as the wind ripped at our defences and water sluiced in.

The storm had searched us out and we were in its heart. Thunder and lightning detonated above our heads. There was no way we could sleep. Then suddenly I heard a voice: someone was talking, and it wasn't David. I felt my tarp guideline twang as someone tripped over it. David yelled, 'Hola?' A voice shouted back, 'Estamos casando' (We're hunting) and moved on. It was unsettling, but their footsteps receded and I started breathing again. I realized I was freezing, saturated from putting up the tarps and now lying in the hammock with rain-water trickling in. I flicked on my torch, half unzipped my hammock and peered out. The ground below us had turned into a brown river.

Pacaraima was a grimy border town high on a hill. But it couldn't dampen our excitement at the thought of crossing into a new country, our final country and the thought of home. None of it felt real or possible, but we clutched at the sensation desperately. We were saturated and cold from running through rain at altitude most of the morning. A self-service restaurant caught our eye. We stepped into the warm and began filling up with a mountain of pork, beef, beans, spaghetti and rice. We would miss these Brazilian gastronomic extravaganzas.

David asked where he could exchange Brazilian *reais* for Venezuelan *bolivars*. He was taken out of the restaurant to a guy with fists full of notes. We had been raiding our accounts over the past couple of weeks, stashing *reais* in the trailer, because if we had exchanged currency at a Venezuelan bank, the official rate would have crippled us.

We ran on to the border, weaving our way through endless lines of Brazilian vehicles belching out acrid black fumes as they waited for their fix of petrol, which was selling at one penny for four litres. No one looked up as we crossed the police check-point. We left the trailer and stepped into a dingy, grey office where a sullen immigration officer with thin, greasy hair looked at his book, wrote something and regretfully stamped our passports. There was no computer, water or loo, just rain, young lads in army uniform fiddling with their machine guns, and scalped grassland stretching far to the horizon.

So this was Venezuela (see Map 8), world runner-up for country with the highest homicide record, the country everyone said we were mad to run through, where we would be easy targets, minced up on the side of the road, where people were being dragged off buses at gunpoint for their mobile phones, where life is cheap. I eyed everyone, every clapped-out old car or rickety bus that jerked past, expecting to be pulled off the road on my next foot-fall, for our lives to be extinguished in a heart-beat. Perhaps this time we really had gone too far?

CARIBBEAN SEA

CARÚPANO

CARIPITO

MATURÍN

R. ORINOCO

ORINOCO DELTA

CIUDAD GUAYANA

UPATA

TUMEREMO

GUASIPATI

EL CALLAO

EL DORADO

Tepui

KILOMETRO 88

LA GRAN SABANA

GUYANA

R. Lawrie

N

50   100   150
0   Kms Aprox
         50   Miles Aprox
                100

SANTA ELENA

BRAZIL

Map 8 – Running Route through Venezuela

Even without binoculars there was no disputing this bizarre bird, with what looks like the blade of an orange shovel stuck in its head

20 Venezuela: the Grand Sabana

'What are you doing?' A bicycle appeared at our side. A cheeky smile lit up the rider's face. 'Look: don't answer that now, it can wait!' He slapped David's shoulder. 'Come and have a cup of tea. You look like you need it! We live at the top of the road. Just follow your nose. We'll be waiting!' With that he was off like a crow on a line, his ragged wings flapping, his spindly legs whirring. We stood slightly stunned. It wasn't the kind of welcome we were expecting in the second-most dangerous country on the planet.

He was called Tewarhi and he was like a magnet, so we let our feet take over and followed him. He lived in a little concrete bungalow with his wife, Morelia, his five-year-old daughter, Anna Paula, and nine-year-old, Violeta. We sat on their doorstep. Plants scrambled from the cracks, and a turquoise water-pipe emerged for a couple of centimetres before tunnelling deeper under the path. Morelia brought us cups of scalding, scented tea, thick with seeds and leaves. Her coal-black curls were making a bid for freedom, grappling with the bands and grips that were unsuccessfully clamping them to her head.

They quizzed us about the expedition. Morelia was a journalist and wanted to write an article about us. It was great reliving our experiences, since for most of the time we had only shared the thoughts that rotated through our heads with one another. She took photos of our shoes, the gaping holes where the fabric we had sewn now flapped off. We mentioned the violence in Venezuela that everyone was warning us of. Their faces grew grave, wrinkles appeared as they shook their heads.

'My Mother always says that I live at the end of the world,' Morelia began. 'I guess I do. The Gran Sabana is a distinctive and distant place, I love it. We live with one foot in indigenous lands and the other foot in Brazil. But beyond our home, Venezuela is not as it should be. There are so many crimes, so many violent acts every day, we lose track of it all. We're so lucky to live here. We feel safe. We can bring up Violeta and Anna Paula without being in constant terror. But elsewhere it is very different. You must take great care when you leave the Sabana. Danger lies beyond.'

We asked them about Kilometre 88 (the first crime hot-spot we would enter), and whether they ever travelled through. 'Yes. But only when we really have to, and only in a bus. I would never travel through on foot,' warned Morelia. She stole a worried glance at Tewarhi. We changed the subject. They invited us to pitch our tent in the garden among the sunflowers and the girls helped us. They were gorgeous, with huge, chestnut eyes and gap-toothed grins. Anna Paula's favourite expression was, *'Creo que sí'* (I believe that), which she delivered in a very authoritative manner. I can hear her singing it now, her little voice chirruping as she smiled up at us, gathering our belongings in her little hands, delighted to be ordering them in our tent. Violeta walked us to the bakery. She hopped from foot to foot as I ordered buns and cakes, and beautifully repeated the words I missed from the gun-shot speaking *señorita* behind the till.

The worry of what lay ahead was consuming us. Everyone we spoke to corroborated Morelia and Tewarhis' concern about our onward passage. Everyone shook their heads, said we were crazy, that we must go by bus. David mapped Venezuela's crime-capitals: Kilometre 88, El Dorado, Ciudad Guyana and Caracas. Our route would take us through all four (we weren't running to Caracas, but we would have to go there to leave the country). We were running into a furnace.

Four-by-fours jostled impatiently to regurgitate their enormous Brazilian incumbents into one of the rash of superstores that infested the roadside. Electrical stuff, furnishing stuff, D.I.Y. stuff, flashy stuff; all the same cheap stuff that attracted Brazilians in thick, sweaty, predatory hordes to the border-town of Santa Elena. Dollar-signs blinded their vision. The artificial discrepancy between their own currency *(real)* and the Venezuelan *bolivar* meant that prices were ludicrously low, and they were salivating in expectation of bargains.

Before leaving St. Elena, we stashed the left bike-tyre and the inside right fork of the trailer with thousands of Venezuelan *bolivars* and our security American dollars. We budgeted on £70 per week for the remaining 35 days of the expedition. We had to collect the shoes that were apparently waiting for us in town. David had tracked Venezuela's Inov-8 agent, Yoselin, and she had single-handedly managed what the entire Brazilian postal service was incapable of doing: she had received our new pairs of running shoes.

I squatted in a lean-to by the side of the road, guarding our belongings, trying to look inconspicuous while David ran off to retrieve the shoes and some last rations. Clapped-out 1970 Fords belched clouds of smoke from their rattling exhaust pipes. Brand-new black Chevrolets and Hyundai trucks gleamed in the scorching sun, their black windows masking the drivers within. A wooden wagon pulled by a skeletal pony wove between the traffic. An elderly man with a thick, ginger beard pissed by the side of the road. Two young guys gestured at traffic, waving something above their heads. Then their two sets of eyes fell on me. I flinched, but it was too late. They were coming, sauntering over and digging one another in the ribs.

'Where are you from?' they asked. They fell about laughing at my response, before they recovered themselves and continued with the cross-examination. 'The UK? So far! What's it like?' But before I could answer, the younger lad pulled out his mobile phone. 'Do you have a phone? Do you have phones like this? What about cars? Are they like ours?'

We had been away from the U.K. for over five years. I had no idea what the latest phones looked like. Even if we had been at home, I doubt I would have been able to answer them. They had the misfortune of stumbling across the least technologically-informed person imaginable. But my answers didn't seem to trouble them. They had found something unusual by the side of the road and were determined to mine me for information, whatever my replies might be. I asked them how old they were and what they were up to. 'José's 13 and I'm fifteen. We're selling petrol, offering a good price,' said Carlos. 'But no one seems to be stopping?' I said. 'Oh yeh they do. Sometimes it takes all day, but someone will stop eventually,' said Carlos. 'What about school?' I asked. 'Left it years ago,' said Carlos, 'No use for earning money, is it? Anyway, I've got a little son. Gotta support him and my girlfriend.' On his phone he showed me a photo of a chubby little baby.

José looked up, his eyes twinkling, 'Do you speak French?' At my answer their eyes grew to the size of saucers. 'English! We've seen it on Facebook. Will you teach us?' I started rummaging around in the trailer for my diary. There were only a few pages left, but it would do and so I began writing some key phrases down. I told them what 'Facebook' literally meant and they giggled. 'What would you like to say in English?' I asked. José was quick with a response: 'I would like a fast car!' After a while he slunk off, leaving Carlos and me chatting. I presumed he was bored with the lesson or me, but he soon returned. 'Look!' he said brandishing a small green pencil and a thick paper work-book with a silver Porsche on the front. I thought it was a new English pad for him, but when I tried to hand it back, he explained: 'This is for you. I saw you had nearly run out of paper. Now whenever you write in it, you will think of Carlos and me!' As we ran off, I kept turning round, waving at the two slight figures as they grew smaller and smaller and finally disappeared behind a bend. I filled the diary and I thought of my two young friends. It lasted me until the end of the run.

David was fraught with worry:

> We're running into the abyss. We are so exposed on the road and there's no cover in the savanna, nowhere to hide. Everybody's worried about us. They keep telling us about all the recent violent assaults that have happened. I'm trying to keep positive despite all the warnings. Our only

chance is to run early, camp early, stay with people where possible, stay hidden and look shit. Then there's the worry of money; the replacement cost of anything is five times its value if we have to use the official currency exchange-rate through a bank.

We camped in an indigenous reserve, the only punctuation-mark in the bare hills we were running through. But the people weren't friendly and didn't want us to stay. I eventually managed to get a reluctant shrug from a young man, who then bolted into a hut. They seemed to be hiding from us. We erected the tent under an open-sided shed, but the *puri-puris* soon found us, riddling our skin with bites.

We resolved to concentrate on the positive stuff: fear would cripple us otherwise. We had six more days, running before reaching the ganglands – six more days in the Grand Sabana Canaima National Park, which had been classified as a World Heritage Site and is home to *tepuis*, some of the earth's most astonishing rock formations. They're flat-topped, towering mountains that rise vertically from the undulating savanna beneath. Like pedestals or *mesas* (tables), as they're known locally, they spear through the sky to dizzying heights. Their skirts support warm tropical growth, while their shoulders burst into cold, rain-drenched clouds. Morelia and Tewarhi told us that the Pemon Amerindians (the indigenous people of the Gran Sabana) had chosen the name *tepui* because it means 'house of gods'.

What fascinated me was the abundance of endemic plant and animal species that has evolved on the tops of these biological islands. A Pemon Indian we met later insisted that they are the oldest rocks in the world – that they remain as the hardy remnants of a previous crust of sandstone that covered the even-older layer of granite which forms the Guiana Shield (which had created the woefully-steep hills we were running up and down). Over millennia the fauna and flora, isolated from others of their kind by the sheer angle of the *tepuis'* cliffs, have evolved into unique and new species. Imagine stumbling across these megaliths It would have been like discovering whole new kingdoms, each one unique and glittering. Not only are their communities distinct from one another and those of the surrounding lands; many of the individual *tepuis* (and there are more than 150) have 'islands' within their island. Features such as sink-holes and enormous caves have provided barriers to movement, so that new species have evolved within these as well.

For us they were distant jewels, stuff of dreams, piercing the backbone of the savanna. But on the ground things had changed. We stopped by a cluster of tents. A group of Pemon were offering guided tours to see a rare ruby river that snaked through a belt of rainforest. David and I had been arguing about whether the grassland we were now traversing had previously been rainforest. 'Yes, of course it was,' he said. 'But over the years people have cleared the trees to graze their animals and see out. It's very sad: we've lost so much.'

We ran on. A cloak of smoke reared up on the horizon. A line of crimson flames licked its way across the cinnamon-coloured grassland. Above it hung flocks of hawks and falcons, eyes darting, wings barely moving, as they snapped up the fire's bonanza of fleeing victims. But this was not a natural fire. An old man limped at the edge of the blaze, now and then beating at an unruly flame with a long branch. Children zipped over charred tussocks, flapping sheets at the flames, giggling. Our nostrils stung with the acrid fumes. We imagined the hundreds of charred bodies, of frogs, snakes, and armadillos, which had escaped the birds' puncturing claws, but not the fire's overwhelming march.

Signs for *Salta Kama* (Kama Waterfall) appeared by the side of the road. The Gran Sabana is famous for its waterfalls; in fact Angel Falls are the highest in the world, rumbling down the remote Auyán Tepui. But the difference with Kama was that we would be able to see it from the roadside. A group of Pemon ladies waiting for a bus by the side of the road giggled as we ran up to them and gestured us onwards. 'Soon, soon, it's not far!' they cried.

Five miles later we heard it. A low rumbling like a freight train, growing closer and closer, louder and louder, until it was blasting the air around us. A river languorously slipped under a bridge a couple of metres away. We watched it sliding, gently eddying, then nothing. There was space where the river should have been. We ditched the trailer and darted down under the bridge and along the bank, hopping from boulder to boulder, working our way across, closer to the 'end'. David was in front, squatting on a rock, craning his neck, covered in spray.

I looked over. The river was free-falling, its bed whisked away, hurtling to crash and curdle with foam and rocks at least 50 metres below, churning like a tormented beast. It was exhilarating. We looked up. We had forgotten where we were, why we were there. A few tourists wandered around a car-park on the other side of the river. There were no barriers, no officials, just us and the beast. We filled our water bottles with the falling river, gulped back ice-cold nectar, refilled our bottles and trotted off.

After 27 miles we found a shepherd's hut centimetres from the road. The door stuck, but after a hefty shove it groaned open. There were old newspapers, rat-chewed plastic, fence poles, wire and a saucepan. A thick layer of dust suggested that no one had passed by in a while. We hung the tarpaulins over its grimy windows in case a motorist caught sight of the light of our stove or a head-torch, and began clearing a space for our tent. Suddenly something scuttled over David's foot. It was the size of my palm, with a halo of hairy legs. 'What the hell was that?' exclaimed David. Repulsed, we gingerly picked up the debris, another one scuttled under our tent. We stood transfixed, flashing our head-torches around the hut, determined to ascertain how many we were dealing with. 'Over there!' I pointed at the corner, from which two more ugly sisters were watching us. We shone the torch on them. Red eyes glinted back. They looked like a cross between spiders and ticks, but were completely flat. 'Do you think they're venomous?'

asked David. 'Don't know,' I replied. And with that we bedded down, hoping our warmth wouldn't lure them in.

During the night I had to worm my way out of our sleeping-bag, unzip the tent, negotiate the random clutter, avoid being bitten by one of the hairy ones, dodge David's barrage of swear words and plunge into the darkness. I was following my nightly ritual; I needed a wee. As I stepped into the darkness, my eyes watered. As far as I could see, way out in the deepest depths of the blackness, millions of tiny, flickering golden lights danced in the savanna. It was as if the stars had fallen from the sky and had chosen the ancient Guianan Shield on which to live their last, twinkling moments. I called David. Our breath condensed in the cold mountain air as we stood spell-bound by the flight of the fireflies, wishing it would never end.

Our next stop was *La Bomba* (the petrel pump/station) which turned up earlier than it should have, but amazingly had food and a room we could kip in. We gorged *empanadas* and chatted to the Indian folk who ran the café. This was the last proper pit-stop before we started the long descent off the Shield and down into the troubled gold-mines of Kilometre 88 and beyond.

We might have looked like penniless vagabonds, but not only were the trailer-frames and wheels stuffed full of cash: we were pulling a pair of Swarovski binoculars worth £1,500, a laptop, camera, Power Traveller solar panels, GPS watch and all kinds of vitals without which we couldn't survive. Somehow we had to rid ourselves of them. The owner of a hostel in Santa Elena said we could leave them with a friend of his in Tumeremo, which lay beyond the first danger hot-spot. We devised a plan for David to catch a bus forward and deposit the valuables with him – at which point we started speaking to an Asian geologist with a silver beard. He had a very pleasant demeanour and when we told him of our plan to offload the gear, he said he could deliver it to Tumeremo himself. We looked at one another, our minds racing. Could we trust this fellow?

He would save us time and money. It would take David two days to catch a bus there and back. We realized we couldn't afford to refuse Silver-Beard's offer. And so we handed a complete stranger our three bags of valuables, which he cheerfully accepted, before speeding off in his white van. We noted his number plate.

The next issue was money. We had already exceeded our budget; also, we were getting thin and we didn't need an excuse not to eat. Then there was accommodation. If we needed somewhere to stay in the crime-ridden towns up ahead, we had to be able to afford it, because sleeping rough could cost us our lives. The only option was to go back to Brazil and change another stash of money. So we left the remainder of our gear with the Indian owners of the café and walked out onto the road to thumb a lift back to Pacarima. In less than a minute a maroon hatchback stopped, and a large, yellow-looking woman beckoned us in. Two other fat ladies filled the car. They were on a road trip through the savanna and were as garrulous as a gaggle of geese, all talking at the same time all the way to Santa Elena, at which point I thought David might actually explode.

Marga, the driver, appeared incapable of using the steering wheel, and her effect on the vehicle was terrifying. As her mouth worked into a frenzy about the rare rocks that inhabited the savanna, her eyes remained glued on us via the front mirror. A vehicle zoomed past, horn blaring. Oblivious to its presence, Marga had wandered to the other side of the road, millimetres away from killing the lot of us. Undeterred, she continued the onslaught, deciding to remove her glasses on a particularly precipitous bend in the road for one of her companions to clean.

Against the odds we made it to Santa Elena and from there caught a taxi, through the immigration, police and army checkpoints back into Brazil. There the taxi waited as David got £400 out of the cashpoint in *reais*, before returning through all three-check points into Venezuela. No one batted an eyelid. Back in Santa Elena, David selected a guy from the hordes of money-changers hanging by the roadside and swapped the *reais* for *bolivars*. For most of the next day we waited for a hitch by a police check-point. No one stopped. Finally a flat-bed truck carried us away and deposited us back at *La Bomba* just as it was getting dark.

We struck up a conversation with an artist who expertly sold lumps of old rock to unsuspecting tourists. Meanwhile a thick-set, blond-haired guy stood at the bar talking to the owners. He was half listening to what we were saying about the run and before long came across to join in. He was Dutch (called Alfredo) and had lived in the Gran Sabana for over 30 years.

'Venezuela's getting worse,' he announced. 'The violence is appalling. The Gran Sabana's the only safe place, but even it is getting enmeshed in the chaos. I'm a guide, I drive tourists between here and the coast, and I couldn't tell you the number of times we've been shot at on the road, it happens too often.'

We had heard all the warnings. Heard the hideous stories. But somehow it was worse hearing it in English. Nothing was lost in translation. 'They'll kill you,' he pointed at David. 'But they'll violate her,' he jerked his thumb at me. David was talking, but his words were swimming unheard through my head. 'What the hell are we doing here?' I thought. 'The expedition means everything, but our lives...' David had the map out. Alfredo was pointing out places we could stay, bolt-holes where people could be trusted, where we could sleep safely. There were some Indians we could stay with after Kilometre 88 and a Belgian, Lutz, after that. This was the kind of information we had been hunting for months. Finally, literally in our last hour we had it. All we had to do now was to ensure no one targeted us during the day.

We stayed the night at *La Bomba* in a small room with rusty beds, one fluorescent light bulb and a gecko. We organized what was left of our stuff and agonised about what we should do. Alfredo's words seared through our minds. 'They'll kill you, but they'll violate her.' We started to question the entire idea of running through these nefarious zones. We were desperate to run the continent, but the chances of a cold bullet through the head, worse still rape, was terrifying.

We started to explore the option of catching a bus through the gold-mining areas. We could jump out once we were through, jump back on through Ciudad

Venezuela: the Grand Sabana

Guayana and then start running the other side of it, making up the missed miles along the coastline. But was the coastline safe? Whatever we came up with seemed to hit a wall in Venezuela's labyrinthine underworld.

We knew what we had to do. We had to run. We had got through so far. We knew the score: run early when the criminals are sleeping; look terrible – that was effortless now, everything was holey and filthy and the trailer and our bags looked awful; hide deep in the forest or in people's gardens; no stopping for birds or wildlife; run marathons or whatever it would take to reach the safe havens; practice the self-defence moves Octavio had taught us all those months ago in Santa Cruz....

> Thank god we met Alfredo (David wrote). He says we have to reach Kilometre 88 and stay there the night. I had to laugh. We're running through an ungovernable war zone and going to stay where the war lords live. As the old adage goes, 'They don't shit in their own back yards!' The problem is when we have nowhere to stay and have to hide in the forest. A hunter with dogs could find us. But you can only be sick with worry for so long.

We ran off early, our bags stuffed with *empanadas* so that we wouldn't have to cook the first night, wouldn't have to expose ourselves with a fire. Police check points punctuated our passage. Argentina and Bolivia had bristled with them, but Brazil had been free of them, so we had forgotten, become blasé. Pre-pubescent lads dressed head to toe in khaki leant on Kalashnikovs. They looked bored, fiddling with their weapons. Were they loaded? We didn't want to find out. A bus stopped, passengers filed out. Everyone's bags were spat out of the hold and searched. Notes were slipped into sweaty hands. We walked past, a couple of cold faces looked up. What were we? We didn't fit the mould, they looked down, let us pass by. We ran on.

A car drove past with a gunshot hole through its back windscreen. People yelled at us, pushed cameras out of half-closed windows. Few stopped. We crossed into Sierra de Lema and the low scrub started to make way for trees. It was a lovely surprise, we hadn't realized we would see more rainforest. We started descending, running hard through thick forest. It was stunning, some of the finest woodland we had seen and it was straddling the road. Perhaps Venezuela's vast oil reserves have ironically protected their forests? Instead of growing crops or raising livestock on cleared forest, the country imports the majority of its food, so its forests remain standing. But then the deforestation is shunted to the countries that Venezuela imports from. Then there's Venezuela's gold mines which are poisoning the forest and providing access for illegal logging. But there was no doubt that the forest just there, just where we were running, was amazing.

We found a gap in the vegetation and scrambled along the banks of a glistening stream to collect water. A few miles further on a sign said *Mirador* (view point). We preferred to find our own, but this time we had no choice. Our eyes saw it and we couldn't prise them away. Our mouths involuntarily dropped, as we gawped in dizzying wonder. Rows of mountains cascaded like waterfalls beneath us. Wisps of clouds clung to their summits. Luscious forest rolled into infinity. It was magical, I had never seen anything like it. It shimmered in the heat haze. We stood, our feet planted on the escarpment drinking the view. Etching it deep into our eyes, so we would never ever forget it, so we could return to it in our dreams.

That view was the drug we needed. We were under its spell, we couldn't stop thinking about it. We began creating expeditions as we ran, planning how we would survive in its mountains, where we would go. We fed off one another's ideas, then ran apart, deep in thought, revelling in the possibilities. Suddenly something large and orange flew high over my head. It perched in a branch for an instance, before hurtling off to another and then disappearing all together. I couldn't believe it, it was a cock-of-the-rock, a bird we had been searching for, that I had given up chances of seeing. Even without binoculars there was no disputing this bizarre bird, with what looks like the blade of an orange shovel stuck in its head.

We ran 26 miles. We knew we couldn't run less, because we would have to run another 26 miles the next day to reach Kilometre 88, then 27 to reach the Indians, then 26 to reach Lutz – and so it would continue until Tumeremo six days later. We waited until we couldn't hear any vehicles and manhandled the trailer behind a tree. It wasn't much of a path, more of an animal trail that dropped almost vertiginously off the side of the road. Safe behind the screen of trunks and climbers we began unpacking the trailer and shepherding it down the sticky trail. We were in the land of giants. Trunks triple the span of both of our five foot ten and six foot four outstretched arms rocketed into a wall of leaves, tens of metres above our heads. The merest chinks of light reached us, reminders us of the scorching sun that fuelled this overgrown greenhouse.

The machete sliced through the odd branch so we could sling our hammocks up, but it was pretty clear, with the trees' canopies successfully stifling light and therefore growth. We roamed off in search of animals. Found spider webs the size of doorways and a tiny olive frog, statue-still, in the leaf litter. A band of iridescent birds chattered above our heads flitting under leaves, now in a hole, now dangling from a branch, forever on the move, forever searching for a fatter grub than the last. We sank into our hammocks, high on the relief of finding forest again and a home that felt safe. At least for now.

A monkey bounded
over to us

21 Mafia Land

Eyes follow us. Two gold-chained teenagers smirk. A black-maned woman beckons to us, her son screams, 'Here come the *gringos*'. We wince at the attention and hide in a shred of dark shade under a sign, hanging, just, by one rusted nail. What have we done?

It took us four and a half hours to descend into the pit of Kilometre 88. It was grim, worse than we could have ever have imagined. It was like walking into the set of *Dusk-'till Dawn,* only we weren't part of the show and all the characters were eyeballing us like lambs to the slaughter. I looked down, determined not to catch anyone's eye as Alfredo's words rang in my ears, 'They will kill you and violate her.'

First reaction? Get out. Run through, find somewhere else to sleep. The prospect of staying was chilling. But now we had arrived, we had very few options; we had already run a marathon, it was stinking hot, the sun was literally frying our skin, we were exhausted. The next safe bolt-hole was a marathon away, there was no way we were going to run another one today.

Rusty Chevrolets rumbled slowly past, their boots big enough to hide a body. Guys were slumped over bottles of beers by a petrol pump. An old man was hawking something in the faces of motorists loitering outside a Chinese supermarket. We needed to make a decision about where we were going to stay, fast. A large pink sign read, *Hotel Paraíso* (Paradise Hotel). Everything about it read dodgy, but we couldn't see an alternative. David darted across the road to check it out. He was back within minutes, 'It looks rough, but it'll have to do. Let's go quickly.'

We dived in, heaving the trailer and ourselves out of sight. That night we ate chicken stew at the 'Three Sisters'. They were huge black Colombians. One laughed nervously as she played with her little grandson. A silver four by four screeched to a halt and a stocky, heavily tattooed Hispanic woman jumped out. She asked for a parcel, the nervous sister shuffled away, soon to return with an A4 black leather purse. The Hispanic woman flashed us a smile, 'May the gods bless you,' we hoped they would and bolted our stew.

That night we heard gun shots. The Arawak family, whom we would take shelter with the following night, would tell us that the town is run by The Syndicate. Shootouts are a regular activity. You have to play by the mafia's rules and pay to stay safe.

At four thirty in the morning we made our escape. Under the shroud of darkness and a low loitering fog we felt our way out of the hotel and up the road. A skeletal dog growled, a few light bulbs leaked orange into the night and a neon green bar sign flickered. We saw a man curled up under a wooden bench. I hoped he was sleeping, not dead. David started filming, mouthing hushed words to the camera. A man on a motorcycle was watching us; we hid the camera and ran. All the shops were boarded up, but still advertised their wares of gold detectors, gold rings, gold to sell and gold to buy. A woman was pulling down the shutters of her shop. The thick smell of pastries wafted out. We couldn't resist it. She offered us dense sugared coffee, it was foul, like treacle, but we necked it, along with sweet *empanadas*.

She grinned all pink gums, explaining that she had come across from Columbia long ago with her husband, lured by the promise of jobs, houses and security. Now he was dead, but she had her daughters and was a grandmother. 'Would you like to go back?' I asked. 'Hell no! Many are talking, saying it's safer there than here these days. I have sisters and brothers over there and my elderly mother. But I won't go back, no, not with my daughters here. I've got my shop, see. I'm ok. For other's it is different…' and she trailed off.

It was getting late, the street was starting to fill. We needed to run, needed to get out. We charged past gardens, fields and forest. A woman was selling fruit juice from a wooden veranda whilst jigging her plump baby on her lap. She ladled spoonfuls of mango and guava liquid into plastic cups, as her fat hens pecked around our feet. A black car stopped in front of us. We stopped too, pretended to tie our shoelaces. Waiting. Desperate that it would go, leave us alone. I can't remember much else: we just ran, fast and hard, desperate to find the Arawaks, for the day to end.

An open-sided barn stood at the road's edge. Our 27 miles were up; this should have been it. Behind it, grass sloped down to a stream before rising up to a wooden house and woodland beyond. There were about five other buildings neatly appointed in the compound. I walked down a path in the direction of a singing voice, '¿Hola, hay alguien en casa?' (Hello, is there anybody at home?). A short, stocky man appeared from the back of a shed. I began to explain who we were, what we were doing; the normal spiel. But this time it was crucial, they had to let us stay, we had no other option. I took a breath and paused, '¿Qué piensas?' (What do you think?)

He looked at me. My stomach churned. Then slowly a smile crept across his face and it remained there, lighting his broad nose, high cheekbones and large mouth. 'You speak English?' He laughed. I couldn't believe my ears. His voice was soft and lyrical, filled with that beautiful sing-song Caribbean accent. 'We're Arawaks, from British Guiana. My name's Byron, I live here in our small community with my family and friends. Of course you're welcome to stay with us. You can hang your hammocks in the barn and I'll bring across some juice and biscuits and will brush the floor.'

Later on Simon, Byron's brother appeared. He hopped onto the wall and began talking, two hours later he was still chatting and we were still enthralled. His world was so removed from ours. He lived in the shadows of darkness within a Quentin Tarantino film; dealing with outlaws, dodging death and confronting brutality daily. He was a mix between Muhammad Ali and Daley Thompson. His dark eyes glinted, his teeth flashed as he smiled wryly and transfixed us.

'I work in the gold mines. It's why we crossed the border. I can make thousands of dollars in a day; on a good day that is, others nothing. I make sure our community wants nothing. But you gotta be tough, flex your muscles, stake your territory, grow a set of eyes on the back of your head. 'Cause just like a jaguar pounces, a rival will pounce and gun you down for your gold, if you don't get him first.'

'How do you physically extract it?' David asked. 'Are you panning for gold?'

'No, that easy work's long gone. I get my wetsuit on and plunge into the deep murky river, spend hours pumping silt from the bed through a long tube onto the bank. Then I sift it with mercury, and that's when the gold dust shines. That's when I'm happy!'

'Who buys it'?

'Ah, sheikhs, princes, them from the Middle East and Russia, you know. I don't deal with them direct. There's someone up there in Kilometre 88 who does it for me. We keep away from the government, or they'll have half our takings. No point in legal work down here, the government has no idea what goes on, better they keep away. Most of the guys never see their takings mind, they'll have drunk and pissed it out the same night as they find it and they'll have a girl to celebrate up there from town. Then they have to start all over again, poor as rats, angry too, but they'll be happy for a night. Doesn't interest me, all that; my priority's my family.'

A car stopped in the layby just up from the barn we were chatting in. Simon sprang up, scrutinised the occupants and marched towards them. Before he could get any closer it screeched off, gears grinding, in a cloud of dust. He swaggered back. 'Unwelcome visitors don't stay long here. I'll have them hung, drawn and quartered before they put a finger on any of my people!' He was laughing, but it wasn't a joke. It was clear that this small, powerful man was not muscly for nothing; his strength and guile protected the village.

He continued. 'One day a man crawled out of the forest just down the road there. Don't know how he got out, he was that weak, lost most of his blood, you know. I had never seen a black man so white, like a ghost he was. He was desperate, beckoning at buses, at cars, but everyone sailed past. No one wanted anything to do with him, no one ever does. So I put him over my shoulder and brought him in. He was riddled with gunshots. We bathed his wounds and took him up to the health centre; they couldn't ignore him because we had brought him in.'

He carried on talking about fights, the past, his ideas and neighbours. He said his mother had been raped by the police and his brother killed in Guiana. That it took eight hours on foot through the forest to reach the Guiana border, but that he didn't go back much. Then suddenly he suddenly jumped up from the fence and walked off. 'See you tonight,' he said turning back. 'Come and share some food with me.'

We set off again the following morning with 26 miles between us and our next safe haven. Tin way-markers were peppered with gun shots. We didn't stop long on the changeovers, didn't catch people's eyes, kept plugging away, focused on getting off the road as quickly as possible. It took us a while to pinpoint exactly where Lutz lived. All we knew was that he was close to El Dorado, the real gold mining town. The El Dorado of legends is still supposed to lie sparkling somewhere deep in the forest between the Orinoco and Amazon rivers. We followed a long sandy track to a cluster of buildings looking over a wide, muddy river. A guy was standing behind the bar.

'¡Hola!' I ventured. 'We were told by Alfredo, a Dutch guy, that we could stay here. He's friends with Lutz.' The man nodded. He was young and handsome, with a thick mop of blonde hair and turquoise eyes. He started speaking to us in English. 'This is crazy, what you're doing. You mean you have really run across Venezuela, from Santa Elena?!' We nodded. 'My god. With that thing behind you? It's not possible. Have you really run all the way? Haven't you taken buses?'

'We've run all the way,' David said. The young man shook his head, 'You're really crazy. She doesn't pull the trailer too, does she?' he said motioning towards me.

'Of course I do,' I said. 'We take it in turns and we're not crazy, just determined. It's amazing what the body will do if you push it.'

We asked about food. 'Look, it might look like a restaurant, but it isn't. Lutz came over from Belgium nearly 40 years ago to train the army. Then he started his own operation. The bar is kept full for all the army guys who work here. We want to keep them lubricated, keep them sweet and happy with the operation, the comings and goings. We deal in contraband and mining. We move stuff from one place to another. It works for me, I'm making a lot of money fast. Life's good, easy…'

Before he could continue, a man strutted into the bar. He was wearing olive combat trousers and an army cap. His bare, grizzled chest was like a barrel and riddled with angry red welts. My eyes ran from scar to scar. He looked at us for an instant, snarled and looked away, carefully filling a glass with beer. The young chap spoke to him in German. We could tell they were talking about us, the young guy was animated, the old guy wasn't. 'What do you want?' he barked (we heard him speak English later, but he would only speak to us in Spanish), 'Why are you here in my house?'

So this was Lutz. David explained that we needed a safe place to stay for the night. His ice-blue eyes stared back at him; he wouldn't look at me. Then he took his glass and walked out, leaving David's words hanging in the air. The other guy looked sheepish. 'Look, he'll let you stay, but only for one night. You must leave as soon as you can. If you need a shower, there's the basement over there under the main house. You can go there. But don't go anywhere else. OK? And don't make a noise. Keep your eyes and ears closed and your mouths shut. Right, I need to see my girlfriend,' and with that he was off. Clearly he had said too much to us already.

We shifted our belongings to a hut where the guard hung his hammock. There was a puppy. We tickled its tummy and David sat in the hammock. We looked away from the bar, tried to be inconspicuous. Suddenly we heard a shout. 'Get out of there,' it was Lutz. 'That's where the guard stays, it's not for you. Get out now.' David was fuming. I was scared. We packed all our bags again and walked across the lawn to a couple of shrubs, motioning to Lutz whether we could sleep there. He didn't reply, so we took it as a yes and unpacked again. Why had Alfredo recommended the place? We were in an ants' nest.

David darted across to the shower first. Green paint peeled off the walls. He turned the round metal cogs, heard water gurgling. The pipe spat something out, but it wasn't water. It was a big black cockroach, gaining flight before hitting the floor and disappearing into a crack in the wall. It was my turn next. I stripped off rapidly, there was no screen, anyone could wander in from outside, but I was filthy, desperate. I curled my toes, trying not to stand on the filthy cold concrete, hoping the cockroach didn't have friends. Brown river water splattered over me. There was no cockroach, just a warty toad sitting in the corner.

A monkey bounded over to us. Its lead dangled from a collar studded with gold. We scratched its tummy and it lay back in the grass dreamily. Then a parrot flew to our tree. It was an *hablador* (blue fronted Amazon parrot). It peered down at us for a while and then flapped over to Lutz. He was sitting with his back to us on a bench, bent over, deep in conversation with a man dressed head to toe in khaki with a Kalashnikov on his thigh. A Rottweiler sat between them, panting. It was like a scene from James Bond.

Later on he watched TV at the bar with the Kalashnikov guy. It was a documentary about Hitler. They kept chanting, '*Heil Hitler!*' We were out of our depth. The place was rotten, everything smelt. Anyone could gun us down in an instant, and no one would ever know. Before we could get out of our hammocks, they could heave our bodies into the black river, and send us floating out to sea as food for the piranhas,

We strained our ears: they were talking about us again. Lutz was agitated about us being there. He came over again, telling us we had to leave more room for people to get to the river. They came all night: the army, gold miners; cackling, whispering, lights flashing on and off our hammocks. They were transporting boxes and bags. We dreaded to think what was in them. The drone of flogging outboard engines drew close, before they cut out and more cargo was bundled aboard. Whatever this place was, it definitely wasn't a haven. I couldn't wait until morning so we could get the hell out of there.

The monkey played in the bar and the parrot chatted on the roof. We ran down the sandy track, relieved to be leaving alive. Lutz drove past, sullen-faced, looking through us. The forest had long gone; now we were running through grassland. We only needed to cover 21 miles, which was a huge relief, as we were both shattered. It was a horrible, slow run, as we doggedly trudged forward in the scorching heat. We had exhausted Alfredo's recommendations, but were passing enough farms and scattered houses, so felt confident that someone would let us stay. I asked a wiry old man weeding a vegetable patch if we could camp. He pointed to the wooden gates opposite. They were about ten feet high and padlocked shut. I called out, '¡Hola'!' After a while a tall, dark man appeared walking slowly down the track towards us. He looked like a cross between a Turk and a pirate. I quickly explained the situation: to our great relief he smiled and gestured us to come in, and began unlocking the gates.

His home was a wooden hut surrounded by pigs, chickens, ducks and dogs. Random shrubs sprouted out of the earth yard, and clusters of trees provided shade. We hung our hammocks and began chopping onions and garlic, asking him to share our food. He gave us a large iron pot and the use of his gas cooker, then shuffled off to find some eggs. He seemed pleased to have company. He said he had a house in Tumeremo, where his wife lived, and that he would go back there during the week. 'She won't come here. Doesn't like the countryside. But this is where I like to be. It's peaceful. Sí Señor.' That was the phrase he used after every sentence, 'Sí Señor' (yes sir). It was like a mantra.

Faded posters of Chavez and Maduro looked down at us. The man was fanatical about Chavez, said he loved him, that he was the father of the nation. It was clear that the only reason Madura had a look-in was because Chavez had chosen him as his successor. He said that Chavez gave the country folk food, looked after them, that without him they would have nothing.

We heard singing. Three Columbians arrived from the bush. They had been putting in fences on the farm and were carrying hammers and a post-driver. One wore a jaunty straw hat perched on the front of his head. He was 37 and handsome, smiling easily as he offered his hand, introducing himself as Ricardo. Then came David. He was shy, looking down as we spoke, although he kept sneaking a glance at us when he thought we weren't looking. Finally there was Daniel, a gangly, grinning, 17-year-old. They all sat down and the conversation became much more animated.

'Eighty per cent of people living here are Colombian,' Ricardo explained. 'We fled the government and the Farc. The Farc killed my father three years ago.' He paused, looked down and coughed. 'Anyway, you were asking about the economy, how it works?' We nodded. 'Well, the government sets a rock-bottom, fixed price for all food and commodities. But no one will sell at that rate, because no one would make any money. So the shopkeepers (they're mainly Chinese around here) buy everything up for nothing, then hoard it away into barns and sell it on at a much higher unofficial price. Prices can change by the hour, but never downwards, always up. Inflation's spiralling. And they'll only ever sell small amounts. They need to keep demand high, so prices stay high.'

The news at home had been full of the shocking story that it was impossible to wipe one's bottom in Venezuela, because of the dearth of toilet paper in the shops. The tabloids were feasting on the bonanza. The reality was less sensational. According to Ricardo and his mates, there was loads of paper, and everything else for that matter, but supplies were just sitting in warehouses, waiting for prices to rise.

Meanwhile *Sí Señor* was shaking his head. 'It's not true. Chavez (he bowed his head in reverence) looks after me and the simple man. I can buy chickens and potatoes four times lower than the market price.' Chavez, he said, was working hard to keep the vote of the countrymen. The government-subsidised commodities were reaching *Sí Señor* and others like him, before the vendors got hold of them. No wonder they treated Chavez like a superstar.

Daniel, Ricardo and David lived in the house opposite *Sí Señor* and invited us to lunch. Daniel cooked, while asking us to translate words into English, carefully repeating them, quickly storing them in his head. He had olive skin, a cheeky dimple and a *joie de vivre*. He offered us green mango, cut up and salted, with a squeeze of lime. 'Have you tried this? It's delicious!' he laughed. It was surprisingly good. He then jumped into the branches of a tree, swinging his long legs up (he was nearly as tall as David) and balancing high up on a branch. He pulled down a couple of pods like over-grown broad beans. 'This is *guama*. It's really soft and sweet.' He pulled open a huge, leathery pod and picked out a white, fluffy bean. He sucked the sweet skin off, revealing a large, shiny, brown bean inside and extracted more beans for us to sample. They required a lot of sucking for very little reward.

They asked a lot about our culture, technology and the prices of things, then the inevitable children question. Ricardo was astonished we hadn't yet produced a family, insisting we should get on with it! Children bloom in the centre of South Americans' hearts. Wherever we ran, people would notice their absence in our lives and feel it necessary to point out this fundamental void. It didn't worry us: we appreciated their frankness, their unflinching ability to call a spade a spade.

We had been chatting and eating ravenously for a good two hours. David had already fallen asleep in his chair and it looked like the others were making movements towards their afternoon siestas too. So we said our thank-yous and strolled back to *Sí Señor*, where a red-legged tortoise ambled under our hammocks, into which we retreated. 'I'm fattening it up,' explained Sí Señor. 'The flesh is very tasty. At Easter it'll sell for good money'.

The following day we reached Tumeremo and the Ministry of the Environment. Nestled under the secretary's desk, were all our valuables. Our man had come up trumps. After much deliberation the boss allowed us to stay the night in one of the Ministry rooms. Having a kitchen was a serious bonus, so we trotted off to the market to buy kilos of exotic vegetables and fruits. A guy in the internet café gave us a free punnet of ice cream when we told him about the run.

As we sat in the town square, an Indian, no more than four feet tall, stood in the middle of the road, turning slowly round and round. He wore a rucksack made from two batons of wood bound by string. Cars, bicycles and people wove round him, as if he was an inanimate object – a tree or a lamp-post, not a human. He looked totally disillusioned, as if he had just stepped out of his forest home for a few minutes, and when he had returned he had found it replaced by this: hundreds of people forging through the digestive pipes of town, with shops selling more gold and more gold detectors, fast-food restaurants; chaos.

That evening David fried steaks and drenched them in a cream-and-pepper sauce, then steamed piles of veg. It was all delicious. But water was a problem. As I attempted to wash the dishes, a trickle of brown liquid dribbled from the tap. Apparently the rivers were polluted nearby. The water-lorry was never far away. So we bought a 25- litre water-jug, like everyone else did, for 50 pence.

Running provides you with a lot of time to think, to muse and to wonder and as we wound our way up the continent, we had been talking about having a baby. I was 35, and, as all the South Americans we met kept reminding us, I didn't have masses of time. Although I love children, love teaching and inspiring the little critters about everything that flies and crawls and sprouts, I had never felt an overwhelming urge to have a child of my own. The natural world means everything to me: it fills my heart and soul. Adding another sprog to the mix wasn't going to help the environment. David didn't share my doubts. He pointed out that the ultimate goal of every animal and plant on this planet is to procreate and produce the next generation of chicks, calves, tadpoles, cubs and foals that would ensure the parents' DNA succeeded. If we went ahead, we would just be following our own biological instincts.

Now, the more we discussed and wrestled with the idea, the more I grew excited about it. But how much could my body take? I was already demanding it run over 20 miles every day, often a marathon. I never slept the night through, often had to survive on four or five hours' sleep, generally didn't eat or drink enough. A balanced diet wasn't in our vocabulary; we ate what we could, when we could. Could my body take on another human being? We thought about those hunter-gatherers, trotting across the vast plains of the Rift Valley. Surely the women folk had to keep on the move, even when they were pregnant? If our bodies had evolved to accommodate running and pregnancy, perhaps what I was asking of mine was nothing unnatural?

We needed advice, from someone who had run serious mileages day-on-day and yet managed to conceive. Paula Radcliffe and Kelly Holmes sprang to mind. I emailed them an unusual request, but one which might perhaps tickle their interest. They never replied, so we had to work things out on our own. We decided we would give it a go, in this the last month of the run when I was super-fit and my body used to the daily quota of miles. If I did suffer from morning sickness or anything else, it would just be a matter of bearing it for the last couple of weeks.

That night, for the first time in our eight-year relationship, we threw caution to the wind. We lay in silence afterwards, contemplating this momentous step, of setting our lives to follow a new path.

A flock of orange-winged Amazons crashed into a tree by the road

Orange-winged Amazon
Amazona amazonica

22 Our World Moves

We threaded through the square before dawn, past the women sweeping away the debris from the day before: plastic drinks-cups and polystyrene dishes pushed into heaps with long, palm-leaf brooms: traditional met modern with one flick of the wrist. A long line of cars was already snaking from the petrol station, with the drivers desperate to fill up before the supply ran out.

We wove our way through green hills. It was 25 miles to El Callao, another mining town full of jewellery shops, but we were relieved to reach it, and celebrated by buying some cane sugar juice from a stall at the side of the road. Then we sat in the central piazza. Red lettering flashed 'Hotel' on a white sign attached to a decaying concrete tower-block. It looked terrible, but it was all I could see within the immediate vicinity. We were missing wild camping, but the countryside was increasingly cultivated and we needed a safe place to sleep. I couldn't muster the energy to search further. I rang a bell. A nose appeared around the door, belonging to a young man dressed in full Eighties splendour. 'What do you want?'

He reluctantly allowed me to step in and bustled off to his counter, where he grabbed his phone and started flicking through the screens with his long slim digits. I heard a snort; a woman was sleeping on a mat by his feet. I waited, growing more and more annoyed. 'Do you have a room?' I asked. He drew his gaze from his phone, pulled at the gold stud in his right ear and said, 'Yes we have a room, but there's no shower. There's no running water, in fact.'

I hesitated, but only for an instant. I doubt he had ever met a more desperate potential client. It would have to do, but I would try beating him down on price. It didn't work. He would give us his cheapest room, and we could take it or lump it. So we took it. The linen hadn't been washed and the beds sagged in the middle; the loo stank. He knocked on the door. 'Follow me, I'll show you where you can collect water.' He sauntered down the corridor. A trapdoor had been removed from the floor to reveal an orange river sloshing below the hotel lobby. 'There it is. Fill your boots!'

We contemplated the situation, as we dipped an old plastic jug in the bucket of river water and slopped it over us. It would probably be easier (definitely cheaper) to buy a bottle of petrol than a bottle of water here.

The next town was Guasipati. David narrowly missed being ploughed over by a car. The car hit the trailer, but by a stroke of luck, the trailer bounced into the tree. There was no space in which to escape the oncoming juggernauts, vans, trucks and cars, all hurtling past at breakneck speeds. A car flashed us, then hooted. The passenger was wildly motioning for us to pull over. We ignored him, needing all our powers of concentration to stay alive. Another mile down the road we recognized the car waiting in the layby. We couldn't avoid it. Two men jumped out. The older guy had a grey moustache and was nice-looking, with a self-assured demeanour, introducing himself as Eduardo. The other man had a surplus of long, straggly blond hair that was starting to turn grey. He wore wrap-around shades and a goatee, and had an odd, wooden manner, gathering us into a full embrace as his 'brothers' and announcing he was called Valentino.

'Welcome,' said Eduardo. 'We know all about you and have been waiting for your arrival. We would like to escort you into town.' This was very flattering, but we wanted to run at our own pace, contra-traffic. They nodded disconsolately, clearly upset not to be accompanying their prize. Then Eduardo jerked his head up, 'We'll wait for you on the outskirts of town. We can escort you from there.' He was excited again. They seemed to have hatched some kind of plan.

The run was interrupted by parrots. A flock of orange-winged Amazons crashed into a tree by the road. Their wings flashed citrus-green and flame-orange as they frolicked with one another. We were transfixed. When the little black car appeared a few minutes later, we followed, as it flashed its way up a hill and down into the centre of town. I could see a large crowd of people milling by the side of the road. Above their heads they were holding a sheet, with writing on it. Other people were waving flags. A car overtook us; faces craned out of the windows grinning and cheering, and Eduardo and Valentino started hooting.

Among the Venezuelan flags I spotted a Union Jack. Our names were emblazoned on the sheet with the word '¡*Bienvenido!*' (Welcome). I felt my legs move into an extra gear, our feet pounding the road, our arms straining, hands interlocked, sprinting now, buoyed by the onlookers, running high on the cheers. Tears streamed down my face. A huge wave of emotion was enveloping me.

The mayor walked forward and formally congratulated us. Everyone was taking photos. People asked us to pose with them individually. We milled about, thanking everyone, drinking the water that was continually thrust into our hands. An official photo was requested. Valentino stood at the front with his fist bonded to his chest. The mayor stood by his side, and we squatted around them. David's face was largely obscured by a Venezuelan flag, but no one seemed to notice.

We finally made our escape, long after we had exhausted our stock-pile of Spanish small-talk. Eduardo and Valentino chugged off in front of us, with Cheshire-cat sized grins, ushering their catch to the museum where they had arranged for us to stay. It was a peculiar place, being the former house of a mountain of a black woman who had a penchant for music and hats. A bouquet of must seeped through its rooms, and a fine layer of dust coated the many ornaments and random possessions on show. No one appeared to be maintaining the place, and as if to acknowledge this, a door dangled off its hinges. The house did, however, have a beautiful garden in a central courtyard bursting with colour and foliage.

Eduardo manhandled us through the house. Apparently the former owner had been very important. It seemed critical that we realized what a hallowed roof we would be sleeping under. 'Look at this hat. Do you see this one? And what about this great one? Handsome, no? She liked to wear very many colours. A woman of many styles. A chameleon, perhaps you would say. And do you see that photo? That was when she met the mayor. She was very famous in the end.'

My legs were aching, my feet were in tatters. I started yawning. Eduardo seemed oblivious of our plight. David had grown ominously silent. I hoped he wouldn't explode at our tedious host. How on earth were we to extract ourselves? My mind was racing. I muttered something about needing to go to sleep early that day. That we had been running long miles back-to-back for weeks, that it was taking its toll. He gazed absently at me, before turning to the next yellow meringue hat. I decided nothing short of blunt reality would work, 'Eduardo, this is beautiful and very interesting, but we're exhausted. We need a shower and then we must find some food and sleep.' He stood with a photo of 'Mrs Hat' in one arm and a vinyl record in the other, his mouth slightly agape, his moustache twitching.

We all ate *la hallaca* a type of local *empanada* traditionally eaten at Christmas, made of maize and filled with chicken, raisins, olives and capers and cooked in a plantain leaf. It was delicious, with lashings of garlic mayonnaise. Then we piled into the car and headed to the radio station, a primary school to give a presentation, Valentino's tree nursery and finally to his friends, Rubi and Luis, for supper where they unveiled platter after platter of local dishes that they had made especially for us. A large group of comrades had assembled, and all too soon the conversation moved from food to the real passion of their lives; politics.

Luis was running to be the equivalent of an MP at the forthcoming election. Life-sized posters of Capriles, the main rival to Chavez, hung from the veranda walls. A handsome giant of a man sat by me, wearing a yellow, blue-and-red striped tracksuit, the colours of Venezuela's flag. People wore them a lot. Venezuelans, we found, were seriously patriotic (as were people throughout South America). The giant, who was the town's new mayoral candidate, told us that the gold-mines were run by the government and were totally corrupt. It felt like we were in a clandestine rally, with Capriles' eyes burning down upon us. I imagined ears straining in the shrubbery.

Rubi's friend was pregnant, and we started talking about child-rearing. Apparently most women in the country deliver via C-section. 'The doctors persuade them to,' she explained. 'Because they receive cash for each operation they do. Women wait on trolleys outside the operating rooms until the money arrives from their families, then the operation can go ahead.'

We finally made it back to the museum. Eduardo showed us a mattress and promised to meet us in the morning. Valentino insisted that he would accompany us for the first fifteen miles of the day's run. We swallowed, but had to agree and arranged that he meet us at half past four in the morning. When we moved our bed, black ants poured from under it. One nipped me on the eyelid. The mosquitoes also seemed particularly jubilant at the arrival of two new bodies and attacked us wantonly.

Valentino was late, and when he finally turned up, wore an ankle-length trench coat and wellington boots. We looked at him in disbelief. He made it to a café to eat breakfast, and then ran about 150 metres before realizing that 15 kilometres might not be much fun, and decided he would find us later.

A few miles down the road, a Brazilian couple who lived in Ciudad Guayana jumped out of their car, asking us what we were up to. 'You must be careful. This place is dangerous. You can't trust anyone. They'll have you in an instant, gun you down for your phone. You'll see. They did it to me two years ago. Minding my own business at home, I was, when suddenly a guy ran in demanding money, my watch, my phone. Next thing I knew he was stabbing me. I hid under the bed. It was the only place that I could get away from his knife. But the blood was running thick. I was lucky to survive. Luckily she (he motioned to his pint-sized wife) found me. Look…' He pulled up his T-shirt; thick crimson welts scored his chest. 'Twenty-eight stab wounds in all. The doctors thought I was a goner.'

We weren't out of the woods yet. It took us five straight days of running to cover the 104 miles to Ciudad Guyana. This, the biggest city on our Venezuelan route, was a huge milestone for us, because when we left it, only nine marathons in nine days would stand between us, the Caribbean Sea and victory! If we could survive this last leg, we would also have nailed the last of the major crime hot-spots of the run.

I felt amazingly well as we stormed around roundabouts and down major carriage-ways into the city. We could accelerate quicker than the cars, so it became a game to out-run them, and whenever the traffic jammed, we would pound down their outside overtaking at break-neck speeds. We were super-fit and high on adrenalin.

The guys who had arranged our shipment of shoes to Santa Elena had flown from Caracas to meet us. They arranged for us to stay in a pretty boutique hotel, treated us to lunch and organised a load of press conferences. It was all great fun, but the next day reality bit when we arrived at our new hotel – an establishment more within our price-range, but in a far less salubrious quarter of town.

The taxi-driver hooted at a high metal gate. A woman in a glassed reception-house nodded and the gates rolled back. We were quickly ushered to a small, neat room and lay back on the massive, crushed-purple-velvet bedspread in relief. But when I opened my eyes I was shocked to see myself staring back from the ceiling. Why was there a colossal mirror stuck to the ceiling? Why would I want to see myself in bed? Most off-putting! My eyes roved the room, 'Oh my god,' I said, 'there are mirrors everywhere!' David was chuckling. Suddenly it dawned upon me. We were staying in a love hotel!

We intended to stay five nights in Ciudad Guayana. We had been planning the break for weeks to allow us a decent stab at the media side of things, and also to organise the run we were planning to hold in London, which was to celebrate completing the expedition. What we hadn't bargained on was a sojourn in Venezuela's premier Purple Palace. Nor, it seemed, had the *Señora*. Unlike her usual discreet guests, who cleared out of their allotted cubicles within an hour or two, we loitered. At least four times a day we would have to ring the bell at the gate intercom on our passage to or from the internet café. At which point the *Señora* would audibly scowl, eventually wriggle her oversized buttocks from their cosy perch and waddle over to the gate-release button. She would then waggle her sausage-sized finger with its scarlet claw and impart some words of woe: 'It's very dangerous out there. You shouldn't wander the streets. Just yesterday there was a murder. When are you leaving?' At which we would nod or shake our heads, whichever was appropriate, and dive into the ghetto. Her words did affect us, for everyone was warning us about the district. We were genuinely concerned about what lay beyond the love-nest, but our room was cheap, the internet was close and we couldn't cope with the palaver of moving again. Also, there was a market just across the street.

Vegetables and fruit, barbequed chicken-legs, ice creams, clothes, shoes and toys filled the stalls, and the stench of fish filled our noses, as did the stink from the oily detritus of rotting food and plastic that belched around the stall-legs and tree-roots, lapping against flip-flopped toes. But if we breathed through our mouths and bought early, we could quickly, cheaply and efficiently eat and then trot off to work.

Our daily pattern of work, sleep and eat was only twice interrupted. The first time was when a couple next door was bonking so furiously that the furniture in our room jiggled around the floor. The second, when we awoke to the entire room shaking. 'Oh my God, who have they got in this time?' I grimaced. 'Everything's moving. This is ridiculous.' When the shaking hadn't stopped after ten minutes, but was getting progressively more violent, with even the mirrors starting to shudder, we decided we would have to complain to *La Señora*. 'What the hell…?' David's words trailed off as he prised open the door, 'Come and look at this!' Half-naked, jewelled and gartered, laced and bonded couples were frantically prancing about the parking lot as the entire complex shook. This time the earth had really moved for all the hotel's lovers, as an earthquake shook the town.

Magnificent Frigatebirds
are circling above us like
a meeting of giant bats

Magnificent Frigatebird
Fregata magnificens

KJ ome

23 To the End of a Continent

'Ow!' I hiss through clenched teeth. A searing pain is surging through my knee. It's like a red-hot poker stabbing me every time I try to run forward. My brain's finally catching up. What am I going to do? What are we going to do? What the hell, why is it happening now? Nine more days. That's all we've got. We've been on the road for 441 days. I just need my knee to hold out for nine more little days and we'll have done it. We can't fail now.

But my knee didn't know that. It wasn't listening, and this time I couldn't see how I was going to con it. David was bending over me, one hand pressing on my back, the other gently unfurling my clenched fist, pushing Diclofenac pills into it. I was massaging my knee, desperately trying to will it back to health. We were on the main carriageway out of Ciudad Guayana. Cars surged past in a never-ending cloud of stinking fumes. We had only run three miles from the hotel, and now here we were; two crumpled figures contemplating the death of their dream only 200 or so miles from the finishing line.

We had no contingency plan. We had just eaten up all our spare time in the city. We were due to arrive in Carúpano on Sunday, 20 October. If we didn't run a marathon every day from this point, we wouldn't get there in time. 'Give me the trailer,' said David. 'I'll take it from now on, until your knee eases up. Let's rub some Ibuprofen gel on it and then bandage it. We're carrying all this first aid around, so we might as well use it.'

Nothing seemed to work. I was in agony. Every step forward fired a shot of pain down my leg. I limped along the road in a slow, silent, shuffling jog, gritting my teeth, crying out when the pain was too overwhelming. There was no get-out plan, I had to win through. I imagined Sir Ranulph Fiennes battling on with frostbite in his toes, nose and fingers. He had conquered immense pain; now it was my turn. I had to find the switch in my head that would control pain and turn it off. 'Mind over matter,' I murmured to myself. 'It doesn't hurt. It's just a warm, pleasant sensation. Keep running.'

Back in Trinidad David had carved off part of a finger with an electric planer. I had never seen him so tormented: he couldn't sleep; he was in agony. An old man who was working in the boatyard with us had instructed him to tap into his life-force, saying that once he had found it, he would be able to override any physical hardship. It sounded a good idea, but finding the force was more complicated. I thought about meditation, of Leo in Porto Velho who could remove himself from the earth for an hour or more each day. That was what I needed to work on. If I could calm and discipline my brain, perhaps I could switch off the pain.

Running at my pace crippled David. So he would press ahead and then wait for me to catch up. But now the running was taking twice as long, which meant more hours on our feet in the fierce sun. During one of those long, painful, teeth-gritting days which seemed to last for ever, as I trotted, limped and cried myself through a marathon, a lorry-driver stopped by the side of the road and asked if he could take his photo with us. Having seen that I was limping, he grabbed all the drink and food he had in his cab and plunged them into our arms. 'You need these more than I do,' he said. 'Anyway, I can stock up in a few hours at the next town. I just hope that knee of yours gets better. Perhaps I'll see you again, I go backwards and forwards three or four times a week on this road. Well, good luck.' And with that he was gone, leaving us with all his treasures.

Such kindness was a priceless tonic during those hideous, pain-stricken days. The sugar and liquid fuelled me, but it was the man's actions and words that really spurred me to keep going. Two days later, we had almost forgotten him when suddenly the honk of a lorry woke us from our reverie. 'Katharine, David,' he shouted across the car-roofs zooming past. 'Great to see you!' He was calling us over. 'I've been carrying these around in the hope that I'd see you again.' He placed two packets in my hands, 'They'll help your knee...' I was flabbergasted. The pain-killers were a vital addition to our dwindling supplies. He then presented us with a clutch of drinks and sandwiches that he had been buying especially for us each day in case he saw us, patted us on the back and disappeared up the road – our unlikely guardian angel brightening another wretched day.

We stopped for the night by a river in an Indian village and waded into the chocolate water in the dark, mud squishing between our toes, allowing the cool waves of the current to envelop us. The banks were thronged with people. A group of men and young boys squatted beneath the branches of an enormous mango tree playing cards. Children darted between the huts, weaving through the groups of chatting elders, hiding and then pouncing on one another. Car doors were left open, with pop tunes blaring out. A huddle of teenagers danced on the bridge. Lights twinkled, snuffing out the stars. A group of girls bobbed towards me giggling. I drifted on my back splashing my feet at them. They grabbed my wriggling toes, exploding into hoots of laughter. Part of the mob sheared off and tickled my armpits. The girls were gorgeous, wide-eyed and innocent. I forgot about my knee, about the parlous situation it had put us in, and allowed my eyelids to drop as I gently drifted, cocooned by the laughter of the children.

Sleep didn't seem to be a priority, but somewhere before midnight, forms started to wriggle out of the water, away from their groups, towards their beds. We had been allowed to spread our tent on the wooden boards of the central meeting-hut. No one joined us, so in the morning I peeked around the side of it, to see if I could spy where the villagers spent their nights. Bodies hung everywhere, swaying in their cloth hammocks, the soft exhalation of breath rising above the lapping of the river.

David had texted José, a friend of Eduardo's who we were due to meet in Maturín: 'We're getting desperate, José. Is there any chance you could bring some medicine for Katharine, please?' Maturin was miles away, and José worked full-time, but a couple of miles after the river, a jeep swerved into a lay-by and out popped a neat little fellow: José. 'Greetings and congratulations!' he slapped our backs. 'You're nearly there! We're all very excited about your arrival in Maturín. Here are some pills and cream for Katharine. I went to the chemist. They wouldn't give you anything without a prescription, but my doctor agreed to see me and prescribed these drugs.'

By the time we collapsed into the turquoise seats at Radio Maturín, we'd clocked 31 miles on the GPS watch. José had put on a magnificent greeting-party for us. A throng of students and friends cheered in a car-park. They had made banners, emblazoning them with wildlife and plants of South America, and used leaves to write our names. The task must have taken them ages. They were dancing and shouting, I could hear our names being chanted. The same feeling that had surged through me on our arrival into Guaspati now rushed all over my body, pricking it into goose-pimples. I shivered, blown away by their generosity, striving to bite back the tears that were streaming down my face.

Six of the students decided to run with us into the centre of town. The others piled into cars which wrapped around us in a protective sandwich. Heads hung out of windows filming us, bunting wavered from the rooftops, and everyone hooted. It was chaos. Cars everywhere stopped to see what the fuss was about, and pedestrians leapt into the road to take photos. The girls gradually peeled away from us, diving back into the cars, leaving us and the trailer to run it alone.

The radio interview was fantastic. The DJ was really clued up about the run. Her only mistake was in announcing that we were running South Africa, rather than South America! And my only mistake was not insisting upon a shower. But first we had to talk to a college, then visit an orphanage. This was one of the most charming and enthusiastic groups we had ever addressed. Afterwards they showed us around the fruit and vegetable garden; hands pulled at our shorts and faces grinned up at us. They presented us with a wooden statue of a hummingbird feeding from an orchid that they had created themselves. It was beautiful. We felt completely humbled.

It wasn't until later that evening, when we returned to José's house, that I finally had a shower. It was too late. My bum had exploded into a series of red, raw hillocks that radiated in an ark from cheek to cheek from the accumulation of sweat and filth. The pain in my knee hadn't receded, either; if anything it had got worse. It was only pure adrenalin that had allowed me to sprint through town with the 'Josés'. If only we hadn't stopped for so long in Cuidad Guayana . . .

I had felt on top of the world roaring into that city; so fit, with every part of my body humming and oiled. But after seven days of rest I malfunctioned. Perhaps a ligament in my knee had become misaligned? Perhaps I strained something when I was sprinting into town? We had had niggles before, when we had taken more than two days of rest, so we had been careful: two days became the maximum. We should never have made an exception so close to the finishing-line.

I plugged on. At the start of each new day my knee would feel OK, and I would cling to the hope that it had somehow recovered. But then, after a few miles, a dart of pain would jab through it and I would be back clenching my teeth and running painfully slowly.

From Maturín we headed for Carapito, after which the scenery exploded into life. It was like running through the Blue Mountains of Jamaica; woods dressed the hillsides and rivers disappeared and reappeared, gurgling through the valleys. We were feeling safer, too, less scared about being knocked on the head. Near the top of one winding hill we emerged into a village. I noticed a shop-sign in someone's window, pushed my arm through the thick iron bars that wrapped round the house and pressed the bell. After about five minutes an elderly woman appeared from behind a door. Her hunched shoulders seemed to overwhelm her spindly neck and head, leaving only two piercing, turquoise eyes that bore down upon us. We bought fizzy drinks and sat on her concrete step, downing the nectar while she picked up some knitting and lowered herself into a metal chair behind the bars. David pondered the *Señora's* predicament as we wound up the hill from her house: 'It seems the way Venezuela deals with crime is to lock the goodies up behind bars and let the baddies free to roam outside!'

Next day we hobbled out of our tent and up the hill into a little restaurant where a woman was baking fat, gummy maize breads (*arepas*). A huge moth flew through the flames of the oven, crashing onto the floor. When David picked it up, it gripped his fingers: it was bigger than his hand and floral, like the curtains of a stately home. After a while it flew out, as did we after a breakfast of monstrous *arepas*, with deep-fried pork. Not exactly the most technical running food, but really tasty.

We had to run 30 miles to catch up on some of the short days we had been accruing. At nearly six o'clock, just before dark we spied a *balneario* (swimming pool complex). A bunch of teenagers loafing about in a small wooden hut agreed that we could stay and so we jumped into the pool, keeping our heads under the water to avoid the rapacious mosquitos.

That evening my period arrived instead of a baby. We were disappointed. It would have been lovely to have conceived; also, it would have shaped the next stage of our life. I lay back on the hard concrete floor deep in thought (our roll mats were pretty ineffective by now). At least we were camping legitimately and wouldn't have to worry about being discovered in the dead of night by some irate hunter. We allowed the chirring orchestra of frogs to wash over us and closed our eyes.

'Who's there?' barked a voice metres away from our feet. We awoke with a start. Our minds raced. Where were we? After a few seconds, the swimming-pool and the encounter with the teenagers flooded back into our consciousness and we explained to the voice. There was a long pause and after a few more exchanges, the man's hostility dissolved and he said we were welcome to stay. His footsteps receded and we were once again left alone with the animals of the night. 'That's something I won't miss when we stop, living on tenterhooks all the time, said David.' I nodded, but was too exhausted to reply and closed my eyes again.

> We're contemplating the unimaginable: finishing in two days (David penned). I feel blurry about it. For me at least we have a clear goal and course whilst running. Finishing throws everything open. Other people always seem to have a good answer for what they want to do next. I don't. We just need to make sure we get the run done. To banish the other churning thoughts from our heads.

The next day we ran into Casanay. We had achieved 33 momentous miles up and down the State of Sucre's coastal range, rising at times to 1,040 metres and descending to 300 metres. It had been incredibly tough. I was in pain after only three miles, and was soon shuffling, limping, even hopping sometimes; it was the only way I could get through the miles. Like David I'm pig-headed and couldn't contemplate giving in. It was awful for him, too, he felt so hopeless. Apart from rubbing Ibuprofen spray on my knee, there was nothing he could do. Bandages came off and on, providing some support, so we kept adjusting them. There was no way we weren't going to finish now – but then again, we still had 27 miles to run. Was it a step too far?

Street lights were flickering on in Cassanay. Small pools of amber dotted the centre of the road, leaving the houses huddled in shadow. Cheers rang out from a barn, cockerels were springing in the air and lunging at one another. The crumpled figures by the side of the road seemed to be getting more and more drunk with each village that we passed through. After a few inquiries we found a *posada* and couldn't believe our luck on reading: 'Restaurant, rooms and swimming pool.'

A long, eight-foot wall surrounded the hotel, with magenta bougainvillea blooms scrambling over it. We pushed the green gates open. A woman was sweeping leaves from the doorway of a little reception-room. Her black hair was dolloped upon her head in a nest of curls. Another woman sat behind the desk gazing at her yellow fingernails. 'Do you have a room, please?' I began, but I didn't let them answer. 'We're so excited. We've run 6,477 miles to reach you, from the very tip of South America. We never thought we would make it. If all goes to plan, tomorrow we'll dive into the Caribbean Sea! We'll be the first in the world to have done it!'

Two puzzled faces blinked back at us. The sweeper gulped. The woman with the nails stared into the distance hazily: something appeared to be registering, but she shook her head, dispelled the thought and resumed examining her claws. We waited. Silence. After the pause had become unbearable, David proffered, 'Do you have a room, then?' On safer territory, the sweeper nodded. 'Nails' pulled out a large black diary and began flicking the pages carefully. 'Yes, I think we can make up a bed for you. A room for a couple is it?' she asked wearily, relinquishing her brush. 'That would be great,' David said sunnily. I was defeated and decided to remain mute. We followed the sweeper into the vaults of the concrete edifice.

'Isn't there a room on the basement level?' David suggested, 'It would be much easier for us, what with the trailer and all these bags.' She stopped and peered down her long nose at him, 'No. This is it. You can take it or leave it. Doesn't bother me.' She pushed against a fire-door that creaked open. The room stank of cigarettes. Piles of sheets and towels lay scattered across the floor. 'I'll see if Daniela wouldn't mind bringing you up some clean linen. Here's your key.' Before we could ask about the swimming pool and the restaurant, she had bustled out. It took over an hour for Daniela to bring the basic items. Daniela was 'Nails'.

It appeared that the cheerful pair were the sole employees. As for other residents, we didn't see another soul, save the poor, dejected capybaras, macaws and *agutis* that slunk around in an earth pit below one of the concrete walkways. David asked about the pool and food, 'Oh no. The pool was drained last year. Hasn't been filled since. Lot of work, that. Much easier without it.' David reminded her of the other question. 'Don't be silly! No one eats here! No one comes, so there'd be no point in a restaurant, would there?'

It appeared that on the last night of our expedition we had stumbled into Venezuela's answer to Fawlty Towers; probably a fitting finale to our 15 months on the road! But we couldn't blame the hotel for another wretched night's sleep. Clouds of worry drifted through our heads: we couldn't stop them, even when we were biting at the gates of victory.

> Katharine's adamant she'll get there tomorrow (wrote David). I wonder how? She's in trouble. We have hill after hill to run up and we haven't slept in days. It's the biggest day of the expedition, but it's promising to be a disaster.

The familiar beeping jolted us from bed. It was three o'clock in the morning, Sunday, 20 October 2013, the final day, the 450th of the expedition. We must have slept, then – at least for a couple of hours. I pulled on my skirt and long-sleeved top. For a few seconds we had forgotten that this was anything other than a normal Sunday morning. Then it dawned upon us, 'This is it! The day we've been longing for. I never thought it would happen,' I grinned at David. 'Yep,' he replied. 'Everything we do from now on will be for the last time. Let's get it done!'

The hills were oppressive, as was the sun. But the countryside was beautiful. My knee creaked, as though it would shatter into a million pieces if I insisted on pushing it forwards. Tears began to blur my vision. David was by my side. I was inconsolable. I felt defeated. I desperately needed to run free, unimpeded, feel a spring in my step, run well and fast. 'If only it could work just for today,' I pleaded – to David, myself, the sky, whoever was listening.

We heard hooting. We looked back. Cheering faces were dangling out of car windows; people were clapping, flags billowed from sun-roofs. It was José. He had brought his family and work colleagues all the way from Maturín. 'You're amazing!' I shouted. '¡Son asombrosos!' They tumbled out of the cars, hugging and kissing us. They had brought coconuts, too. I sipped the icy liquid, closed my eyes, forgot the pain and the disappointment. The world dropped off the cliff at our feet, spiralling away down thorny hills. 'Soon you'll see it,' they shouted as they sped away. 'Soon you'll see the sea.'

We wound our way up and up towards the turquoise sky. It had rained yesterday, but today was blue and the sun burnt through the cacti lacing the road and danced on the tarmac that met our feet. At the top of a craggy summit we saw it: the Caribbean Sea, stretching deep into the horizon. 'Oh my God!' I cried. 'We're going to do it!' I looked up at David smiling; we were so close now.

And slowly, oh so slowly, the miles disappeared. We summited the coastal range and started descending, running down and round hairpin corners, free-falling off the mountain- side. A cavalcade was waiting for us. José's lot were there again, cheering from the side of the road. They held flags and banners, and our sponsors' and trusts' flags too. We rigged them up on the trailer. 'Seven miles, that's all you've got! We'll show you the way, down to the best beach in Carúpano.' They were laughing as they revved off.

'This is it! We can do it, Katharine.' David was hugging me. 'Do you want the trailer? We've shared its load for nearly 15 months. It's only fair that you run to victory with it.'

I stood between the familiar bamboo arms, fastened the old belt and started running, following the Josés who were leading the way shouting and clapping. Crowds started gathering by the roadside. People were stepping out of shops, stopping their cars in the road, getting out to see what all the commotion was about. An old man darted into the road in front of us with a huge camera. 'Perhaps José found a professional photographer for us after all?' I grinned at David. 'He looks a bit doddery though. Wonder where José picked him up? I'm not sure he's going to survive this chaos!'

We were on fire, riding the goodwill wave that was surging through Carúpano. I couldn't feel my knee any more. I had lost all sensation. David was sprinting beside me in tandem. We were running along the coast now, passing rows of rainbow-coloured pirogues, watching waves tumble over the sand. 'What's wrong with these beaches?' I gasped. 'Where the hell are they taking us?' I may have been on an adrenalin rush, but it wasn't going to last forever.

José and the gang were gesturing, pointing ahead to a track that veered off to the right. They swung down it, disappearing. I was pulling the trailer through sand now. I could taste the sea on my tongue. Up in front people were dancing and the *Josés* were waiting, holding up a banner, '¡*Felicitaciones!* Congratulations, you've done it!'

We're clutching them in our arms, kissing them, thanking them. Now David's holding me and we're running, running for the last time. Sand cakes our feet and now sea water's gushing over them. We dive in through the surf. I gaze into the sky. Magnificent frigate-birds are circling above us like a meeting of giant bats. Brown pelicans are bobbing like bath toys. These are our birds, the ones we sailed with, when we dreamed of running South America.

David grabs me, he's hugging me, we're kissing and I'm crying. I can't stop. Relief floods us. Fifteen months ago we were in the icy Southern Ocean. Now somehow we've arrived at the other end of the continent, with the sun beating down upon us. We look down. We arrived here on nothing but the four small feet that are walking us out of the water and carrying us home.

Epilogue

Katharine became the first woman in the world to run the length of South America, and David the first man to run the continent 'unsupported'. Katharine probably completed the second-longest run in history undertaken by a woman. Together they became the first people to have run the Amazon Basin, the entire country of Bolivia and Chile's *Carretera Austral*.

A third of the run was barefoot (or in barefoot shoes) and a third on rough tracks. Their longest running-day was 36 miles (58 kms), their longest running-week 192 miles (309 kms) and their average running-day 20 miles (31 kms). During their final burst to reach the Caribbean they ran the equivalent of nine marathons in nine days. They ran for 332 days and went through ten pairs of shoes each. Non-running days amounted to 113, and were spent arranging logistics, planning, acquiring food and kit, and presenting. Two hundred and seventy-one nights were spent in the wild. Five days were lost to injury and illness.

The trailer weighed between 60 and 140 kg, depending on food and equipment. It was re-built by David three times during the run, and pulling was shared equally between the two runners, except during the 423 mile (681 km) *Rua de Onces* section in Brazil, where Katharine and David each pulled a 100kg trailer, due to the volume of food they required. They each expended at least 4,000 calories per day, but often didnt manage to replenish it!

The couple presented to 2,583 students in Spanish and English, including 30 institutions in South America and eleven in the UK on their return. They gave over 100 television and radio interviews. They wrote 35 articles and blogs for *The Ecologist,* the *Independent* online, *Soy Maratonista* and *Patagonia Magazine*. They also raised money for all their charities: *Asociación Armonía*, Birdlife International and *Conservación Patagonica*.

David and Katharine recorded 453 bird species and registered 6,154 individual birds, including many that are endangered. Their bird-transect indicated that Brazil had the greatest diversity and number of species, followed by Bolivia. They identified 17 living species of mammal, and numerous species of bat. They saw at first hand the ecological threats of road-building, urban development, deforestation, over-grazing and fencing; but they also encountered extraordinary wildlife and stunning wildernesses, and basked in the warmth of encounters with fellow human-beings in all the countries they ran through.

HRH Prince Charles kept his word, and met the couple after the expedition, congratulating them on their mammoth run and their work for nature-conservation. Two months after their return to Uruguay Katharine became pregnant, and gave birth to a baby boy, Theo, who sailed home with them. After digging their boat out of the mud, they nearly sank on their way north, had to make an emergency stop in Brazil and then battled head-winds, sea-sickness and an enthusiastic little boy as they headed home on a two-month, non-stop voyage across the Atlantic. Baby Beth arrived soon after to complete their new family. Katharine is writing a book about their circumnavigation of South America which preceded their marathon run.

Appendices

Trusts and Foundation which supported The 5,000-Mile Project:

Transglobe Expedition Trust
Sculpt the Future Foundation
John Muir Trust: Bill Wallace Grant

		Item	Sponsor
Kit List	Footwear	Transition trainers (small heel)	Inov 8
		Barefoot shoes	Vivobarefoot
		Gaiters	Inov 8
	Clothes	Rainproof breathable Shell running jacket	Berghaus
		Fleece	Berghaus
		Gloves	Patagonia Inc.
		Running tops	Yew Clothing
		Socks	Inov8
		Bra	Boobydoo & Patagonia Inc
		Buff (chafe protection)	Inov8
		Running leggings	N/A
		Running shorts/skirt	Patagonia Inc.
		Cap	Berghaus
		Lightweight warm waterproof hat	Berghaus
		Light cotton trousers (non-running)	Berghaus
		Light long cotton sleeved shirt (in camp)	Patagonia Inc.
		Lightweight down jacket for Patagonia	Patagonia Inc. & Berghaus
		Waterproof over trousers	Berghaus
	Shelter	Lightweight tent	Hilliberg Nallo 2gt
		1-season sleeping bag	N/A
		3-season sleeping bag	N/A
		Inflatable air mat (x2)	Klymit X frame
		Silk Liners	N/A
		Foam sleeping mat (x2)	N/A

		Item	Sponsor
Kit List		Hammocks	Hennessy Deep Jungle Asym
		Rainfly Tarpaulin (x2)	Hennessy Hex Asym
		Ex-Army Bivvy Bags	N/A
	Cooking	Water purification pump	LIFESAVERS
		Water Pump filters	LIFESAVERS
		Water Bags (dry weight)	MSR 10ltr Dromedary (x2)
		Bladder Pack 2ltr (x2)	Inov8
		Lightweight universal uel cooker	MSR
		Fuel bottle 500ml	MSR
		Stove service kit	MSR
		Aluminium pan	MSR
		Eating utensil	N/A
		All weather lighting device	N/A
		Cup	N/A
	Medical	Micro Expedition first aid kit	N/A
		Snake venom extractor	N/A
		Blister pads	N/A
		Zinc tape	N/A
		Cool spray	N/A
		Insect repellent	N/A
		Immunisations/malarial prophylactics	N/A
	Other (misc)	Ultra-light binoculars	Swarovski EL 8x 32
		Waterproof Overboard bags (x3) to carry equipment	N/A
		Rucksack 25lt	Inov8
		Quick-drying towel	N/A
		Sunglasses	N/A
		Water bottle	N/A
		Cheap watch	N/A
		Knife	N/A
		Machete	N/A
		Pepper Spray	N/A
		GPS Watch	N/A
		Compass	N/A
		Needle and thread	N/A
		Spanish mini-dictionary	
		Spanish Verb book N/A	N/A
		Female sanitary device	Mooncup
		Sun cream	N/A
		Write in the rain notepad plus pencil	N/A
		Diary (x2)	N/A
		High vis reflective vest	N/A
		Duck tape 1m	N/A
		Whistle	N/A
		Sponsors flag	N/A
		Dyneema rope 5m	TBC
		Bird guide (for each country)	N/A

		Item	Sponsor
		Wildlife Guide (Chile & Argentina)	N/A
Logistics	Pre-Post Expedition Transport		N/A
	Shipping costs from UK/US		N/A
Trailer	Recycled / found parts		N/A
Comms	En route comms		
		Mini Laptop	N/A
		Iridium Satphone	N/A
		Mobile Broadband	N/A
		Network charges	N/A
		Sat-mail address	N/A
	Website	Domain name registration plus annual fee	N/A
		Maintenance	N/A
		Newsletter service	N/A
	Audio Visual	Ipadio phone blog	Ipadio
		Compact camera	N/A
	Energy	Solar charger	Power Traveller
Insurance	Health Insurance		N/A
	Travel Insurance		N/A

Mission Statements of the three Charities supported by The 5,000-Mile Project

ASOCIACION ARMONIA
To conserve Bolivia's birds and their habitats by empowering local people.

BIRDLIFE
The BirdLife Partnership strives to conserve birds, their habitats and global biodiversity, working with people towards sustainability in the use of natural resources.

CONSERVACION PATAGONICA
Works to create national parks in Patagonia that save and restore wildlands and wildlife, inspire care for the natural world, and generate healthy economic opportunities for local communities.

RECICES

Rocket Fuel

An easy, delicious and energy-packed treat constructed from the following ingredients*:

- Chocolate
- Cream
- Nuts
- Raisons, plus or minus an assortment of dried fruit
- Biscuits (without palm oil or soya)
- A tot of brandy or sherry (if you like)

(*The quantities are up to you. The resultant mixture should be spoonable, not runny.)

It's more a case of assemblage; melting, crushing and chopping, than it is cooking.

Summer Porridge

- Oats
- Milk (we used powdered)
- Plain yogurt
- Raisins
- Grated apples.

Add all the above ingredients together to produce a thick mixture that will puff up and sweeten overnight outside in winter (or in a refrigerator)